CAMBRIDGE URBAN AND ARCHITECTURAL STUDIES

General Editors

LESLIE MARTIN
Emeritus Professor of Architecture, University of Cambridge

LIONEL MARCH
*Professor, Graduate School of Architecture and Urban Planning,
University College of Los Angeles*

◇◇◇◇◇ ◇◇◇

10 THEO VAN DOESBURG

VOLUMES IN THIS SERIES

To my parents

10 JAREN STIJL 1917 - 1927

Voor nieuwe tijdschriftjes hebb... niet erg bemoedigend, scepticisme. Zoo gaat ook nu we met eenige aarzeling schrijven ov... nieuw maandblad, voor de moderne beeldende kunsten onder de redactie van Théo van Doesburg. Di... heet « De Stijl ». De naam wordt den lezer in een raadseltje van blokken op den omslag opgegeven, ... an onze zetterij geprobeerd heeft hierboven ... nabootsinkje te maken.

(Haarl. Dagblad 1917).

Les artistes du « Stijl » s... des cubistes purs, des cubistes qui en certain qu...ons, veulent aller plus loin que les cubistes français, t... le maître Pablo Picasso entre autres, dont l... garde un certain carac-tère de plasticité.

Le « Stijl » n'admet pas c... Le cubi-me, qui a bien fait r... encore en certains milieux, n'en demeure pa moins fort vivace et dépit des attaques dont il est l'objet. Ceci mérite l'attention. Il n'entre pas dans notre idée de l'analyser ici. Nous voulons simplement constater qu... cette interprétation moderne de la vie, donne déjà, — en architecture par exemple — des résultats que même une profane (sans parti pris) saurait apprécier. Ceci également mérite l'attention.

Lumière, Nov. 1919.

Dat kunstenaars zich vermaken met, of zich vergeten in het opstellen en verkondigen van theorieen is de dwaasheid van den krompoot, die zich op glad ijs waagt, maar het brengt nog humor in de wereld. Dat ze echter waarachtig probeeren om in lijn en kleur en in beeldende en bouwende plastiek hunne philosophie-tjes te verwerkelijken is een dwaasheid, die niets beminnelijks meer heeft, omdat het 't aanzien geeft van een pretentieuse propagandakunst, waarvan de onmacht van het woord nog eens dik onderstreept wordt door die van het kunnen.

Ook deze strooming is een teeken van onzen tijd vol van tijdelijkheden, een tijd, waarin niets duurzaams schijnt, en ook deze *mode* zal tijdelijk blijken... zelfs bij personen, die thans met haar pro... en, zal ze voor-bijgaan, hopenlijk om ze te ontwikkelen, want daarvoor is bij deze rechtlijnige geaardheid no ruimte, zoo ze althans voor sommigen geen einde beteekent.

C. J. Blaauw in « De Telegraaf 1920. »

Das Triumphgeschrei der Stilgruppe Architektur und Malerei aus ihren eigentlichen Mitteln : ehrlich, ein-fach und sachlich, erscholl voll Widerhall in europäischen Ländern. Die rasche Verbreitung der konstruk-tivistischen Erkenntnisse ist wohl hauptsächlich eine Folge Doesburgscher Taten, dessen philosophische Gründ-lichkeit die neue Bewegung mächtig gedeihen liess. Hinzu kam der Umstand, dass diese Erkenntnisse gewis-sermassen in der Luft lagen, wie das gleichzeitige parallele Vorgehen z. B. russischer Künstler beweist. Eine Zeitschrift « De Stijl » die von Theo van Doesburg selbst geleitet wurde und ein von ihm verfasstes Werk : « Grundbegriffe der neuen Kunst » haben seinen Erfolg verstärkt. Theo van Doesburgs Theorien, welche m. e. viel schärfer umrissen sind als die Meinung... B. Mondrians, haben trotz und wegen einer gewissen Einseitigkeit — stark gewirkt.

Harry Scheibe, in « Form » (1926).

Wir haben hier nur die Konstatierung zu unter...then, dass die Stellungnahme Doesburgs unbeirrt und früh erfolgte : 1917 — also zu einer Zeit, in der man in Deutschland etwa das Poelzigsche Schauspiel plante.

Dr. Giedion, Zürich in « Cicerone » (1927).

DE STIJL
LE STYLE
DER STIL
THE STYLE
1917
1918
1919
1920
1921
1922
1923
1924
1925
1926
1927
1928

THEO VAN DOESBURG

Painting into architecture, theory into practice

ALLAN DOIG

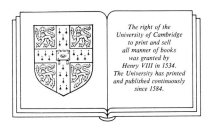

The right of the
University of Cambridge
to print and sell
all manner of books
was granted by
Henry VIII in 1534.
The University has printed
and published continuously
since 1584.

CAMBRIDGE UNIVERSITY PRESS

CAMBRIDGE

LONDON   NEW YORK   NEW ROCHELLE
MELBOURNE   SYDNEY

Published by the Press Syndicate of the University of Cambridge
The Pitt Building, Trumpington Street, Cambridge CB2 1RP
32 East 57th Street, New York, NY 10022, USA
10 Stamford Road, Oakleigh, Melbourne 3166, Australia

First published 1986

Printed in Great Britain by
BAS Printers Limited, Over Wallop, Hampshire

British Library cataloguing in publication data
Doig, Allan
Theo van Doesburg: painting into architecture, theory into practice.–
(Cambridge urban and architectural studies, 10)
1. Doesburg, Theo van   2. Architects–
Netherlands–Biography
I. Title
720'.92'4   NA1153.D6

Library of Congress cataloguing in publication data
Doig, Allan.
Theo Van Doesburg: painting into architecture, theory into practice.
(Cambridge urban and architectural studies, 10)
Bibliography
Includes index.
1. Doesburg, Theo van, 1883–1931–Views on architecture. 2. Stijl.
I. Title. II. Series: Cambridge urban and architectural studies, no. 10.
NA1153.D64D65 1986   720'.92'4   85-19493

ISBN 0 521 32213 8

BAS

Contents

7119651

Illustrations

Preface

Until about 1923 the magazine *De Stijl* was the clearing-house for the theoretical work of the group De Stijl. As the editor, Van Doesburg was the central political figure and guardian of the party line. By 1925, with the departure of Mondrian, the last faithful member, the journal became Van Doesburg's private statement of principles. One of those basic principles, which had been maintained since the foundation of the group, was the fundamental unity of all the arts and the realisation of that unity in the *Gesambtkunstwerk*. This principle had led Van Doesburg increasingly towards the practice of architecture, and it is the history of that development that I wish to reconstruct here.

The magazine *De Stijl* was intended to be an international point of contact and thus contained articles in English, French, and German as well as Dutch. The artists of the group had various national backgrounds, Dutch, Belgian, Hungarian, and fringe members who were French, German, and Italian. The public and private correspondence naturally shows varying degrees of competence in these languages, which presents problems with quotations. French and German quotations have been kept in the original, and original orthography and grammar have been retained except where it causes confusion. Some of the idiosyncrasies of language actually contribute greatly to the sense, in Dada-influenced writings, for example. Because it is a lesser-known language, all quotations originally in Dutch have been translated. Unless otherwise footnoted, all those translations are my own.

This book in an earlier life was my doctoral thesis of the same name, submitted in 1981. While being prepared for publication a considerable number of new books and articles appeared, for the most part to mark the centenary, in 1983, of Van Doesburg's birth and I have tried to take account of this material where it affects my argument.

I am greatly indebted to a number of public bodies and individuals for help and encouragement received along the way. The Dutch Ministry of Science and Education provided a scholarship, the Technical University, Delft, a fellowship, and the University of Kent a research grant. Professor Peter King of the Institute of Modern Dutch Studies, Hull, provided endless help and encouragement. Mr Thom Mercuur, Franeker, Friesland, and Mr Dirk Rinsema opened their homes and collections to me, and the late Vicomte de Noailles his villa in Hyères. Joop Joosten

of the Stedelijk Museum, Amsterdam, the Nederlands Documentatie-
centrum voor de Bouwkunst (N.D.B), Amsterdam, Wouter van der
Horst, It Bleekerhûs Museum, Drachten, Friesland, the Stedelijk Van
Abbemuseum, Eindhoven, and the Musée d'Art Modern, Strasbourg,
have all been extremely helpful, and above all I wish to thank Jean Leer-
ing and Wies Leering-van Moorsel, the heirs of Mrs Nelly van Doesburg.
The Van Doesburg Collection and Archive have been bequeathed by the
Leerings to the Dutch State and are administered as the Schenking Van
Moorsel by the Rijksdienst Beeldende Kunst, who gave me the oppor-
tunity of cataloguing the collection itself. At the R.B.K. Drs Robert de
Haas, Evert van Straaten, and Marianne Kentie were all very generous
with their help.

Further, the production of the thesis was facilitated by the extremely
efficient typing and proof-reading of Dr and Mrs J. T. Grantham and Dr
P. J. Ford. Many thanks are also due to William Davies and Margaret
Sharman of Cambridge University Press for their patience and meti-
culous care. For that I am most grateful and wish to stress the fact that
any mistakes in the text are entirely my own. I should like to thank
Dr Stephen Bann for his support, encouragement, and many helpful
suggestions throughout my research. I sincerely hope that the result
proves worthy of all this help.

For all these great debts there is still one more, the largest of all, and
that is to my wife Belinda. The final transformation of thesis into book
was thanks to her.

Canterbury ALLAN DOIG
13 January 1985

Introduction

At a crucial moment in his career as an artist, Theo van Doesburg focused his attention on the tectonic, or 'structural', qualities of painting. Formal experiments in two dimensions soon led him to consider the third, and a painterly conception of architecture emerged. In 1929 he looked back to the early years of De Stijl in an article called 'The Struggle for the New Style':

It is unquestionably the *architectonic* character of their pictures which finally enabled the more radical painters to convince the public that their endeavours were serious, and not only to *influence* the developing architecture but also to dictate the way towards collective construction.

In 1917, however, things had not got as far as collective construction, although certain painters, in collaboration with architects (Van der Leck with Berlage, myself with Oud, etc.), were attempting to transfer their ideas about painting . . . into three-dimensional space, instead of onto canvas. The idea of a universal stylistic idea was already latent in the attempt to forge an organic link between architecture and painting.

Van Doesburg, more than any of his contemporaries, consistently tried to bring about a union between architecture and painting on such a fundamental level as to revolutionise them both. By the early 1920s a considerable amount had been accomplished, and he felt justified in continuing his reminiscences with the following summary:

1921–23: *Architectural* projects were now being executed in rapid succession. The most important ones were Rietveld's work in Utrecht, Jan Wils's garden city, *Daal en Berg*, in The Hague and Oud's large, neat housing complexes for workers in Rotterdam.

Theory was turned into practice; the country was given a new impulse, a new mentality as to material structure.[1]

An inspection of this interface between painting and architecture involves a search for the most fundamental source of form and style. Not surprisingly such a search can quickly expand to encompass stained glass, sculpture, and eventually even typography, film, music, and poetry. This was Van Doesburg's all-consuming passion, to analyse the arts to the point of identifying their fundamental means of expression, to reduce, or perhaps better to distil them, and then to experiment with all manner of ways of recombining the essential primary elements to create a purer artistic result. The analytical stage in this process is

1

familiar to those who know the work of Piet Mondrian and it has long
been seen as the central idea in De Stijl theory. The experimental stage
in the process of recombination, on the other hand, has been viewed
as antithetical to Mondrian's slow, patient, and undeviating search for
the fundamentals of form and style.

Van Doesburg's varied experiments, with a resulting appearance of
inconsistency, have troubled an otherwise rather comfortable view of
De Stijl as a consistent, not to say orthodox or even homogenous, body
of theory and artistic production. Van Doesburg was aware, from the
earliest days of De Stijl, of the difficulties involved in presenting a united
avant-garde front as a revolutionary cell of artists, while at the same time
participating in the most diverse artistic activities. In order to distance
himself from some of his more outrageous experiments he assumed two
pseudonyms, Aldo Camini for his simultaneous writings, and I. K. Bonset for his Dada poetry.

Although not a pseudonym in the narrowest sense, the name Theo
van Doesburg had also been assumed. He was born Christian Emil Marie
Küpper on 30 August 1883 in Utrecht. As has become well known
through the writings of Joost Baljeu, Wilhelm Küpper may have been
registered as the father, but Christian Emil Küpper believed strongly that
his mother's second husband, Theodorus Doesburg, was his natural
father.

Van Doesburg's earliest ambition was to be an actor, but when his
aspirations turned increasingly towards painting, the disapproval of his
parents led him to decide at the age of eighteen to leave home. One of
the earliest known paintings by Van Doesburg is a naturalistic painting
of a dog, dated to 1899. From these early laboured essays as a self-taught
painter, he quickly (and characteristically) became totally absorbed in
what seemed to be the infinite expressive possibilities of the medium.
The first entry in his diary (like so many of his original documents, it
is kept in the Van Doesburg Archive, National Art Collections Department – *Rijksdienst Beeldende Kunst*, The Hague – hereafter referred to
as R.B.K.[2]), begins: 'If life touches me then I feel the need to return *this*
touch by means of paint or words' (3 May 1902; Van Straaten, p. 26).
Not long after, he explained the nature of that 'touch':

Passion. Harmony has passed through me. It is the harmony of life *in* colour.
Now I have a god. Harmony. I want to reveal him in form and colour.
  Colour is God.
  God is colour. [Diary I, 10 September 1902; Van Straaten, p. 26]

From very early on indeed, spiritual, religious, and (broadly speaking)
philosophical notions were basic concerns in Van Doesburg's art. The
early works themselves at times achieve a certain intensity, particularly
in his self-portraits, but on the whole he had both technical and formal
difficulty in penetrating beyond the material world to reveal the essential
'touch' or 'Harmony' he felt. The artist, in Van Doesburg's conception,
was a creative genius and mediator between Harmony and man; the
artist can create and order experience through colour.

Form and style in art were, somehow, to form the bridge between the material and the spiritual world. During the first decade of the century, that is during the first decade of Van Doesburg's intensive artistic activity, the form and style of his paintings were not exceptional. His intentions far outstripped his hard-won technical achievements and his formal development. As before, his intensely vital artistic drive made him 'feel the need to return *this* touch by means of paint or words', but at this stage he had to resort to words to indicate the necessary line of development for art to be able to create this bridge between the material and the spiritual. His diary entry for 1 August 1905 cites the accomplishment of a fellow Dutch painter:

I have seen a 'bride' by *Thijs Maris*.
    This bride listens to her own soul. She anticipates the touch of her lover. Here Thijs Maris depicts the unconscious process of anticipating the touch of love.
    The less reality in form, the greater the reality in Spirit, because the spirit is without form. [Van Straaten, p. 28]

The search remained intense. The diary entry for 3 April 1907 reads:

In art we must conquer the material *with* the material. . . . I am always reproached for being too demanding. But truly I do not demand much. I do-not-seek-much-I-seek-something that is almost nothing: Spirit. [Van Straaten, p. 29]

Form as spirit, or rather form as an iconic presence of spirit, was a frequent theme in his writing, but despite his belief that 'less reality in form' was the most effective revelation of the spirit, his explorations in this direction during these early years were limited to the distortions of caricature and the growing influence of the experiments of the Impressionists. Van Doesburg did meet with a degree of artistic success, however, and in the spring of 1914 he sent three paintings to the Salon des Indépendants in Paris.

On 1 August 1914 Van Doesburg's world was shattered. The tale is poignantly told in letter number three, dated 18 November 1914, of his 'Letters to Bertha':

Only in the last while, since 1908, have I been able (and then only very briefly) to push aside the curtain that kept my spiritual existence hidden away, and show the world what I have in me. I had chosen a name for the fight (Theo van Doesburg) . . . I had to win. . . . Within a small circle I had a good reputation. I had planned a daring spiritual campaign across the whole of the artistic and philosophical map of Europe. This was a possibility only whilst Europe cherished the works of Peace.
    Do you not preach the brotherhood of all men of all nationalities through Art?
    Did I not preach Love as a basis for all forms of Art. Yes I did. . .
    But now for the tragedy of this confession, Bertha! I was just on the verge of rounding up the whole old world of art and its intellect, and taking it all on board, when as suddenly as a grenade can bring horror, the *thought* hit my mind of the *possibility* of a European war. (For me that means the conquest of the spiritual and noble world by the filthy hypocritical world.)
    Already I felt that I had been *personally* conquered by the possibility of this war which would destroy all beauty and culture.
    I had had too much trust in higher nature and the spiritual in man. There

I stood, suddenly confronted by raw Reality. Not Art, not love, not wisdom, but grenades, grenades, grenades!

Once again I sang, though not as before . . . through Love, 'The Song of the Wild Beast' (Eenheid 1 August 1914 [published in *Eenheid*, no 218, 8 August]). I could feel them approach, so I warned of all the horrors of this disaster. I posted the article one hour before the mobilisation and said goodbye to everything: my ideals, my passions, everything.

Can you imagine how I felt?

Can you imagine what it was like for me to be a soldier? [Van Straaten, pp. 37–38]

Around the same time Van Doesburg suffered another loss when his marriage to the poet Agnita Feis collapsed. The 'letters to Bertha' were written on the Belgian front. They were never posted and most likely 'Bertha' was a literary character invented as the object of a poetic catharsis.

The crucial change in both Van Doesburg's artistic and theoretical work occurred between 1914 and 1916. There are sketches dated, perhaps in retrospect, to 1914 which are completely abstract. Van Doesburg's enormous personal collection of sketches (now in the possession of the R.B.K.) gives a complete picture of his painstaking development through these early stages and includes a sketch of a church, with the unlikely dating 1914, that is very close in spirit to the well-known Mondrian sketches, c. 1914–15, of the church at Domburg. Whether or not that particular sketch by Van Doesburg is correctly dated, there are many other works dating from 1915 and 1916 which demonstrate a similar linear, analytical, neo-Cubist tendency. His development away from natural form towards an elusive spiritual essence had entered an entirely new stage. In a review of the 1915 autumn exhibition of the Independents (*de Onafhankelijken*) in Amsterdam, he defined the three great periods of art:

I. The expression of the visually perceptible, or nature: *Realism.*
II. The expression of the psyche *by means of* the visually perceptible: broadly speaking, *Naturalism.*
III. The expression of the spiritual without the natural as an aid, with no other means than the pure elements of painting – colour and line: *Spiritualism.* [*De Avondpost*, 20 November 1915]

Not surprisingly Van Doesburg's theoretical development in his critical writings betrays a similar evolutionary pattern. His earliest publications were concerned with the study of the main lines of historical progress in art, and with drawing conclusions from that study for application and guidance in his own advancement and that of modern art in general. In 1915 and 1916 Van Doesburg wrote two decisive theoretical tracts: 'The Development of Modern Painting' ('De ontwikkeling der moderne schilderkunst'), a lecture in 1915; and 'The New Movement in Painting' ('De nieuwe beweging in de schilderkunst'), a series of articles of 1916. These consolidated the results of his own early experimentation and study of historical developments, and brought forward a thoroughly worked out theory from which a completely new style could emerge. In the earlier work he discussed the basic means of the arts and the necessity of a purification of those means for the new style. In the later work he developed further the ideas concerning art as the balanced relationship and proportion amongst those elements. These purely abstract relationships were for him the only acceptable content for art, and as a result the natural subject had to undergo a complete 'transformation' to achieve such a 'universalised' aesthetic balance. In 1926 he summed up this early development in the introduction to his article 'Painting: from Composition to Counter-composition':

In 1912 I published my first paper entitled 'Specimen for a New Criticism of Art'. I attempted to place my own development in the context of the general development of art and came to the recognition that the universal was the new content of art and that the straight line was the new expressive means. In my eyes these two elements would lead the way to the new style.

I rounded this period off with *Girl with Buttercups*, a composition abstracted from a naturalistic form. When I was released from military service in 1916, I set up *De Stijl*, and did that not without enthusiasm. . . . In an article 'From "Nature" to "Composition"', published in *De Hollandsche Revue* in 1918 [*sic*], I drew my ideas together and demonstrated through a series of illustrations progressively abstracted from a subject how I moved from a realistic composition through such a series to arrive at a painterly composition.[3]

The ideas discussed in the articles written prior to 1915 were primarily concerned with painting since that was, after all, Van Doesburg's profession, but his concern was by no means exclusively with painting. As he wrote in 'From "Nature" to "Composition"':

Architecture as well as painting and sculpture, and for that matter even music, literature, and dance, display certain common features. We can see that architecture is gradually turning away from the arbitrary and picturesque, the capricious and disorderly, and is turning towards constructive necessity and mathematical order, in a word the monumental. For years the same has been true of painting and sculpture. The result is that all the arts in the final analysis have *the same problem* to solve, whether on their own or together.

This problem is the problem of *balanced relationship*, of creative harmony.[4]

Between 1915 and the early part of 1917 Van Doesburg came into contact with a number of artists, architects, and even a poet who were in sympathy with his ideas. The central figures were Antony Kok, Bart van der Leck, Vilmos Huszar, Georges Vantongerloo, Piet Mondrian, Robert van 't Hoff, and J. J. P. Oud. In their enthusiasm for his, at this point, very generalised theory of abstract art, they were willing to range themselves behind the magazine *De Stijl* in order to contribute more effectively to the already furious debate between the advocates of naturalism and abstraction in art, and to do so with the added force of a unified radical cell. While the unity on this very generalised theoretical level would last, problems arose very soon when it came to particular applications of the theory, the developmental line to be followed, and the specific tactics to be used in the fight against naturalism. Their general agreement allowed them to produce a group *oeuvre* despite their many aggressive arguments which have recently caused some critics to question whether they can be called a group at all.

Beyond this general level it is impossible to define precisely what is meant by the phrase 'the De Stijl theoretical position' (which, it must be stressed, did not find its sole well-spring in the early theoretical work of Van Doesburg). Professor H. L. C. Jaffé, in his seminal work *De Stijl, 1917–1931: the Dutch Contribution to Modern Art*, tends to equate 'De Stijl theory' with 'Mondrian's [specific] theory' since Mondrian produced the paintings which have become accepted as the stylistic paradigms of the movement. On the other hand, the movement De Stijl could easily be equated with the journal *De Stijl* and hence the specific theoretical position of its editor Van Doesburg. But that would be to deny that Mondrian's works after 1925 and Oud's housing at the Hook of Holland have the status of De Stijl (that is *De Stijl*) objects just because they did not always enjoy the favour of the editor. To equate the magazine and the movement in such a way is highly questionable, not to say unacceptable. But, for all that, Van Doesburg did provide the impetus and almost evangelical conviction which brought the artists of De Stijl together as a movement and set the course, however briefly, towards certain commonly adopted goals at a crucial point both in terms of their personal careers and in the development of modern art as a whole.

Considering Van Doesburg's special position within De Stijl and therefore European modernism, it is important to analyse his theory, to locate it within its broad intellectual tradition in order to understand his art more fundamentally, to watch the way he was able to bring his discoveries in painting to bear on the question of style in modern architecture, and finally to recognise the ramifications of this for his eventual practice of architecture. Such a study as this is the biography of an idea, which is quite different from a personal biography. It addressed itself to the 'why', 'how' and 'what' of artistic production, relegating the 'when', and to some extent even the 'who' to a subsidiary role. Thus, the question of the respective contributions of Van Doesburg and Van Eesteren to the design of the Paris Models will be superseded by the questions: how were those ideas developed; why, in terms of the theory, did the architectural designs take those particular forms; and how in practice was the theory in the end 'translated' into form? The story of modern architecture is not just the story of personal accomplishment, it is the story of the origin and development of style, and on this point Van Doesburg would, in principle at least, have agreed whole-heartedly.

The notion that theory can be 'translated' into form was entailed in Van Doesburg's belief that art, religion, and philosophy express the same truths in different modes. In 'Thought – Vision – Creation' ('Denken – aanschouwen – beelden'), written in October 1918 and published in the December issue of *De Stijl*, he formulated the idea and at the same time made a clear reference to the group's work:

Pure thought, in which no representation is taken from passing phenomena, but instead number, measure, proportion, and abstract line appear, reveals itself conceptually (as reason) in Chinese, Greek, and German philosophy, and aesthetically in contemporary Neo-plasticism. [p. 24]

That art and philosophy were capable of expressing the same content was a commonly held belief, even amongst the rivals of De Stijl. On the opening page of *The Symbolism of Art (De symboliek der kunst)*, published in the same year as Van Doesburg's article, Just Havelaar phrased it as follows:

Art reveals the world-view, or feeling for life of the artist and of mankind, through the forms of nature. Just as philosophy does, art expresses the relationship between man and his world – just like philosophy, but in another mode, because it expresses itself in images and within the sphere of emotion.[5]

The two writers obviously had very different attitudes to nature, and this was enough to make them ideological enemies, but they were in full agreement that art and philosophy have the same subject, and both men relied on the same source for their ideas. That source was Hegel, who was currently enjoying great popularity in intellectual circles through the work of G. J. P. J. Bolland, Professor of Philosophy in Leiden, and the professor's former student Dr A. Pit.

In Hegel's Introduction to his *Philosophy of Fine Art* there is a passage strikingly similar to that just cited from Havelaar:

Fine art is not art in the true sense of the term until it is also thus free, and its *highest* function is only then satisfied when it has established itself in a sphere which it shares with religion and philosophy, becoming thereby merely one mode and form through which the *Divine*, the profoundest interests of mankind, and spiritual truths of widest range, are brought home to consciousness and expressed.

Later in the book, Hegel further developed this idea of forms or modes of expressing the divine or Absolute Spirit, and concluded that:

The differences which are perceptible in these modes of presentment are due to the notion of the absolute Spirit (Mind) itself. Spirit, in its truth, is essential substance brought home to itself. It is, therefore, no essence which lies outside and in abstract relation to objectivity, but rather is, within the compass of that objectivity, the re-recollected presence of the substance of all objects within finite spirit. It is the finite which grasps its own essential universality, and, in doing so, grasps essential Being in the absolute sense. The *first* mode of this comprehension is an *immediate* one, that is to say, it is a sensuous cognition, a cognition in the form and semblance of the object of sense-perception, in which the Absolute is presented directly to the understanding and feeling. The *second* form is that of the *conceptive* or imaginative consciousness. *Last* of all, we have the *free thought* of absolute Spirit.[6]

The same categories can be found in Van Doesburg's article 'Thought – Vision – Creation', but there they are not used as different modes appropriate either to art, religion, or philosophy. Most ingeniously, he has used them as categories or rather developmental stages in art. Moreover, he maintains that 'my own development in the plastic arts has moved through these stages during the period of the past twenty years'. These stages he called: 'concrete thought' as embodied in representational or 'physio-plastic' art; 'deformative thought' as embodied in 'ideoplastic' art; and 'pure abstract thought' as embodied in pure abstract art. In 1919 he published *Three Lectures about the New Plastic Art (Drie voordrachten over die nieuwe beeldende kunst)* where he illustrated these *Three Creative Moments of a Composition* and described

them as 'impression, expression, and plasticism' (p. 93). The three paintings (figs. 1, 2 and 3) show a development from a Cubist still-life, according to Van Doesburg still an immediate presentation of the sense object; through an intermediate stage where references to nature all but disappear, as in his geometrical works (fig. 4); culminating in a Neo-plastic painting 'in which no representation is taken from passing phenomena . . .', thus rising to the level of pure thought.

Hegel had reserved the first category of immediate representation of the objects of perception to Mind as appropriate to art and denied the capacity of art to rise beyond perfect representation to conceptive consciousness, let alone to abstract thought itself. The same sort of restriction was placed on the function of art by Schopenhauer, whose work was being studied and occasionally cited by Van Doesburg and Mondrian during these early years of *De Stijl*. Schopenhauer's conception of the viewer in pure, will-less contemplation of form sparked Mondrian's imagination in particular, and although Schopenhauer never completely divorced the notion of painting from a representational subject, he did anticipate the possibility of a highly abstract art:

The product of plastic and pictorial art does not present us, as reality does, with something that exists once only and then is gone forever – the connection, I

2 Theo van Doesburg, *Composition*, 1918 (gouache, 26.6 cm × 25.4 cm) Stedelijk Museum, Amsterdam (A6672); an almost identical version is reproduced in *Drie voordrachten* (p. 93) as the second in the series of *Three Creative Moments of a Composition*

3 Theo van Doesburg, *Composition XIII*, 1918 (oil on wood, 29.2 cm × 29.8 cm) Stedelijk Museum, Amsterdam (A29685); reproduced in *Drie voordrachten* (p. 93) as the third in the series *Three Creative Moments of a Composition*

4 Theo van Doesburg, *Still Life*, 1916 (whereabouts unknown); reproduced in *De Stijl*, I, no. 5 (March 1918), plate X

mean, between *this* particular *matter* and *this* particular *form*. It is this connection which is the essence of any concrete individuality, in the strict sense of the word. This kind of art shows us the *form* alone; and this, if it were given in its whole entirety, would be the *Idea*. The picture, therefore, leads us at once from the individual to the mere form; and this separation of the form from the matter brings the form very much nearer the Idea.[7]

Van Doesburg took the argument one step further, claiming that the Idea itself could be reached if the form were entirely divorced from the 'matter' (that is to say the individual circumstances), and thus it would be possible to go beyond the mere example to the rule itself; the 'universality of the concept', which was for Schopenhauer the preserve of philosophy alone, would be conquered by art. Havelaar accepted Schopenhauer's more conservative view, but was willing to admit the enormous expressive capabilities of art, writing of 'the manipulation of signs and symbols in the creation of plastic form for spiritual life, the illustration of idea. "Idea" as thought alone is conceived, but not yet born' (p. 114). However, Havelaar upheld, as did Bolland and Pit, Schopenhauer's conclusion that art 'never quite reaches its goal', that it can never reach perfection. There are limits to its expressive capacity. Paraphrasing Schopenhauer, Havelaar acknowledged that in man's dreams he becomes a great intuitive artist, sometimes creating images whose changing colour and rhythmic line conjure up extremely strong emotions. He continued, claiming that 'Kandinsky's art, being devoid of subject, is related to this kind of experience, but in that way also oversteps the bounds of the capabilities of art' (p. 15, n. 1).

On the other hand, even at this early stage in the development of his theory, Van Doesburg saw art, religion, and philosophy as parallel and in themselves fully adequate descriptions of the world. During the course of his 1915 lecture, 'The Development of Modern Painting', later published in *Three Lectures*, he divided the historical development of painting into three main periods analogous to his three categories of expression in art. In the first, the means of art (colour and form) are appropriated to some practical end, that is for some religious purpose; in the second, art becomes more independent when the means are explored more for their own sake than for the sake of narrative; but in the third period art becomes totally emancipated from the forms of nature. In this total abstraction of form from nature there was:

the disappearance of the object from painting, pure, cleansed art: the expression of our spiritual sensations by the composition of line and colour. Thus painting became what music has been for centuries – the pure subjective organ of man's genius.

Formerly, nature provided the means to clarify the Idea; the portrayal of nature became the form of the Idea.

In Kandinsky's work, Form and Idea flow together and we may well say that the Idea is the Form. [p. 27]

In the third period of development, art could actually reach its ultimate goal. He affirmed the possibility of an *absolute* art as opposed to Havelaar, Pit, Bolland, Schopenhauer, and Hegel. For Van Doesburg, there was no question of art ever being superseded by religion or philosophy as Mondrian believed along with the philosophers. Art could provide a direct presentation of the Idea as the fullest embodiment of truth. In 1915 Van Doesburg had already arrived at the conception of painting as 'visual philosophy', but he did not go as far as the Theosophist M. H. J. Schoenmaekers was to go the following year in *Principles of Plastic Mathematics*. The influence of Schoenmaekers on Van Doesburg did not come into its own in this respect until the developments beginning with his Dada-istic anti-philosophical stance in 'Caminoscopie' in 1921 and continuing through 'Painting and Plastic Art' ('Schilderkunst en plastiek – elementarisme') of July 1926.

As a completely adequate parallel to philosophy, art allowed the mind to grasp the absolute, or, as already quoted from Hegel concerning the Spirit: 'the finite . . . grasps its own essential universality, and, in doing so, grasps essential Being in the absolute sense'. The history of this process of enlightenment had been primarily the history of philosophy for Hegel, while for Van Doesburg it increasingly became the history of art. However, in both cases the history of the world disclosed a rational process and had an ultimate goal. This historical argument led Van Doesburg to the conclusion that the artists of De Stijl were the conscious instruments of an irresistible, almost inevitable, historical development. It has been protested that 'what is wrong is to impute the logic of the historians to the actors and perpetrators of the deeds' when discussing the history of art,[8] but for Van Doesburg history was inherently logical. It had its goal in the development towards abstraction as a revelation of Absolute Spirit. He was only acting in the role of midwife at the birth of the inevitable new style.

The revelation of Absolute Spirit allowed the finite mind to grasp its own universality, letting it transcend the tragedy of being bound by the particulars of the physical world and returning it to the realm of absolute balance and order. In terms of artistic production this meant the removal of the subject or narrative (particulars or accidentals of the physical world) from the work. The proper 'subject' of art is art itself, and the elementary means of art – line, form, and colour – are not to be used for any other purpose than to reveal harmony and balance within the new art of relationships. The whole history of art as explained in 'The Development of Modern Painting', his 1915 lecture, shows the irresistible movement towards abstraction. The argument was to be further elaborated in *Classic – Baroque – Modern (Klassiek – barok – modern)*, written in 1918, and again in 'The Will to Style' ('Der Wille zum Stil') of 1922, where he maintains that 'instead of the theory of rise, expansion, and decline [and to him a swing towards naturalism was a decline], I prefer the concept of a continuous evolution. This continuous evolution is one of the spirit in life and art, but in space and time it takes the form of rise, expansion and decline.'[9] In this he agrees with Schopenhauer's idea of 'true history', which sees beyond the vacillation of the course of events to the repeated application of a single theme by the human race as a whole, in much the same way as one individual applies reason to solve a particular problem. A proper application of this 'true' principle would extend man's 'narrow present of perception' to his vastly larger past experience and 'only in this way does he have a proper understanding of the present itself and can he also draw conclusions as to the future'.[10] This was precisely Van Doesburg's aim in his often-repeated detailed exegesis of the history of art, for example in *Three Lectures*: on a sound historical basis (Lecture I, 'The Development of Modern Painting') he established a theoretical structure (Lecture II, 'The Aesthetic Principle of Modern Plastic Art') for a style of the future (Lecture III, 'The Style of the Future').

In summary, he posited that art, religion, and philosophy are not only expressive of the same content, as for Hegel, but that Hegel's three levels of thought could be seen as three stages in art. The third, and highest, level of thought, that is pure abstract thought, is fully and adequately expressed in pure abstract art, that is in Neo-plasticism. In this stage of art, pure-form-as-Idea could only be reached by the rejection of narrative content and all natural references, and by the purification of the means of art by using line, colour, and form for their own sakes according to the necessity of their own intrinsic qualities, their *zelfs wille*. Finally, his analysis of the history of art revealed that this development from naturalism to abstraction is the abiding 'theme' in the logic of 'true history'.

Although Van Doesburg was familiar with the works of Hegel and

Schopenhauer and includes them in a list of books available to sub-scribers to *De Stijl* (in the April 1919 issue), his understanding of their philosophy was gained primarily from secondary sources. It has often been remarked that Theosophy had also had a considerable formative influence on De Stijl, most particularly on Mondrian. Interestingly Bol-land, the greatest contemporary exponent of Hegelian ideas in the Netherlands, attempted in his 1910 book *Schelling, Hegel, Fechner and the Newer Theosophy (Schelling, Hegel, Fechner en de nieuwere theosophie)*, to place Theosophy in a direct line of inheritance from Hegel. This was based primarily on the similarity of their respective concepts of Ideality and the development of spiritual awareness.

The clearest statement of what Bolland's aesthetic philosophy meant in terms of the arts themselves and their history was not written by Bolland himself, but by his former student Pit, who introduced his little book *Logic in the Development of the Arts (Het logische in de ontwikkeling der beeldende kunsten)* by saying that:

In this work some five essays, in which the products of the plastic arts are des-cribed as manifestations of a growing self-awareness, have been adapted from versions published in *The Journal of Philosophy* [*Het Tijdschrift voor Wijsbegeerte*]. These essays were the result of the study of the philosophy of Hegel, stimulated by the lessons of G. J. P. J. Bolland. Obviously I have fallen into the use of langu-age peculiar to my teacher. Of course that use of language, by which he has been able to render Hegel's profound ideas intelligible for a Dutch audience, leaves no room for improvement once the audience has been able to catch the drift. However, in my experience the language remains an insurmountable diffi-culty for those outside Bolland's circle who still brave reading his works, or those of his students.[11]

As the direct consequence of this density of language, members of De Stijl sometimes misunderstood Bolland's position, as will later become clear.

Pit's digested version of Bolland's argument was concerned with the cycles of the history of art and, as he himself said in his introduction, he saw works of art as symptoms of the level of self-awareness of their period. For example, the art of the Middle Ages was concerned with the creation of images of natural forms as symbols of divine intention. For the men of that period nature 'bears witness to God' (p. 15). Individual artists are submerged in the *Zeitgeist* in a collective struggle towards common goals. One could, claimed Pit, speak of a collective conscious-ness (p. 57). His basic definition of architecture likewise described each style as a 'moment' in the architectural 'train of thought', to speak in terms of the *bewustwordingsproces*, or style coming to conscious expres-sion. 'One need not seek any further for the reason behind endless change in styles of architecture than the endless movement of thought itself.' The fundamental nature of architecture which does not change is that it consists of planes held in proportional relationship (see pp. 69–71). It is 'space-determining thought', and as such is realised by mass, plane, line, and points in space – a conception of architecture close to that of both Van Doesburg and Berlage.

Havelaar's ideas on architecture, especially its relationship to painting, had caught the attention of Oud as early as 1916. In September of that year, Oud wrote an article about the importance of modern painting for architecture, where he drew upon what he understood to be philosophy of Bolland, and the critical writings of Van Doesburg, Erich Wichman, and Havelaar.[12] A concise summary of his ideas, which were in this respect of most interest to Oud and Van Doesburg, is in Havelaar's 1918 book:

We have already remarked that symbolical art is architectonic art; the art where the idea of 'style' evolved into the conception of an anti-naturalistic 'stylisation' [in the sense of the anti-naturalistic expression of an 'inward idea', or Platonic form – see Havelaar, p. 39]. This is an art which emerges from a rhythmical expression. (All architecture is in this sense ornamental.) We have already seen, and will presently even more clearly see, that such an art only arises when the general level of cultural life has built up with sustained spiritual tension towards the exalted dream of one all-embracing concept of the world. The culmination of symbolical and stylised art is in architecture. No longer is architecture first and foremost the creation of the isolated individual; it is the creation of the whole of mankind at this particular stage in its development. Each monumental spiritual act is a collective spiritual act. [p. 42]

In his article, Oud developed the argument in terms of architectonic painting which has rejected narrative or subject in favour of pure visual structure. This was much farther than Havelaar pursued, or indeed, was prepared to pursue, the argument. Oud had divided art into two broad types, direct representation or naturalism, and the architectonic or symbolical. The first was seen as an outward sign of materialism, even utilitarianism, and the second was a transcendental art concerned with 'essentialisation' as opposed to pure abstraction. Havelaar, and Pit, agreed with Oud and Van Doesburg that narrative is not the job of the plastic arts, that it must not be allowed to overshadow the plastic expression. Havelaar deplored the anecdotal nature of Hogarth and the illustrative or allegorical preoccupation of others (p. 117). Pit, in his turn, claimed that 'the products of some nineteenth-century painters, whose works astound the populace because they illustrate nice stories, prove only that the maker was mistaken in his choice of instrument, that he picked up an artist's pencil mistaking it for an author's pen' (p. 63). However, both Pit and Havelaar strenuously denied the possibility of an absolute art devoid of subject which was the avowed goal of Van Doesburg and Oud. As Oud wrote towards the end of his article: 'thus painting appears freer and more abstract, and develops from a *programmatic art* to an *absolute art*'. According to the philosopher and the critic, art essentialised nature, it was not in opposition to nature. The development for them was rather one from naturalism to transcendental realism. Havelaar disapproved of the Impressionists because

They had pretensions to absolute 'painterliness'. The evolution of art right up to Breitner is, formally speaking, to be understood as an evolution from the abstract, plastic line towards the sensuousness of colour, from the symbol to the sensation – as a slow, but steady growth towards absolute painterliness.

5 Willem Maris, *Zomerweelde – In the Lush Growth of Summer* (oil on canvas, 76 cm × 100 cm); auctioned in October 1943, present whereabouts unknown

Absolute painterliness is virtually divorced from reality. It brings to mind Willem Maris's statement . . . 'I do not paint a cow, I paint the light.' [pp. 89–90; fig. 5]

Van Doesburg's intention was similar to Maris's. His art was transcendental, that is, it dealt with ideals rather than attempting to reproduce visual phenomena from Nature.

This means (in terms of our example): the cow as draught-animal, as source of food, as product for sale; in a word: the natural animal disappears and becomes for the formative artist a complex of formative aesthetic accents, in colour-relationships, formal relationships, contrasts, tension, etc.

This was quite a different thing from a Platonic ideal, and Van Doesburg recognised the fact. He wanted to take the 'absolute painterliness', which Havelaar had disliked, to its ultimate conclusion:

The formative artist sees the cow also in combination with open space, the play of light on her flanks, he experiences the hollows and the prominences as *sculpture*; he sees the parts of the body between the forelegs and the hindlegs not primarily as belly or breast but experiences them as *tension*. He sees the ground on which the animal stands as *plane*. He sees no details, since features of the object do not interest him. The artist experiences animal and environment in organic cohesion. Should the animal begin to move, there will be new experiences for the artist. He observes a definite periodicity and a repetition of unequal movements which he experiences as *rhythm*.[13]

The elementary means of painting were to be used to produce icons of the elements of visual experience in their relationships. The stages of development towards such an art can be seen in *Three Creative Moments of a Composition* (figs. 1, 2 and 3) or in Van Doesburg's series *The Cow* (figs. 6a–d).

6a–d Theo van Doesburg,
original clichés for *An Object
Aesthetically Transfigured*:
(a) *Photograph*. (b) *Form
preserved but relationships
accentuated*. (c) *Form abolished*.
(d) *Image*, 1917, as published
in *Grundbegriffe der neuen
gestaltenden Kunst*,
Bauhausbücher 6

a

b

c

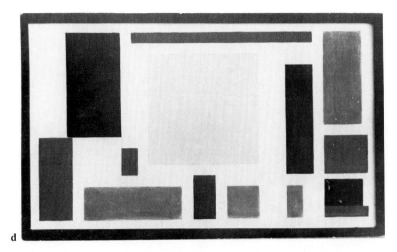

d

When Thijs Maris, Willem's brother, died in 1917, Van Doesburg defended him against the bitter attack of Bernard Canter, editor of the journal *Holland Express*. Canter, like Havelaar, disapproved of such attempts to reach an 'absolute art'. Van Doesburg's open letter replying to Canter drew to a close with a reference to the same quotation from Willem Maris: 'You say that Jacob [a third Maris brother] painted cityscapes, Willem, cows (certainly not just cows – also light) – precisely so, but Thijs painted spirit and in so doing used a minimum of reality.' Canter published the open letter and further provided an editorial reply in which he noted that 'Mr Van Doesburg is soon going to found a new periodical called *The New Style*. Hopefully this defence of Thijs Maris is not a sample of what his new style is, otherwise it is to be feared that his choice of words will not be able to assure him the public that his good intentions deserve.'[14] The first issue of *De Stijl* appeared the next month.

Canter, Havelaar, and the more traditional critics and philosophers had no sympathy for art which was all form and no content. For Havelaar, the harbinger of the new age was Puvis de Chavannes, whom he likened to a latter-day Giotto in his figurative and very linear style (p. 91). This attitude was shared by many artists involved with the periodical *Wendingen*, most particularly R. N. Roland Holst, who himself produced murals for Berlage's Stock Exchange in Amsterdam. Roland Holst's treatment of the human figure, as seen in his design for a stained-glass window for the Dutch Pavilion at the Paris Exhibition of 1925 (fig. 7), shows obvious similarities to the style of Giotto, and of course the influence of Puvis de Chavannes.

Van Doesburg relied heavily on the German art historian Wilhelm Worringer for support in the argument concerning form and content. Lecture II ('The Aesthetic Principle of Modern Plastic Art') of *Three Lectures* was modelled to a great extent on Worringer's book *Abstraction and Empathy (Abstraktion und Einfühlung)*. Van Doesburg delivered the lecture at a meeting of the professional architectural association 'Archi-

tectura et Amicitia' on 20 December 1916 and an aggressive debate ensued. The debate was continued in the periodical *Architectura* and Van Doesburg prefaced his defence with two quotations from Worringer's book:

1 The primal artistic impulse has nothing to do with the rendering of nature. It seeks after pure abstraction as the only possibility of repose within the confusion and obscurity of the world-picture, and creates out of itself, with instinctive necessity, geometric abstraction. It is the consummate expression, and the only expression of which man can conceive, of emancipation from all the contingency and temporality of the world-picture.

2 The essence of cis-Alpine art consists precisely in the fact that it is incapable of expressing what it has to say with purely formal means, but that it degrades these means to bearers of a literary content that

lies outside the aesthetic effect, and thereby deprives them of their own specific quality.[15]

Unlike Van Doesburg, Worringer did not insist that the whole of history was moving steadily towards abstraction; he preferred to see historical development as a 'circling orbit' around the two poles of abstraction or spiritualism, and empathy with nature, or materialism.

This dualism of nature and spirit was strongly echoed in *Philosophische Kultur* of 1911 by Georg Simmel, a German sociologist. According to him: 'Architecture is the only art in which the great struggle between the will of the spirit and the necessity of nature issues into real peace, in which the soul in its upward striving and nature in its gravity are held in balance.'[16] Architecture expressed the triumph of man over the forces of Nature. If through time and decay the building were to fall into ruin, this would become an icon of man's futile struggle towards immortality. This is the enduring theme of history in Simmel's view, and would be absorbed into Van Doesburg's theoretical position of a modern humanism more profound than what he saw as the egocentric humanism of the Renaissance.

Simmel's dualism between 'the will of the spirit and the necessity of nature' was one which had important consequences for the useful arts such as architecture and industrial design. In Van Doesburg's estimation, the useful arts were in their turn central to the new humanism and the practical re-building of Europe after the devastation of the Great War. In order for the Spirit to find expression within the restrictions of the necessities of nature, obviously the conditions of both the aesthetic and the practical realms must be satisfied. The laws of form and line, the elementary means of art, must be followed in the most direct solution of the practical problem to achieve an expression of the Spirit's victory over the limitations of nature. Man could virtually become a prosthetic god. It is of crucial importance, however, to distinguish Simmel's and Van Doesburg's position from functionalism:

The handle belongs to the enclosed unity of the vase and at the same time designates the point of entrance for a teleology that is completely external to that form. It is of the most fundamental interest that the purely formal *aesthetic* demands on the handle are fulfilled when these two symbolic meanings of it are brought into harmony or equilibrium. *Yet this is not an example of that curious dogma which makes utility a criterion of beauty.* For the point at issue is precisely that utility and beauty come to the handle as two unrelated demands – the first from the world, and the second from the total form of the vase. And now, as it were, a beauty of a higher order transcends both of these claims and reveals that their dualism ultimately constitutes a unity that is not further describable. Because of the great span between its two components, the handle becomes a most significant clue to this higher beauty. Till now, art theory has hardly touched on this kind of beauty which contains beauty in the narrower sense merely as one of its elements. Formal beauty, together with all the demands of idea and life, is incorporated by what one might call superaesthetic beauty into a new synthetic form. Beauty of this ultimate kind is probably the decisive characteristic of all really great works of art; the fact that we give it recognition divorces our position sharply from any aestheticism.[17]

Simmel used the handle as an example only because it is the simplest of the whole class of objects inhabiting these two realms, the spiritual and the material. The design of that class of objects, instructed by the formal discoveries made in the art of painting, was to be the basic means for the creation and expression of the spirit of the age. Man could raise himself from the tragedy of slavery to Nature, and rediscover the paradise of dominion over Nature. Van Doesburg was to adopt these ideas in the following version: to conquer Nature, the requirements of both the practical and spiritual realms had to be fulfilled. Exploration was being carried out in industry towards the satisfaction of material and production demands, while experiments were being carried out in the free art of painting towards the satisfaction of spiritual requirements by the aesthetic manipulation of the elements of pure form.

The ways in which form could be manipulated were the subject of Heinrich Wölfflin's 1915 book *Principles of Art History (Kunstgeschichtliche Grundbegriffe)*. In it he described two fundamental approaches to form in painting, the linear and the painterly.

The great contrast between linear and painterly style corresponds to radically different interests in the world. In the former case, it is the solid figure, in the latter, the changing appearance: in the former, the enduring form, measurable, finite; in the latter, the movement, the form in function; in the former, the thing in itself; in the latter, the thing in its relations. And if we can say that in the linear style the hand has felt out the corporeal world essentially according to its plastic content, the eye in the painterly stage has become sensitive to the most various textures, and it is no contradiction if even here the visual sense seems nourished by the tactile sense – that other tactile sense which relishes the kind of surface, the different skin of things. Sensation now penetrates beyond the solid object into the realm of the immaterial. The painterly style alone knows a beauty of the incorporeal. From differently orientated interests in the world, each time a new beauty comes to birth.[18]

In terms of style these approaches corresponded respectively to the Classic and the Baroque. The Classic was concerned with the static build-up of absolute form, the Baroque with movement over the whole surface of the composition. The Classic was a closed composition with horizontals and verticals echoing the edges of the canvas, while the Baroque emphasised the dynamic of the oblique, opening the composition and rejecting the contrived rigidity of Classicism.

The idea of movement in painting, Jaffé rightly concludes, was to culminate in Van Doesburg's Elementarism and cause his split with Mondrian. Jaffé quotes a passage from *The New Movement in Painting* in his book *De Stijl, 1917–1931* and concludes that since life is in constant movement, as posited by Van Doesburg, De Stijl itself must also be kept in constant movement. Jaffé finally states that Van Doesburg's conception 'was not the result of his dispute with Mondrian; it had already been expressed in 1917, in his *New Movement in Painting . . .*'.[19] That little booklet had first been published as a series of articles dated May to August 1916. The quotation cited by Jaffé used precisely the same terms as those found in the lecture 'The Development of Modern Painting' written in October of the previous year, but during the short intervening period which corresponds with the publication of Wölfflin's *Principles of Art History*, the terms have gained entirely new significance. In the earlier lecture Van Doesburg defines 'this continuous transformation' as 'the *movement* [*beweging*] or evolution of art'[20] and thus speaks of this 'movement' in a purely historical sense, whereas in the book *The New Movement* he has begun to speak of movement as the 'subject' of painting after the manner of the Cubists who 'see their model-in-movement as a self-transposing multiple construction in space'.[21] Significantly, the Cubists do not figure in the earlier argument, and Mondrian had no reservations about the earlier sense of movement as development. Even in the entrenched position of his later years Mondrian still maintained that 'Neo-plastic work is deduced from life, of which it is at the same time, from continuous life, which is "culture", evolution'.[22] Jaffé is correct in stating that it was movement which was at issue, but he does not distinguish clearly between movement as a subject in painting and movement as changes of style in painting.

As has already been noted, the intervening period between writing 'The Development of Modern Painting' in October 1915 and 'The New Movement' in May 1916 significantly corresponds with the publication of Wölfflin's book. Movement as the 'subject' of painting, not in the superficial way in which the Futurists attempted to paint a moving subject, but the 'model-in-movement' of the Cubists, and especially the idea of the primary elements of painting themselves setting the whole canvas in motion, were the ideas which captured Van Doesburg's imagination at the time and were later to have significant effects on his painting and architectural projects.

Wölfflin's method in Chapter I was to outline first the linear, second the painterly, and then to arrive at section three the 'Synthesis' (the opening lines of which have been quoted above on p. 20), where he stated a basic argument which was closely related to Van Doesburg's. Wölfflin denied the idea of perfect imitation:

As even the most perfect imitation of the natural appearance is still infinitely different from reality, it can imply no essential inferiority if linearism creates the tactile rather than the visual picture. The purely visual apprehension of the world is *one* possibility, but no more. By the side of this there will always arise the need for a type of art which does not merely catch the moving appearance of the world, but tries to do justice to being as revealed by tactile experiences. [p. 29]

Van Doesburg rejected imitation outright. Art should not be subject to Nature but to its own independent, intrinsic laws of form. His argument proceeded dialectically from Classic (thesis) to Baroque (antithesis) to Modern (synthesis). In December 1918 he completed a definitive statement of the argument in his other booklet, *Classic – Baroque – Modern*:

It is not absolutely necessary to bind these three stages to particular periods in history as happens with the dogmatic theory of art. We must take this description as broadly as possible and not in such a restricted sense. Thus every work of art where the harmony between essential being and phenomena, or between

Spirit and Nature, is expressed by means of natural form, as for example the human figure, *is* Classic even if it is a contemporary work. Each work in which the capriciousness of passing phenomena has the upper hand *is* Baroque, even if it is a contemporary work; whereas if there has been an attempt to create a balanced relationship between Spirit and Nature, or between the Universal and the particular, purely by the use of the essential means of art and not the manner of Nature, the resulting work *is* Modern in the fullest sense of the word.[23]

The categories introduced here after a study of Wölfflin were significantly different from the three stages of art which Van Doesburg had discussed previously in *Three Lectures* (see above, pp. 7–12). The basic principle which did not change was his definition of the essential characteristic of Modern art.

In *Three Lectures* Van Doesburg began his historical narrative with the Italian 'Primitives' Cimabue and Giotto. Their painting, he maintained, was primarily illustrative of the religious sentiments of their period, and to this end they had entirely subordinated the basic painterly elements: 'The "what" was given pride of place; the "how" was secondary.' Here the subject ruled the means of artistic production and the main purpose of Van Doesburg's argument was 'to bring you to see, in contradistinction to modern painting, what a scanty position painting's *free end* [*zelfs wille*] held' (p. 6). His history of art was entirely concerned with the increasing pre-eminence of this *zelfs wille*, until in its final expressive purity it would reveal the absolute inner essence of life, thus becoming a concrete example of the reconciliation of the material and the spiritual.

The relationship of these ideas to those of Kandinsky is easily established. Van Doesburg might as well have quoted the passage on the 'how' and the 'what' straight from *Concerning the Spiritual in Art*:

In such periods art ministers to lower needs and is used for material ends. It seeks its content in crude substance, because it knows nothing fine. Objects remaining the same, their reproduction is thought to be the aim of art. The question 'what?' disappears; only the question 'how?' remains. By what method are these material objects reproduced? The method becomes a rationale. Art loses its soul.
The search for the 'how' continues.[24]

Secondly, *zelfs wille* is a concept closely related to Kandinsky's idea of 'inner necessity'. Jaffé described this 'law' as 'alien to everything that Mondrian was striving for', that is, objectivity, and it would be expected that this would also hold true for Van Doesburg. Herbert Read would emphatically agree, having stated that 'the test, the standard of judgement, is always subjective – in this Kandinsky identifies himself with the expressionist theory of art. "That is beautiful which is produced by inner need, which springs from the soul".'[25] Read had previously implied that Kandinsky was already aware of Worringer's *Abstraction and Empathy*. In the foreword to the 1910 edition Worringer speaks of the re-establishment in artistic practice of the abstract artistic volition 'not arbitrarily, but from inner developmental necessity'.[26]

Abstraction for Worringer was first and foremost a revelation of the inner thing-in-itself as it was for Van Doesburg and Mondrian, whereas for Kandinsky it was a revelation of inner (psychological) man. One critic tried to reconcile these two positions by demonstrating that they are not incompatible since each is 'a revelation of a more fundamental reality'.[27] That the question arises at all is a consequence of the fact that Kandinsky tried to capitalise on both the subjective and objective sides of the argument. For him 'internal necessity' was comprised of three elements: first, art is the revelation of the individual artist and hence subjective; secondly, it is the revelation of the spirit of the age, which can be construed as objective; and thirdly 'every artist, as a servant of art, has to help the cause of art (this is the quintessence of art, which is constant in all ages and among all nationalities)'. Subsequently he underscored this third element: 'the pure and eternal art is, however, the objective element which becomes comprehensible with the help of the subjective. The inevitable desire for expression of the *objective* is the impulse here defined as "internal necessity".'[28]

A further similarity between Van Doesburg and Kandinsky was that they both considered the concept of the essential means of art, the *zelfs wille* of Van Doesburg and the 'internal necessity' of Kandinsky, to be a central theme of the history of art and his own work to be at the apex of historical development. But, unlike Van Doesburg, Kandinsky's primary concern was not to demonstrate a compelling unidirectional movement from naturalism to total abstraction; he merely wished to demonstrate those aspects of abstract expression which had been realised to varying degrees. Van Doesburg, by contrast, attempted to place the whole weight of history behind his argument, to give an air of inevitability to the accomplishment of his artistic objectives.

The general consequences for painting of the concept of the essential means of art are relatively easy to imagine. This will be studied in some detail particularly in connection with Van Doesburg's work in stained glass. The consequences for architectural design are not quite as obvious, but will become a theme central to the analysis of Van Doesburg's architectural projects. The problem was posed and to some extent a general direction was indicated by Wölfflin:

Painting *can*, architecture *must*, be tectonic. Painting only develops its own peculiar values where it emancipates itself from the tectonic: for architecture, the abolishment of the tectonic scaffolding would be equivalent to self-destruction. What in painting belongs of its nature to tectonics is only the frame, but the development proceeds in such a way that the picture parts company with the frame: architecture is specifically tectonic and only decoration seems to comport itself more freely.

Nevertheless, the weakening of tectonics, as the history of representative art shows, was accompanied by analogous processes in architecture. While it seems far-fetched to speak of a-tectonic architecture, the notion 'open' composition as opposed to 'closed' composition may be used without objection. [p. 149]

The distinction drawn here is between visual and actual tectonics, or structure, a distinction which was to find direct echoes in Van Doesburg's introspective criticism related to his first architectural

projects in co-operation with Oud in 1917, and its consummate realisation in the Aubette a decade later.

Experiments with the elements of pure form in painting and stained
glass established a basis for Van Doesburg's development towards an
elementary 'style of the future' for architecture. From tectonic painting
developed a constructive architecture; from an ideal and utopian theory
developed a practice which, although initially modest, became increasingly influential in the 1920s. Van Doesburg's experimental activities
continued, despite personal setbacks, until the end of his life. On 12
February 1931, Arp, Giacometti, Herbin, Hélion, and Kupka gathered
at Van Doesburg's newly-built house at Meudon where they named their
new group 'Abstraction-Création'. Less than a month later, on 7 March,
Van Doesburg died of a heart attack in Davos, Switzerland.

Letter of 24 May 1919
from Van Doesburg
to J. J. P. Oud and his wife

Dear Bob and Piek (or Piet),

. . .

What is so beautiful about the new creativity [Neo-plasticism], lad, is that *all of us* in *everything* we do are working on a single problem. If everyone realised this they would forget about their individuality to a large extent. They would no longer be of the opinion that they could each still achieve something else for themselves. If they accomplish something other than this Single Problem, then it just goes to prove that something is wrong. The French and Italians don't realise this either. The more I read their periodicals and the more letters we exchange, the more I am convinced that for the most part they represent the decayed old intellectual attitude. We, on the other hand, are rather the primitives of a new intellectual attitude . . . . We actually stand apart [from other radical groups] in a certain sense. We are in fact '*isolés*', and it is the source of our power to remain so. We can't by any means consider making alliances with the enemy (as Wils and Huszar). . . .

. . . I got a completely different view of Mondrian through his theosophical confessions [last week]. It is terribly difficult to put it in writing, but in short he believes that after our work nothing more can develop. This work is developing as the highest stage in the plastic arts – and then comes the sixth sense. *La peinture est finie!* . . . I defended the idea that we are the transition towards something else, just as Cézanne provided a transition towards our art. Everything is in a *Mouvement perpétuel*! Mondrian is actually a dogmatist, and in terms of his dogma (with all due respect!) he doesn't know what to do with the fourth dimension. . . . He did admit that I was much more advanced in my work and theory, but maintained that the *Plane* was the single and absolute consequence of all creativity. He is indifferent to many subjects such as architecture, communism, etc. When he left I had a vague impression that he had indeed opened up theoretical and cultural possibilities, but still that he had in practice got bogged down. Perhaps his move to Paris was necessary in order to open up new possibilities in his work – to freshen it up. His last works have no real composition. The division of the plane is in a single module, which are therefore just ordinary rectangles of equal size.

[*Composition*, 1919]

25

Contrast can only be achieved by colour. I also find this work a bit opposed to his theory . . .

One thing and another have given me a lot to think about. For myself, I feel that many still don't realise that only a radical stance can realise our aims, and I believe that those of little faith who must feel the 'wounds' in the body of God before they believe that those wounds were made for the sake of truth, are not our true brothers.

Oh well, we'll just go slowly onwards. . . . Thank goodness my hay-fever is just about over. Now mate, all the best to you and your wife, from the two of us,

Your friend,
Does

[letter in the Van Doesburg Archive, R.B.K.]

Part I

1

◇◇

The early years of *De Stijl*: national and international contexts

Theo van Doesburg declared in the introduction to the first issue of *De Stijl* that it was the object of the magazine to unify the modern trends of thought which had been developing internationally, and to a great extent independently, in artistic, architectural, and even farther afield in literary and philosophical circles. Advances were being made separately in all these areas to pave the way for the new cultural epoch, but the ultimate goal could not be achieved until these independent advances were brought together into one self-consistent movement. Tracking Van Doesburg's inspiration and the lines of influence originating in all the various sectors of this vast watershed of ideas involves a wide-ranging study of the sources both at home in the Netherlands and beyond, in France, Italy, America, and Germany before the outbreak of the First World War.

In the years preceding the founding of *De Stijl*, Van Doesburg had been successful in publishing articles and letters in various Dutch periodicals and thus was able to reach a sizeable public with his revolutionary ideas. Although he found a number of supporters for his approach, he found no suitable organ where he and his sympathisers could concentrate their efforts to provide a solid basis for a front line of attack on his many opponents. He had become increasingly convinced that a radical cell must have a focus for its activities where its unity and discipline could be demonstrated. Deviations from an established party line would threaten the fragile existence of a small formative radical cell in a generally liberal-minded and individual-orientated artistic climate. Had Van Doesburg allowed too much individualism within the collective and adopted a less stringent editorial policy, the group would have been quickly re-absorbed into the established stream. In his eyes, this stubborn individualism was preventing the emergence of a new universal style as a reflection of the new age. In terms of his historical argument derived from the Hegelian tradition, the birth of the new universal style was a historical necessity.

A new periodical was needed to champion the new universal style. Peace was just coming into sight again when Van Doesburg founded *De Stijl*. His editorial introduction, which launched the enterprise, was the distillate of years of practical and theoretical work, a statement of intent, and as one reviewer quite rightly expected, 'a declaration of principles'.[1] As Van Doesburg outlined in the introduction to the first issue, the purpose was in the first place to stimulate an awareness of the new directions in art, and by theoretical exegesis make the public more receptive to those trends. By way of logical argument, the ripening style was to be put forward as a manifestation of a purer relationship between the spirit of the age and the aesthetic means of expression. The various arts had each made a certain amount of progress in this direction and the editor of *De Stijl* intended to unify their achievements, and extract from them a general critique of art and society. He was not interested in what society saw in art, as expounded by the critic or layman, but in what art had to say about society, as expressed in the introspective writings of the artist. In the contemplation of the problems of art, he could cull a theoretical position from his practical accomplishments. Ultimately he could formulate a new vision of the world and lay it before the public along with its social consequences and the possibilities it opened up for reform. The socialisation of art required the artist to renounce his personal strivings on behalf of a higher universal and ultimately social end embodied in a new universal and organic style. Van Doesburg's editorial introduction continued:

[This periodical] will thus prepare the way for a deepened artistic culture based on a *collective* embodiment of the new awareness of plastic art. As soon as artists in the different branches of the plastic arts come to the realisation that in principle they are all alike, that they all speak a *common* language, then they will no longer cling jealously to their individuality. At any rate, they will not *in any way* serve a universal principle with a restrictive individuality. Serving a universal principle, they will automatically generate an organic style. In order to *spread* the new idea of the beautiful, not a social, but a spiritual community is necessary, and that spiritual community cannot arise without the sacrifice of ambitious individualism.

Only from a new relationship between artist and society arising from the consistent application of this principle can the new plastic beauty reveal itself, in all things, as *style*.[2]

He obviously had no intentions of founding yet another artistic social club with an official voice. He wanted rather to bring together those artists who had, until then, been working in comparative isolation towards a common goal, the new international style.

Review copies of this first issue of *De Stijl* were sent to various established periodicals. The response was strong, and on the whole sceptical. The editorial in *Bouwkundig Weekblad* complained that

In *De Stijl*, clear argument gives way to the introduction of several fancy phrases, vague generalisations which are for a thinking man not simply to be accepted without question . . . What is 'plastic' consciousness? What is the spirit of the age? What does all this mean? Is there no explanatory material [*significa*] needed for these peculiar terms, such as exists for legal or mathematical language?[3]

Van Doesburg's prose, it is true, is particularly dense (having been influenced by the language of Bolland and Pit) and the full theoretical position was by no means explained clearly and concisely in the editorial introduction, but then that is hardly to be expected. The clarification of the theory, this *significa*, was the *raison d'être* of the periodical itself; it could not be accomplished in one article. On the other hand, Van Doesburg had come a long way towards a precise and highly elaborated answer to the taunting questions of his critics. All of the most important aspects of this *significa* had already been worked out, at least in outline, in his copious articles of the past few years. Whether or not the reviewer was aware of Van Doesburg's other publications and lectures, he held out little hope for the success of the *De Stijl* venture: 'it is too bad; it could have been good, but *De Stijl* is travelling the same road as many brochures and *Signalen* in which modern ideas are being expounded'. The implicit comparison of the artists of *De Stijl* with the neo-Symbolists and neo-Impressionists grouped around the periodical *Het Signaal* was hardly appropriate because they represented the very 'pseudo-modernism' which Van Doesburg so strongly condemned.[4]

Comments in *Architectura* were coolly limited to a pre-publication announcement in their 8 September issue. The new periodical was not much better received in *De Wiekslag*, which had itself been recently founded in May of the same year. It was the journal of the group of painters known as 'De Onafhankelijken' (the Independents). Van Doesburg may have expected a somewhat more sympathetic hearing from this source since the 'Independents' had some of the earliest Dutch abstract artists in its membership, not to mention the fact that he had been a founder member in 1916. He thought well of both theoretical and practical work which had been produced by members of the group. For example, Erich Wichman (mentioned incorrectly in *Architectura* as a member of De Stijl) contributed 'New Directions in Painting: Cubism, Expressionism, Futurism' to the series *Pro en contra* (IX, 1, 1914) which had impressed Van Doesburg, and the year before the founding of *De Stijl* Van Doesburg had dedicated a short book to one of the central figures of the group: *The Painter De Winter and his Work*. Though Wichman was a co-editor of *De Wiekslag*, it was the editor-in-chief, Alex Booleman, who reviewed the first issue of *De Stijl*. His reaction to their initial efforts was similar to that of the reviewer in *Bouwkundig Weekblad*.

We of the Independents cannot help but applaud such an attempt. Therefore we will continue to follow the endeavours of *De Stijl*, although we have reason to doubt that they will achieve their declared aim in consideration of the editor's unclear introduction. An introduction amounts to a declaration of principles, and as such must not at any rate be wanting in clarity of thought.[5]

Even if he remained sceptical, Booleman was at least willing to wait for further results. That is not to say, however, that he reserved judgement entirely. In his rather extended critique of the introduction, he found serious fault on a number of points centring around Van Doesburg's idea of the role of the artist as theorist and critic. Van Doesburg declared that the artist was far in advance of society as a whole in the creation of a new conception of beauty. The professional critic not only failed to make the public more receptive to this new conception, he tended to be hostile to it himself. In such a situation it was up to the artist to take over as critic and theorist in order to put his own case before the public. Booleman disagreed, saying that the artist could create a new conception of beauty, but that the public consciousness of that beauty was a function of social development and could not be brought about by what might be seen as the addition of footnotes to works of art, even by what Van Doesburg chose to call the 'truly modern artist', whatever that might mean. The most effective way to reform aesthetic notions was through the work of art itself. The work of art which had to depend on a body of theory was to that extent a failure. Artists forced to write about their art were simply admitting the deficiency of their proper means of expression.

Booleman had complained about the lack of clarity in Van Doesburg's use of language, and that certain principles on which the journal was founded had no basis in fact. The final assault, however, was reserved for Van Doesburg's insistence that artists spoke a universal language and must sacrifice their individuality to the collective effort. The ferocity of Booleman's objection, with an impassioned defence of the 'strongly personal language' and the supreme individuality of the artist, is evidence enough of his heavily expressionistic leanings. Despite all the incorrect hypotheses and inherent fallacies he saw in the argument, he denied being unsympathetic to the magazine. On the contrary, the other articles in the issue contained a good deal of interesting material. It seems that essentially he objected to the editor.

Van Doesburg's reply took the form of a letter to the editor-in-chief, dated 30 January and published in the March 1918 issue of *De Wiekslag*. There he did not defend his own editorial policies, he immediately took up the offensive, attacking Booleman for the discrepancy between his stated and applied editorial policy. *De Wiekslag*, said Van Doesburg referring to Booleman's editorial introduction, was founded with the intention of providing space for artists of any persuasion to address the Dutch public. It was to be a free, unbounded liberal periodical. In practice, Van Doesburg found, Booleman was over-indulgent with his editorial remarks and footnotes, effectively slamming the door behind his guests. In other words, the liberalism of the magazine was a sham, and many of the correspondents of *De Wiekslag* whom Booleman had denigrated in his liberal footnotes actually provided the real justification for its existence.

De Wiekslag, *Bouwkundig Weekblad*, and *Architectura* were the official publications of the most influential artistic and architectural societies of the day. As the mouthpieces of such large heterogeneous groups, they were bound to accept an open-ended editorial policy. In opposition to this, *De Stijl* was openly and unabashedly sectarian with Van Doesburg serving as watchdog for the purity of its ideological content. In his position he was dictatorial and unafraid of conducting outright purges to ensure that purity (as will become abundantly clear in his dealings with Huib Hoste).

What was to become the prime example of the liberal periodical was officially announced in December 1917[6] and made its first appearance

in January 1918. The editorial secretary of this new magazine was
H. Th. Wijdeveld, who launched the first issue as if in prophetic
revelation:

Like the harbingers of an era in which we shall return to a purer vision and
concord will be found, many tidings come from the world where the seekers
abide – brief messages from those who, with a calm gaze and steady pulse, lead
the inquiry and set the trends; but there are also the strange sounds of those
who are feverishly ransacking the Californias of artistic expression as in a gold
rush for hidden treasures.

It is a matter of finding a balance between thousands of ideas gyrating in
terrifying acrobatic feats on the highwires and tightropes of art's development,
but how often they fall into the abyss of oblivion.

Here are our pilgrim wanderings [*wendingen*] through all these artistic statements and our gracious compliments to those trends which vigorously pioneer
the approaching harmony. Here alongside architecture in its new development
of pure structure, we acknowledge the full glory of the emergence of the Fantas-
ists playing guilelessly with the treasures of rationalism. Here we enter the
domain where rigid wall masses are transformed into supple architectonic forms
which playfully follow the cadence of spatial development.[7]

The periodical being introduced was appropriately titled *Wendingen*, 'a
monthly for building and decorating from "Architectura et Amicitia"'.
Van Doesburg summed up the new offspring of *Architectura* in a searing
article in *De Stijl*:

The periodical *Weathercock* . . . appears under the pseudonym *Wendingen*, which
describes its contents perfectly (its motto: 'you never can tell', or 'wherever the
wind blows, there go I'). It is the Dutch continuation of the periodical *Der Ring*,
founded in Düsseldorf in 1908 and edited by the architect Lauweriks (a periodical
which smelled strongly of Vienna and the Werkstätte). On this axis, *Wendingen*
makes its Cubistic revolutions. . . .

Whether the developments can justifiably be called *Cubist* remains to be seen.
Cubism is the optical/mechanical consequence of the Latin spirit and culture,
is it not? Considering that fact, then, the magazine, wending its own kinky way,
appears rather to have Expressionistic wiring. It is a beast with Cubo-
Expressionist scales and a Symbolist-Expressionist tail. A product of the Baroque
in modern form, but born too late, tame, and not at all dangerous. Even Roland
Holst before long will be trusted by the little beast.[8]

Van Doesburg pretended that it was not necessary to take *Wendingen*
very seriously, and indeed it is mentioned only half a dozen times by
name in *De Stijl*, but what he considered its dishonest liberalism and
downright eclecticism were repugnant to Van Doesburg, and in direct
opposition to the aims of *De Stijl*.

In his opposition to these major official publications, Van Doesburg
made potential enemies of the most powerful critics, artists, and architects in the Netherlands. In the association 'Architectura et Amicitia'
alone, the membership as of 1 January 1918 included such distinguished
architects as K. P. C. de Bazel, Dr P. J. H. Cuypers, W. Kromhout, J.
Gratama, M. de Klerk, P. Kramer, J. L. M. Lauweriks, J. M. van der Mey,
M. Brinkman, P. J. G. Klaarhamer, the writer and artist R. N. Roland
Holst, and what may come as a surprise, Jan Wils. Berlage himself was
the honorary chairman of the society.[9] With Jan Wils on the list, it is

obvious that members of these organisations were not *per se* enemies either of Van Doesburg or *De Stijl*, but Van Doesburg's willingness even to risk the opposition of such powerful groups was a daring enterprise. In fact it was not just a risk, he had purposefully set out to polarise approaches to architecture – to make it impossible to sit passively on a fence. For him there could be no compromise amongst a thousand individual approaches. He aimed to singularise the *De Stijl* position by keeping it untainted by any eclecticism whatever.

During the year prior to the founding of *De Stijl*, Van Doesburg had also participated in the founding of more heterogeneous groups, 'De Anderen' and 'De Sphinx'. Both were dedicated to abstraction, but were strongly affected by Expressionism. However, he was at least able to find support here for his insistence that 'nature' and 'art' were two separate realms. On the other hand he was unhappy that so much artistic power was being dissipated in so many different directions, despite the fact that the artists had 'united' into a group. In his review of the first exhibition of 'De Sphinx', held in Leiden between 18 and 31 January 1917, he complained that:

The painting represented here is of many different characters and therefore not of a positive character. The leadership of this young but highly active club is made up of different elements. There is something to be said for this, but also a great deal to be said against it. The positive side is that the visitor gets an overview of coexistent directions. The negative side is evidenced by the fact that everything this kind of club achieves is diluted, because the members who neither feel anything for, nor understand anything of the work of the other members, are motivated only by *self*-interest and not by any common goals.

A movement which has a fixed goal can concentrate its power, and in so doing can become as much a cultural as an artistic force. At the present time, self-interest can only harm the common good: the renaissance of Plastic art and its socialisation.[10]

If he could not find powerful support for his artistic endeavours in terms of numbers, then Van Doesburg decided to seek it in the establishment of a small, disciplined radical cell united behind a single purpose. Thus driven to found yet another group, he won converts in many different aspects of the arts, and gradually De Stijl was welded into the spearhead of an ideal. His stress on the socialisation of art helps to explain his insistence on the inclusion of architects in the movement. Architecture provides the envelope for, and therefore shapes, the everyday life of the people. In this way it could be used as a powerful instrument of reform. Life within art was the end, and architecture provided the 'environmental canvas' for the exploitation of the new means. Attacking the problem of the socialisation of art, the architectural efforts of the group were to be concentrated on experimentation with the dwelling, constantly thinking beyond the private house to the multiple dwelling.

The socialisation of art was naturally bound up with the success or failure of the critic in making the public receptive to the new concepts. Van Doesburg had opened his editorial introduction speaking of the 'new awareness of beauty' which was being shaped by the artists of the new generation who were readjusting the boundaries of consciousness. He continued his argument with the assertion that neither the public alone, nor the critics, could free themselves from the shackles of the old way of seeing. This was a repetition of what he had written in 'The New Movement in Painting' in the August 1916 issue of *De Beweging*:

A great vitality of spirit is needed in our time for this adjustment of the boundaries of consciousness. Why? Because the development of painting in the twentieth century is characterised by an ever-increasing tempo. History provides proof that the people of each epoch are always a few steps *behind* Art, instead of keeping *abreast* of it. They possess too little spiritual vitality, and are too conservative as far as the traditional conception of painting is concerned, to be able to pace the growth of their idea of art to the tempo of artistic development.

Criticism, whose business it is to make good the shortcomings of the public understanding, stands on the same level as public opinion, if not lower, and wallows hopelessly within the bounds of an old and comparatively worthless conception of art. Meanwhile, Criticism attempts to ameliorate its own failures at the foot of the artist. What a travesty! Was Criticism not intended to inform and direct the artist and not the other way round? In all honesty should Criticism not cease discussion of works of art whose aesthetic value is *beyond* its comprehension?[11]

Of course, critics in general were not very happy with these remarks, but some, most notably Bernard Canter, recognised this as a fair assessment of the situation. Canter was editor of *Holland Express*, a weekly publication with strongly religious and nationalistic overtones. It was the official policy of the weekly to encourage abstract tendencies in painting, but mostly within an expressionistic, or even symbolist framework. In Canter's review of Van Doesburg's paintings on show at the first exhibition of 'De Sphinx', the painter was congratulated for his expressive force and his moral rectitude in refusing to compromise his principles for monetary gain. Further, Canter was willing to recognise his own failings as a critic when confronted by certain examples of the new art, and he wholeheartedly welcomed the participation of artists themselves in critical activity, in order to clarify the basis of their revolutionary art.[12]

The basic separation between those critics who were willing, and those who were unwilling to hand their duties over to the artist, Van Doesburg found, was their attitude to abstraction. Canter was sympathetic to abstraction in art, and was willing to admit the limitations of his own understanding of the phenomenon. On the other hand, the architect C. J. Blaauw was, in Van Doesburg's terms, representative of the critic who had failed to keep abreast of the changes in art, thus remaining a prisoner of an outdated conception of painting. Blaauw published an article entitled 'A Concrete and Final Word in Reply to the Recent Abstractions of Mr Van Doesburg' in the 10 February 1917 issue of *Architectura*. The article was an attack on Van Doesburg's position as outlined in his lecture 'The Aesthetic Basis of Modern Plastic Art' (later to be published in his book *Three Lectures*), held on 20 December 1916 before a general meeting of Architectura et Amicitia. Wijdeveld published a summary of the meeting, including the lecture, in the

13 January 1917 issue of *Architectura*. As before, contention arose primarily over the role of the artist as critic. Wijdeveld summarised Van Doesburg's contentious ideas as follows:

The time came when naturalism in painting was supplanted by the plastic, and the art critics (mostly laymen) no longer knew what to say, because their yardstick, Nature, was nowhere to be seen.

  Therefore the public stood on the side of the critics, distrustful of the new movements. Mr Van Doesburg described it as a happy turning point that artists now speak and write about their own work.

Blaauw's reply, in the form of an open letter, urged the reading public of *Architectura* not to recognise Van Doesburg as the true champion of modern painting, ironically enough because of Van Doesburg's arguments on behalf of abstraction. From Van Doesburg's point of view, the logical and historical necessity for the movement of art towards the formal and abstract was of central importance to his programme, and the critical elucidation of this historical progression was the only way to enlighten an artistic public trapped in the mimetic conception of art. A clear knowledge of the new art 'based on a pure relationship between the spirit of the age and the means of expression' was the only liberation for the public from its prison of antiquated ideas, allowing it to stand fully conscious and receptive before the new way of seeing.[13] The new awareness on their part and the growing communion with the modern artist would stimulate a more profound artistic culture, which would develop not according to rules of taste imposed largely from outside, by critics who were involved in art only on an intellectual level, but according to a self-consistent logic discovered by direct experimentation with the pure means of art themselves. For this new experimentation leading to a deepened artistic culture, a new mental attitude was demanded of the artist. Just as the natural scientist must discipline his personal fantasies by a cool objectivity, so must the experimental artist sacrifice his narrow search for an individual revelation, and turn himself outwards to join the new communion in the attempt to uncover the universals of art. Van Doesburg held on to this idea of painting to the very end. In *Art concret* he wrote: 'L'évolution de la peinture n'est que la recherche intellectuelle du vrai par la culture de l'optique' (p. 3). Such research demanded a collective effort in the study of the universal language of art and the development of a new relationship between society and the artist. Where the Symbolists and Expressionists were struggling towards self-fulfilment in personal revelation, Van Doesburg's goal was to co-ordinate the work of a team of artists for the socialisation of art in the realisation of a new architecture based on the elementary language of form.

  However, the stark reality of contemporary Europe had for years placed choking restrictions on experimentation and development. During the first long years of the war it seemed that cultural advancement had ground to a halt, and the artists of the Netherlands were left clinging to the ideas, and struggling with the unfinished work, of the revolutionary artistic movements which had uncompromisingly confronted pre-war Europe. Van Doesburg summed up the situation in his book *Three Lectures*, decrying the fact that in the wake of the war many artists 'reverted to one or other outdated style, or stayed safely within the set canons of one of the new modes of expression. They affected Cubism, Expressionism, Impressionism, Symbolism, Romanticism, yes even pseudo-Classicism' (p. 87). There were others, however, who had the courage to continue the logical development beyond those earlier movements. In painting, Mondrian, Van der Leck, and Van Doesburg had all made independent progress towards the further purification of their art. They did not allow themselves to become wholly transfixed by painting alone. Van Doesburg especially kept abreast of advances in many other fields, in particular the philosophy of Bergson, socialist thought, the movement in literature from Mallarmé and Rimbaud through to the Dadaists, and the ideas coming out of the Werkbund culminating in the Cologne exhibition of 1914. He recognised all of these as potential contributors to the growth of the new artistic culture. *De Stijl*, although it was the Dutch contribution, was to be so effective because of these international roots and the continuing international contacts.

During the war nationalism was the order of the day and Van Doesburg's internationalism brought him under attack. Dirk Roggeveen, a neo-Impressionist and member of 'De Sphinx', claimed that the artists of De Stijl were actually in the pay of the Austro-German culture-machine, and that Van Doesburg especially was the champion of German culture and ideas. However literally Roggeveen meant the accusation, he was serious enough to close with: 'Enfin, in spite of it all, we remain Dutchmen and I love my country too much to allow us to be bowled over [*overschetteren, sic*] by any foreign culture.'[14] On the part of De Stijl, the criticism was taken seriously enough to warrant a reply. Oud took up the call on behalf of Van Doesburg, protesting that material aid from foreign sources had never been sought and, more to the point, that the motive for the inclusion of foreign members was not to further German, Austrian, Italian, or French ideas as such, but 'that on the contrary, the editor is working to advance the *international* character of modern art *in the most general sense*; and that it is remarkable that *this movement originates in Holland*'.[15] His stress here on the Dutch origin of the movement is not for narrow nationalistic reasons, but to defend it from those who, like Roggeveen, saw it as an attempt at cultural invasion and occupation.

In the first year of *De Stijl*, the international content was provided primarily by Gino Severini. Elzas, Van Doesburg's assistant during the design of the house at Meudon, quoted Van Doesburg as commenting that:

The early death of the poet Guillaume Apollinaire took away a committed defender of the will to produce a new art but, filling his place, Gino Severini wrote to us enthusiastically: 'J'ai toujours dit que nos recherches étaient un retour à l'école (qui n'est pas l'Académie des Beaux-Arts) pour cela vers l'art *anti-individualiste et collectif*!'[16]

The parallel between Apollinaire's contribution to Cubism through his critical writings, and Severini's contribution to the defence, explanation, and publicity of *De Stijl* is a singular honour, coming from Van Doesburg. Severini's credentials as foreign correspondent for the periodical were indeed immaculate. The work he produced as a painter was a successful blend of Cubism and Futurism. His close participation in the avant-garde circles of Paris provided a contact for the Dutch group with the artistic giant of Europe just rousing itself from the initial shock of the war. Both Severini and Van Doesburg were re-thinking the artistic accomplishments of the pre-war period, and Severini's articles for *De Stijl* were very much in the spirit of the editorial introduction; on the basis of experimentation with the means of art, he set out to produce a new critique of the role of the modern artist.

In an article appearing in the second issue of *De Stijl*, Severini initiated the series 'La Peinture d'avant-garde', in which he drew heavily on his Cubist and Futurist experience, but produced an interesting new synthesis in terms of a machine aesthetic. Whereas the machine had previously provided the subject-matter of his art, he now proposed the more abstract notion of mechanisation as a new means for the construction of a more profound reality. Artistic production in these terms became analogous to invention: 'En continuant jusqu'aux extrêmes limites ces raisonnements, il serait facile de créer une esthétique qui, pour être logique, devrait supprimer le mot art (ne signifiant plus rien) et le remplacer par les mots: création scientifique, ou industrie' (p. 20). What still distinguished art from real machines was that art was an end in itself, striving towards universals. Great contemporary intellectual achievements were reshaping man's view of society, his world, and the universe. Art was beginning to participate in this reconstruction and to this extent had a philosophical content. The nature of this philosophical content he explained in the following passage:

Tous les efforts des peintres d'avant-garde tendent vers l'expression de ce réalisme nouveau qui, étant tributaire de la sensation et de l'idée, avait été défini par moi dans mon article précédent; réalisme idéiste ... On pourrait l'appler 'idéaliste', mais ... il y a deux 'idéalismes' très différents. Un qui vient de *idéal* et qui est 'l'expression d'un état d'esprit moral ou religieux, synonyme de spiritualisme', et l'autre qui vient de *idée*, et qui est une 'conception philosophique du monde'. (Platon, Schopenhauer, Bacon, etc.) C'est ce dernier idéalisme, prenant sa base sur la matière et sur la forme qui s'identifie avec l'art, c'est pourquoi j'ai cru devoir l'adopter dans cette expression: réalisme idéiste, qui le définit sans possibilité de doute. [pp. 18–19]

The series of articles offered support to Van Doesburg's ideas on a broad basis. The third of the series ventured into a discussion of 'Mesuration de l'espace et 4e dimension', a subject which had already been lightly touched upon by Van Doesburg, and which was to grow steadily in importance throughout the years. The two men agreed that progress in this area was the most important single contribution made by the Cubists: they had developed a means of disintegrating the spatial object and reconstructing it in a temporal dimension, that is to say, reconstructing it from many points of view simultaneously. As the articles continued, Severini explored the work of the philosopher/mathematician Poincaré to confirm a space of '4 or n dimensions', and drew parallels in the world of art. He described the relationship between the philosophical and artistic realms, saying that 'cette 4e dimension n'est en somme, que *l'identification de l'objet et du sujet, du temps et de l'espace, de la matière et de l'énergie.* Le parallélisme du "continue physique" qui, pour le géomètre, n'est plus qu'une hypothèse, se réalise par le miracle de l'art'.[17] In conclusion he confirmed Van Doesburg's stand that it was the duty of the modern artist to go beyond the accidentals of particular phenomena to the universal content, the 'Platonic' idea. For him, as for Van Doesburg, the purification of the means of art was the proper route towards a closer definition of the common language of art. The derivation of the value of the work of art from its uniqueness and originality was a notion of the past; rather, as Severini stated: 'je pense que l'esthétique collective et anti-individualiste à laquelle je viens de faire allusion prépare une époque d'art réalisant enfin l'universalité et le style'.[18] Van Doesburg could hardly have wished for a foreign correspondent who was more fully atuned to his own theoretical position.

Severini continued in the service of *De Stijl*, reviewing the accomplishments of the Futurists and Cubists in an article published at the beginning of the periodical's second year. In that, he pointed to an earlier and highly successful exploration of some of the above-mentioned ideas in the literature of Mallarmé and the Symbolists. He then proceeded to trace those ideas through the work of the Impressionist, Cubist, and Futurist painters. This kind of activity, the contemplation and analysis of pre-war accomplishments, accounted for a great deal of time and effort expended by Van Doesburg during, and immediately following the war, as evidenced by his copious lectures and writings of the period. Under his influence, Oud wrote an article for *Bouwkundig Weekblad* entitled 'Cubism, Futurism, Modern Architecture'. There he emphasised the importance of the new developments in painting for, and in combination with, architecture. He began:

It is becoming clearer and clearer that the new movement in painting is going to develop in the direction of a high and monumental art. Modern attempts appeared to have reached an impasse, but it is beginning to manifest itself again, and at the present time the attention of architects may again be turned that way because this painting is going to be of more importance to them in the future than was the case in the foregoing period.[19]

Proceeding further in his argument, Oud quoted from Van Doesburg's 'The New Movement in Painting' as it appeared in the periodical *De Beweging* in instalments over the immediately preceding months (May to September 1916). The quotation is concerned with the use of pure elementary plastic means as an end in themselves rather than for any mimetic purpose. The painting is not a reproduction, but what Van Doesburg terms a symbol, of the natural object. Oud then re-emphasised the distinction which Van Doesburg had drawn between 'plastic' and 'optical' artistic expression. The latter was defined as conveying emotion by means of a subject with a natural, historical, or allegorical setting. On the other hand the purely plastic expression, in a very Kandinskian sense, gave direct expression to emotion by form and colour. This was the direct transfer of sensation, the contemplation of pure form without the disturbance of a natural subject as interloper. The ultimate aim of art was not the reproduction of nature, it was to create an image of the Idea, the Absolute Idea. Pure form was the proper content of the work of art; the plastic means of art, colour, line, and plane were to be used in the revelation of proportion, balance, and unity. In Van Doesburg's terms, the work was a symbol of the Absolute Idea as conceived in the spirit of the artist.

In producing such a symbol, the artist opened a channel of communication with the spirit of the observer. In the July instalment of 'The New Movement' (*De Beweging*, 1916, p. 62), Van Doesburg wrote that 'Cézanne put together the new alphabet of painting, and the Cubist is forming this into the Language of Plasticism which is only spoken *from* spirit *to* spirit'. Echoing this statement and 'quoting' from *The Beautiful and Art* by Professor Bolland (at the time the main Dutch exponent of Hegelian philosophy), Oud expanded his argument as follows:

Thus painting becomes independent and abstract, and changes from a *programmatic art* into an *absolute art*. It becomes *symbolic* because it presents no fixed reality but only sensations of reality, and the words which Bolland wrote about architecture are also applicable to painting, namely '*dat door haar niet rechtstreeksch geest tot geest vermag te spreken*'.

The Dutch is included here because as 'quoted' it is ambiguous. It can be read either as: 'that through it [architecture], not directly, spirit can speak to spirit'; or as: 'that through it, spirit cannot speak directly to spirit'. From the context of the argument, Oud clearly intended it in the former meaning. Bolland's actual words were:

[Plutarch said of the Parthenon that] the sweet smell of blossoms drifted up from its everlasting beauty which can never be marred by time. It retains its bloom and the soul of eternal freshness. In that way all masterpieces of architecture are signs [*teekenen*] of the spirit without being perfect expressions [*kenteekenen*] of spirituality. Works of architecture are not only material through and through, but are also manifestations of proportion, in which the spirit has become concrete without spirit being able to speak directly to spirit in those determinate forms [*zonder dat uit de vastgelegde vormen rechtstreeks geest tot geest vermag te spreken*]. Architecture is still the pre-eminently 'symbolic' art.[20]

Bolland's meaning was clearly the second of the two possibilities noted above. It is difficult to see how Oud arrived at his interpretation unless he was relying on memory rather than using the text itself.

Oud obviously meant the 'quotation', or rather paraphrase, to support his argument, but such a reading is impossible to reconcile with the Hegelian basis of Bolland's philosophy. The kernel of the misunderstanding lies in the confusion and conflation of philosophical and artistic terms, namely in the use of the word 'symbolic'. For Hegel symbolic art was the lowest, not as for Oud and Van Doesburg the highest, developmental stage in art: 'in *symbolic art* the human mind struggles to express its spiritual ideas but is unable to find an adequate embodiment'.[21] A more careful reading of the enlarged quotation from Bolland reveals that he was in full agreement with Hegel on this point. Because of the material requirements of architecture and in the process of the spirit's becoming concrete, much of the essence of that spirit, or the Idea it conceives, is lost in the work itself. Van Doesburg considered that the spirit of the painter could speak directly and adequately to the spirit of the viewer by means of the newly formed 'Language of Plasticism'. Oud agreed and testified to the perfection of the embodiment of the idea by referring to painting as an *'absolute art'*. Having stated that, he moved straight on to say that is was symbolic. In Hegelian terms at least, that contradicted the immediately preceding statement. For Bolland, art was undeveloped religion, and philosophy was the perfect and absolute religion. Art could never aspire to the adequate expression of the abstract, because then it would have left the sphere of art and become philosophy:

Thus in a single art we shall neither ourselves learn to seek, nor even discover a search for, the true art as the all-embracing and absolute art or art of the absolute, in which the absolute seeks and finds, is sought and found. After thinking through art in general, we shall have to do the same for the individual arts, but without expecting that we shall come to know absolutely in a single art the capabilities of the absolute within us.[22]

The members of De Stijl wished to invert this classification. During the developmental history of art, it had long been bound in the service of religion; Van Doesburg was attempting to bring religion and philosophy into the service of art. Until then, the mimetic in art had confined its content to the particular; if it could be freed from all traces of naturalism, the proper subject of art (that is the abstract idea or universals) could be expressed.

The fact that Oud had quoted Bolland in support of these ideas clearly indicates that the members of the group had misunderstood Bolland's philosophical position, not just used parts of it in the construction of an eclectic philosophy as a basis for their artistic theories. Bolland recognised that he himself had departed from the letter, not to say the spirit, of Hegel's thought when he declared, 'Great is the spirit of Hegel, – but in 1900–1910 pure reason speaks Hollands and Bollands';[23] that is to say, not only had Dutch, or *Hollands*, superseded German as the most philosophically precise language, the particular brand of *Hollands* which had superseded Hegel's German was Bolland's own peculiar *Hollands*. Van Doesburg upheld the validity of this claim and recognised Bolland as an important source of De Stijl ideas when in his turn he wrote in 1919:

The Romans conquered the Greeks, but the Greek spirit conquered the Romans. It is not impossible that it will be the same with the German spirit. One only has to consider the influence that the philosophy of Hegel has had, and still has, on the whole of our intellectual life through the teaching of Bolland.[24]

Ideas, the dialectical method, and 'Hollands-Bollands' (a particularly dense language), were all assimilated from the writings of the Hegelian philosopher. Notwithstanding the misconceptions, there were many areas where the philosopher made valuable contributions to De Stijl theory. Oud could have found many more useful passages for citation, for example:

Imitation alone does not create a work of art. The work of art as a conception of reality is clarified perceptibility of ideality, plus the tangible ideality of sensation and the imagination which dominates the reasoning of the artist. Therefore, the knowledge of the very root of reason shows itself in the artist: the wisdom of art is unreasoned reason, not thought through, undeveloped, and not yet risen to higher power. . . . However, he who in this connection still might think it fitting that there be some repetitions, imitations, and mimicry, and bound up in this some realism and naturalism in art, has not yet considered that the art of architecture has already risen above the imitation of nature. Neither has he considered that there is nothing in nature, nor anything objective which is a given of our perception, which is acknowledged in the musical work – nor are tunes and melodies, chords and harmonies offered up by the fowls of the air. In the kingdom of sound, man must draw the factors, elements, and relationships in the work of art out of themselves.[25]

The ideas found in this passage, namely the support of abstract art, the comparison of architecture and music, and especially the basis of music (and by implication architecture) as elements in relationship, will all find numerous echoes in the early writings of De Stijl. The elements-in-relationship actually amounts to the same thing as the 'words and syntax' of the new Language of Plasticism whose discovery Van Doesburg had attributed to Cézanne and the Cubists. This language was common to all the arts, and it was Oud's purpose in writing his article to begin the reunification of the arts with a co-operative effort in architecture and painting. Painting would open vast expressive possibilities for architecture, and architecture could produce a more conducive atmosphere for the contemplation of painting. The Villas 'Allegonda' and 'De Vonk' were to be the collaborative practical test of this theoretical position.

The lessons taught in the new language of the Cubists which were most important for the architecture of De Stijl were: in the first place, the purification and abstraction of form towards a more contemplative art freed from the fetters of naturalism, temporality, and the mundane; stemming from this was the purification of the painterly means, revealing the possibility for a similar development in architecture; last, but eventually to be given pride of place, was the introduction of time as a new dimension in painting by the denial of the use of perspective based on a single point of view. When the Futurists discovered the new language of Cubism, they quickly began to contribute to the development of its syntax. Antonio Sant'Elia attempted to realise an architecture that until then had only been conjectural.

From mid-1919 Sant'Elia received a great deal of attention from the members of De Stijl. Van 't Hoff dedicated an article to the study of his architecture, concluding that there was a lamentable absence of detail to create a convincing reality, and further that there was some discrepancy between the proper use of material and its structural function. Notwithstanding these shortcomings, the idea as a whole, in combination with the application of new advances in building techniques, placed the work of Sant'Elia firmly within the modern international movement. His complete independence from historical references opened whole new areas of formal possibilities. To drive home this point Van 't Hoff quoted the eight points of the 'Proclamation' from Sant'Elia's Futurist manifesto of architecture. There, the familiar anti-decorative sentiment, the synthesis of the useful and the beautiful where 'the decorative value of the architecture of the future depends solely on the use and original application of the raw or bare or strongly-coloured material', lends yet more support to Van Doesburg's stress on the importance of colour in composing the pure independent means of architecture.[26] Another important point forwarded by the manifesto was that architecture must become a direct reflection of the spirit of man. The Italians, Van Doesburg would claim, had derived this idea from Hegel via Gentile in the same way that the Dutch had discovered it in Hegel via the writings of Bolland.[27]

At the beginning of 1920, Oud reaffirmed the interest of the members of De Stijl in the work of the Futurist architects. He stated that Sant'Elia's greatest contribution to architecture was his struggle against 'passéist' architecture, but he continued with the warning that purely formal experiments of this type could very easily lead to a new facadism as it had for the Futurist architect Chiattone. However, Sant'Elia's method of working from interior to exterior and his complete independence from romanticism and decoration prompted Oud to compare his work with the accomplishments of Van 't Hoff at Huis ter Heide.[28]

The De Stijl attitude to the Futurists found its origins in Van Doesburg's critical writings as early as 1915. While he at first rejected Futurism as superficial, later in his lecture 'The Development of Modern Painting' he recognised its importance as the inheritor of Cubism in its continuation of experiments with simultaneity and space-time. According to him they broke no significant new ground, but in the true spirit of the international movement they embraced all the arts and attempted to divorce art from mimeticism. He was not entirely uncritical of the movement, but he was happy to praise their accomplishments, especially the fact that they were 'a slap in the face of all classical and quasi-modern movements in art'.[29] Van Doesburg's subsequent participation in Dada activities was to a certain extent the result of a wish to do a bit of agitating himself.

In his discussion of the work of Sant'Elia and Chiattone, Oud contended that as opposed to the Futurists' self-conscious and one-sided search for an aesthetic for a limited life-span architecture, the Americans had achieved the same in practice.[30] The influence of American architecture in general, and Frank Lloyd Wright in particular, was mainly through the first-hand experiences of Berlage and Van 't Hoff. Berlage had travelled through America on a lecture tour in 1911, published *Three Lectures Held in America* in 1912, and *Memoir of an American Journey* in 1913. In the last-named, it is easy to see that he had been quite impressed by new developments in American architecture, although he did not allow himself to be carried away in a flood of enthusiasm. The core of his assessment was that the Americans were asking the same questions, and to a great extent were arriving at the same answers as their contemporaries in Europe. The advantage enjoyed by the Americans, however, was that they did not have to fight the ghosts of a strong tradition. Berlage presented these ideas early on in his argument, and then towards the end of the book he returned to re-emphasise them in connection with a publication by Wright:

It has been my intention to present reasonably extensively the ideas developed here, because it is important to hear someone of Wright's stature preaching his ideas on style and its development, and that is important because in the final analysis it seems that the same things which are driving forces here in Europe at the present time are also at work in America. The same ideas elucidated by the same arguments appear both there and here, while it seems from the manner of presentation that Wright has developed these ideas completely independently. Here he names only Sullivan as a precursor of these ideas. A spirit freed from all tradition has taken the floor. That is, of course, not to say that Wright denies any bond with, and thus any dependence on the past. It rather goes to show that he is clearly conscious that the architecture of the past is not to be copied, but to be understood in connection with the circumstances within which it arose.[31]

Having declared their independence from stylistic historicism, the modern movements in Europe and America were working towards a common goal. Their unity of purpose, Berlage considered, lay in their search for a more universal beauty. However, in an extended quotation from Wright is to be found a discussion of individuality as an ideal of the American democracy and the basis of their architectural taste. To reconcile the apparent conflict between the two statements, Berlage read Wright as advocating not the narrow individualism of the styles, but a broader individualism, the individualism of the thinking man, free of this tunnel vision in regard to the past and 'taste'.[32]

The distinguishing marks of this more universal beauty, which Berlage recognised in Wright's work, were not surprisingly themes which recurred again and again in his own writings and which had to a great extent been realised in his own architectural works, albeit within a different stylistic vocabulary. First there was the play of masses and planes against each other: 'as opposed to the more planar character of the old styles, Wright applies himself to the creation of a plastic effect by a play of mass and plane'. (Incidentally, what could be a more concise description of Wils's 'De Dubbele Sleutel'?) In the second place there was the full acceptance of the machine, its aesthetic, and its products, as opposed to the unmodern rejection of the machine typified by Ruskin and Morris. Finally there is the restraint of economy as the controlling principle. According to Berlage, commerce and industry were the sources of the new building types, not, as was previously the case, religion and the temple. In pursuing this train of thought, he discussed the Larkin Building with unhesitating enthusiasm:

The building presents itself as a great, heavy mass, with huge wall-planes at the corners where the staircases are housed. Between the enormous planes and separated by pillars which run the full height, are the beautifully-set windows. The building has a flat roof, the walls are left undecorated, and the pillars alone have a horizontal articulation on the top floor. A single piece of sculpture is set by the entrance. The same sober but pithy treatment of detail is used on the interior, which is clearly the signature of the exceptional artist. The material is brick, red on the exterior and yellow on the interior; the floors are concrete. Together they lead naturally to a straight-angled geometry.[33]

The architects of De Stijl held these values and intentions in common with Wright and Berlage, but as Berlage had already remarked, Wright provided only one of the interesting formulations of both question and answer on these issues. Van Doesburg personally shared Berlage's admiration of Wright's accomplishments, but was not quite so unequivocal in his praise. In his comments accompanying a photograph of the Larkin Building reproduced in his *Three Lectures* (p. 99), Van Doesburg lauded Wright's high level of achievement, but contended that he had not yet reached a truly universal and monumental solution (p. 101).

In the pages of *De Stijl* itself, it was Van 't Hoff who provided the most comprehensive analysis of Wright's work. Although the discussion in the articles 'Architecture and its Development' did not disagree with Berlage's assessment, it did take quite a different tack. He began by describing Wright as one of the few architects who produced sound theoretical exegeses while at the same time going a long way towards realising his programme in practice. This in its turn could lead to further developments towards the delineation of a twentieth-century architecture. Van 't Hoff was particularly impressed by Wright's ideas on composition, and quoted him as saying that 'the architecture must not be "thrown up" as an artistic exercise, a matter of elevation from a preconceived ground plan. The schemes are conceived in three dimensions as organic entities, let the picturesque perspective fall how it will.'[34] Design should proceed neither from a fixed plan, nor from the elevation, but from the section, so that the demands of use and structure can be fully integrated within the rational geometry of that particular building. The series of articles in *De Stijl* continues with a technical discussion of the Larkin Building and Unity Church, and then beyond to survey techniques developed since they were built.

Oud's references to Wright in the early issues of *De Stijl* are much more in the mould of those of Berlage in his *American Journey*. In 'Art and Machine' which appeared in the third issue, Oud described painting and architecture, particularly that of Wright, as moving towards a pure expression of the spirit of the age in the realisation of a machine aesthetic. At this point, like Berlage, he took the opportunity of firing a broadside at Ruskin and Morris. In the next issue, he continued his comments on the machine aesthetic, this time in connection with the Robie House. Here Oud, as Berlage had before him, praised the method of designing from the interior out with the resulting spatial organisation and massing becoming the direct expression of the enveloped function. The play of masses was the origin of the visual effect and 'this inter-

8 J. J. P. Oud, *Design for a
Factory and Offices*, 1919;
reproduced in *De Stijl*, III, no 5
(March, 1920), plate VI

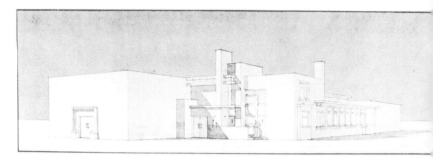

penetration opens new ethical possibilities for architecture on a purely
constructive basis. These means are far greater than those with which
our modern architects, known as the Amsterdam School, attempt to
arrive at plastic form by using fussy detailing.'[35] The primary means
of architecture – structure and the possibilities inherent in the materials
– provide their own aesthetic, not the application of detail and decoration
as a secondary means.

Direct formal references to Wright's buildings can easily be traced in
the early architectural works of the group and indeed this has been
carried out quite thoroughly in more recent criticism.[36] The question
arose whether this did not constitute just another kind of copyism only
in a more modern form. Van Doesburg adamantly denied this. When
he published an illustration of Oud's design for a factory at Purmerend
(fig. 8), Van Doesburg seems to be answering precisely such an accusation, stating categorically:

I think that the houses of the American Wright are so good because no aesthetic
a priori has been applied. The secret of originality is hidden in that approach.

Oud knows this. His design is therefore free of Wrightian influence. It has
no Wrightian connection at all, because it is the consequence of an idea of building already in operation and fully under control.[37]

He claims, therefore, that it is only the rejection of any fixed *a priori*
principle which Oud has in common with Wright. Perhaps it was also
considered that design for function was so consequent and determinate
that there were bound to be stylistic similarities as a result. The precise
aesthetic solution here, however, does not appear to have been so inevitably determined by functional demands as Van Doesburg would suggest.
There are, of course, any number of functionally appropriate solutions
and treatments of material which would not produce quite such a
Wrightian face as appears on the right-hand side of the drawing, for
instance the two quite different treatments of the central and left-hand
sections of the building. To balance this comment, it is also necessary
to remark that as far as Van Doesburg's architectural work is concerned,
similarities to Wright remain on a very general level of intention and
principle, and hardly penetrate at all to stylistic matters.

Oud, Berlage, and later Van Doesburg himself, all remark on the similarity between the work of young America and young Germany. Oud
echoes Berlage's sentiment that the advantage enjoyed by the Ameri-

cans was the lack of a strong, established architectural tradition. In fact, he summarised Berlage's argument so succinctly that it is worth quoting at length:

The works of Wright first became better known after the visit of Dr Berlage to America. In Germany they were known earlier, which cannot be surprising because there exists a great similarity between the strivings of the young Americans and the young Germans before the war.

The distinguishing mark of both movements is namely the urge to unify the material and spiritual needs of the day. In the formative days of young Germany, as with the young Americans of today, there arose the tendency to link up the great technological and commercial developments with art and vice versa. This trend reveals itself in architecture in the search for the aesthetic solution of the modern building problems presented by the department store, the factory, the office building, machine rooms, etc. Especially Behrens and Olbrich (after Messel) achieved eminence in this field.

In this area, German art had the legacy of tradition to bear, which, by a lack of critical discernment, worked counter to the achievement of a pure form of expression. Because of this obstacle, the movement began to crumble, and the struggle towards simplification and purification took the wrong path, in the direction of classicism. Examples of this were to be seen by the score at the Werkbund Exhibition in Cologne, held just at the outbreak of the war.[38]

The Werkbund had created a stir in the Netherlands as great, if not greater than had Wright. The former was a working example of a collective effort with the combined might of art, industry, and trade united to a significant extent behind the ideals of Muthesius. Emerging from the Arts and Crafts movement, the Werkbund over the years freed itself more and more from the craftsy applied ornament of Jugendstil and embraced the machine aesthetic. From the very beginning of the organisation there had been a struggle between the factions supporting what Van Doesburg termed the individualist approach of Van de Velde and the engineer's aesthetic of Muthesius and Joseph August Lux. The Werkbund yearbooks of 1912, 1913, and 1914 (all of which were in the De Stijl library) testify to the continuing presence of the purely decorative element in architectural composition. However, in the work of Behrens and Gropius, and also in the photographs of railway stations, trains and ships, an aesthetic consequent on industrial techniques was being promoted.

Muthesius's book *Culture and Art* was translated into Dutch and published in Amsterdam in 1911. The book produces a strong argument for the co-operation of art and industry as a reflection of the modern spirit. Perfectly describing his ideal for the Werkbund, he introduced a group that (as opposed to the artists of the Jugendstil whose misunderstanding of the modern movement produced the mere appearance of modernity) was already attempting:

to set themselves apart in order to express their own personal lives. Obviously it is only the spiritually advanced who are under discussion here. After all, a culture is always created by the few, by those whose interests are predominantly of an intellectual nature: the spiritual 'producers', artists, the learned, thinkers, and generally the independent souls in all areas of human endeavour. At present they form the core of such a group which is in the process of strengthening and expanding itself in order to unite the far-flung patches of cultural advancement into a great and pure ground on which a noble and pure culture can flourish on as broad a basis as possible.

Such a group, then, should point the way in the direction of the pure spirit and of the straightforward [*zakelijk*] work in every sector and in all expressions of the personal will.[39]

Further in the text he referred to this group as a cultural aristocracy, but in spite of this elitist position the ultimate goal was always a popular, national culture. The machine played the major role in this development because of the volume in which it could produce articles of the highest quality, economical, durable, and aesthetically pleasing even though the machine process led more and more to the stripping away of superfluous decoration which had previously been equated with beauty. The central argument can be summed up in the following quotation:

Besides the social situation, the new economic relationships have contributed to the reformation of our aesthetic insight. The age of mechanisation began about the same time as the rise of the bourgeoisie. Until then the machine had been used only infrequently, and then only in a technically imperfect form, but thereafter it became one of the most important factors in social development. Before long, railways and steamships replaced coaches and sailing vessels. With thousands of whirring axles and flywheels, the factories arrived and flooded the market with innumerable new articles. The whole countenance of our way of life changed within a half-century – yes, it was wholly revolutionised. An enormous quantity of iron was hauled out of the ground and worked into all kinds of forms. Consequently, a new class developed, that of the engineer. The engineers stretched a network of traffic over the earth, they created motorised vehicles, spanned rivers and valleys with bridges, built mighty works in iron and glass, and they designed machines to mass-produce our objects of use by the millions. It is, then, also worth considering the outward appearance of the engineer's creations with which we are surrounded. Here we find the undecorated object of use, without ornament, without any trace of the old decorative aesthetic. Further, we see that we have already become used to these forms, and to a certain extent even find them beautiful. A beautiful ship can certainly be seen from an aesthetic point of view. The roof of a station with its calculated span built only of iron and glass, can surely be viewed with the same eye that viewed the Colosseum in ancient Rome. Who doesn't feel the fascination of the modern bridge made of slender rods of iron, with its giant span and heroic impression; and doesn't the modern electricity station with its rows of gigantic machines awake the same fascination? [p. 87]

Muthesius pitted himself firmly against what he considered to be the fantasies of Van de Velde, and went so far as to single him out as 'the enemy' in his book; however, Muthesius was quite willing to recognise the artfulness and talent which Van de Velde so often displayed (p. 17). His applied decoration was indeed 'modern', that is to say it was not a revival, but it was *applied*, superfluous and self-indulgent. 'This disease [of Jugendstil] was exaggerated and emphatic rationalism' (p. 18), whose decoration served no practical end besides being uneconomical.

On the whole, Van Doesburg sympathised with the ideas of Muthesius, but the two had completely different definitions of Rationalism. At the same time, Van Doesburg could not agree with the antiquated Rationalism of Van de Velde with its romantic notion of the machine and its lip-service to industrial production. As the Cubists had not followed abstraction through to a totally abstract art, so had the Rationalists' practical work only realised the intentions expressed in the theory to a primitive degree. They compensated for their shortcomings in the handling of the pure primary means of architecture by the use of secondary means, applied decoration. Van Doesburg considered that the use of the 'sinuous line' by Van de Velde was the result of his clinging to his individualism and to sentimentality. The consequence for his architecture was that, even after he managed to reach a *zakelijk* form, it remained a personal, and therefore not a universal expression. In 'The Will to Style' of 1922, Van Doesburg acknowledged Van de Velde's contribution to the process of the purification of architectural form, but he made it clear that he had no use for the 'sinuous line' when he condemned Oud for his application of forms reminiscent of those of Van de Velde in his own projects, such as the housing at the Hook of Holland.[40] On a theoretical level, in fact, Oud was much more under Behrens's influence, as evidenced by his praise of the German master for his contribution to 'an enduring dialogue between theory and practice' – praise he had previously heaped on Wright.[41]

The work and message of Behrens was also of considerable interest to those architects who ranged themselves around the periodical *Wendingen*. When he visited the Netherlands in 1922, his comments on the latest developments in Dutch architecture were eagerly sought, and his subsequent arbitration of the dispute between the two opposing groups of his admirers showed all the acumen of the practised diplomat:

The speaker roused everyone's interest when he turned to the contrast between the Rotterdammers and the Amsterdammers, as reflected in the periodicals *De Stijl* and *Wendingen*. A few passages from *Wendingen* (considered by the speaker to be the best periodical) clarified the standpoint of the Amsterdammers: the bondage to the demands of material and the brief must be overcome – the young architect stands above the material, the spirit rises above the physical. While the Amsterdammers talk of the 'classicism' of Rotterdam, in Rotterdam the direction taken by the Amsterdammers is considered 'romantic'. Indeed such a distinction may well be drawn, even though the art of both groups is utterly modern. This touches on the age-old distinction between two approaches: that of logical/mathematical thought, in the spirit of Archimedes, as opposed to sentiment; the machine as opposed to handicraft; the useful as opposed to the personal; construction as opposed to growth. Without wishing to take up sides, Behrens had the impression that the architecture of young Rotterdam, notwithstanding its 'classicism', was in fact rich in romantic beauty, and that the architecture of Amsterdam gives an adequate reply to the demands of modern living.[42]

The interest expressed by the Dutch in the Werkbund and its architects reached its peak at the the time of the Cologne exhibition of 1914. To whet the appetite of the Dutch, there had been a small photographic exhibition of the work of Muthesius in Haarlem just a month before the grand opening of the Werkbund exhibition. The great event took place on 15 May; almost immediately the Dutch began organising excursions, and the 4 July issue of *Architectura* reported that plans were being hammered out for a *Hollandsche Werkbond* 'in the main the same as the *Deutsche Werkbund*' (p. 221). In the months which followed, a series of articles in *Architectura* covered the exhibition in detail for the benefit of those who were unable to attend personally. However, reviews of the Werkbund exhibition were not entirely uncritical. The Germans were accused of cultural imperialism in the name of an as yet unripe 'German style', and in their haste to impress the populace the Werkbund had been reduced to a mere commercial advertising, albeit on a monumental scale.[43]

The Dutch were represented in Cologne by Berlage, Lauweriks, and Van Anrooy, but only on a very small scale. However, these first-hand experiences with the Werkbund sparked great admiration and excitement at the thought of the possibilities offered by such a *Driebond* (a unity of three: art, industry, and trade) to the Netherlands. On 27 June 1914 Jan Gratama, editor of *Bouwkundig Weekblad*, published an article called 'The German Werkbund and its Significance for the Netherlands'. He was terribly enthusiastic and could hardly find praise enough to do it justice. He lauded machine production, industrialisation, and modern techniques, borrowing a battle-cry from another enthusiastic writer: '*with machine and large-scale industry against ugliness*'. The stirring conclusion was:

> Therefore, over and above the directly practical, economical, and useful by-products, the great significance of a Dutch Werkbond is the vigorous modernisation of the Netherlands.
> It is the duty of modern, progressive citizens to unite in a Dutch Werkbond, in order that any backwardness in our culture may be banished, and that in terms of modern civilisation, the Netherlands may again come to stand in the forefront of the ranks of nations.[44]

The day following the publication of these words, Archduke Ferdinand and his wife were assassinated. As the war ballooned, enthusiasm for the Werkbund shrank. What at first appeared to be a great cultural advance now took on the complexion of cultural imperialism. Just a fortnight after Gratama's bubbling review, the designer W. Penaat published an article on precisely the same topic. Although the war was only a few days old, the reaction was startlingly powerful, as shown by his summary of the German attitude:

> 'We shall be able to overwhelm the trade of the whole world for the coming centuries if *we*, Germans, only succeed in impressing our stamp on the civilisation of the world.' You see their train of thought. It points at the same time to the danger that the unchecked development of the German Werkbund might hold for other artistic cultures. The danger is not just imaginary, above all here in our own land.[45]

He tried to remain reasonably objective by listing the pros and cons, remarking on the greatly increased productive power achieved by the unification of the efforts of both artists and industrialists, but he came to the very lukewarm conclusion that, although many professional organisations already existed, perhaps a central co-ordinating body would be of use. This was not to be the last word on the Dutch Werkbond, but for the time being all that remained were whispers. *Bouwkundig Weekblad* announced that on 30 June a meeting amongst industrialists, artists, and other interested parties had taken place and the desirability of founding a *Nederlandsche Werkbond* was discussed. It was agreed, 'whereupon the union was founded'.[46] There was, however, little chance for its survival. By the end of August the profession was in chaos and struggling for its own life. Unemployment was enormous, and materials were scarce, or completely unobtainable as in the case of concrete.

In mid-1917 trade was eased greatly,[47] the Americans had entered the war, and the Kaiser, if not the generals, wished to sue for peace. With room to breathe again, thoughts returned immediately to a *Driebond*, or *Nederlandsche Werkbond*. Nothing lasting had come of the first attempt, but this time Penaat himself brought the suggestion forward in the *Handelsblad* of 21 May 1917. *Architectura* took up the call and canvassed its members with a detailed questionnaire (18 August 1917). In his reply, Berlage showed considerable interest, saying that a *Driebond* would contribute much to the development of industry and culture, but on the whole the reaction was very mixed. This time the *Driebond* was becalmed; it no longer held the fascination it once enjoyed. At the end of 1917 in their annual report, *Architectura* for the first time included a list of members, on which the names of both industrialists and corporations are to be found. It may be that they were attempting to demonstrate their own suitability to act in the role of a *Driebond*. If so, whatever potential they possessed was left largely undeveloped or realised in an extremely unobtrusive manner.

Remarkably Van Doesburg remained silent throughout this debate. One would imagine that with its emphasis on collective work, machine production, etc., Van Doesburg would have encouraged and participated in the founding of such a union. Not only did he not participate, he founded De Stijl precisely when there was again the possibility of a functional Dutch Werkbond. The accomplishments of the Werkbund in Germany, and the principles on which it was founded, greatly interested Van Doesburg, but in the final analysis its failure to maintain a unified front had inhibited its progress towards a pure, and purely modern, style. The ideological purity which he demanded of his colleagues was impossible in such a large, official framework, as evidenced by the clashes between Muthesius and Van de Velde. In view of the relationship which existed between Van Doesburg and the Dutch architectural profession, his participation in a *Driebond* would have been fruitless.

There was no consensus of opinion amongst Dutch architects as to the shape and function of such a *Driebond*. Feeling was still running high over German influence. Organisations which already existed in the many areas which would come within, or fall under the influence of the *Driebond* were jealously guarding their territory. Last, but perhaps most importantly, all the fissures which had been present in the Werk-

bund itself were already becoming apparent in the debate over a corresponding Dutch organisation: there was already trouble over the exact
relationship and balance between the industrialists and the artists, over
the basis of their co-operative effort, and above all over the artistic
freedom of the individual.[48] Wijdeveld, soon to become editorial secretary of *Wendingen*, explained his personal vision of what the organisation should be in the so-called *Driebond* issue of *Architectura*. Above all
else, it had to be national in character for the development of a national
style as the reflection of the Dutch people and as a bulwark against German cultural expansionism. Wijdeveld also defended most staunchly the
individualist approach and characterised the attitude to machine production as follows:

The people demand generalised, mass-produced articles; the artist is in search
of *the particular*, independent of the machine and industry. Yet we must conquer
the great new province of industry, the machine. If we wish to subdue the machine to our own ends, we must first submit to being its slave. In this way the
occasion of the founding of the *Driebond* will be as a battle in the victorious
struggle of rebellious slaves against the machine product.[49]

If this curious credo was to be the foundation stone of the organisation
Van Doesburg could by no means use it to further his own ends.

Following this short burst of intense debate in *Architectura*, the question virtually evaporated. It appears that the complaint of a member
at the next meeting of Architectura et Amicitia, only four days after
the publication of the *Driebond* issue, was justified in stating that 'there
never seems to have been sympathy in the Society for the struggle of
the *Driebond*' and further that the issue itself had been a waste of time
and space. Wijdeveld's only reply was that the gentleman was out of
order and should have waited until question time for his remarks. At
the following meeting of the society on 24 October 1917, Wijdeveld put
forward his concept for a new monthly periodical intended for a more
broadly-based public than *Architectura* itself. 'In the speaker's conception, such a magazine as the one he was describing could best be created
by intimate and practical co-operative work with the practitioners of
the decorative arts, by the limitation of text, and by the widest possible
range of illustrations.'[50] The first issue of *Wendingen* appeared in January
1918. If this was the inheritance of the Werkbund, Van Doesburg wanted no part of it. An examination of the first issues, and a comparison
of them with the *Driebond* issue of *Architectura* and the yearbooks of the
Werkbund, reveals just how much *Wendingen* was created in the image
of that German association. Insofar as they had failed to found a
Driebond, *Wendingen*, as the Dutch offspring of the Werkbund, lacked
the organisational might of its German parent and the advantage of the
official connections with industry. Despite its limitations and its rather
lopsided, individualist inheritance, Wijdeveld saw the ultimate goal of
the two as being essentially the same, namely the unification of the new
directions and possibilities in art for the creation of a strong national
style.

The members of De Stijl recognised the debt they owed to the great experiment carried out by the Werkbund. Behrens in particular had made important contributions to the purification of the elementary means of architecture. He was a pioneer, he had helped to give direction to the new movement, but Van Doesburg and De Stijl were now exploring far beyond the territory first pointed out by the old master. Following Van Doesburg's lead, they sought inspiration towards the new architecture in an entirely new area – the lessons to be learned in the more theoretically rigorous art of painting. In a review of Otto Grautoff's book *Formzertrümmerung und Formaufbau in der bildenden Kunst*, Oud laments,

It is a shame that the writer is not clear how he should work out the developmental section of his argument. Through this shortcoming it happened that he was able with chauvinistic delight to see the spores of this new art just in examples of German architecture, but with the best will in the world we cannot reconcile the facts with his reasoning. Moreover, it must be recognised that at the moment the leadership of the revolutionary movement in art rests not with architecture but with painting, and that architecture has never settled its account with historical and traditional form to the same extent as has painting. The old elements of form are never completely negated in architecture. What happened with architecture in determining modern form was always more a reworking of and abstraction from inherited forms than the creation and determination of form as such. (This holds true to a certain extent even for the work of artists like Sant'Elia and Wright.)[51]

Van Doesburg's work in this area, on the analysis of 'the independent means of painting' and the application to architecture, gave the real impetus to De Stijl's early architectural experimentation. Earlier developments in America, Germany, and Holland had revealed a drive towards simplification and a more elementary means of expression, but true independence from an antiquated formal language could only be achieved by experimentation with the formal means of the 'useless', that is to say free, arts of sculpture and (much more important in Van Doesburg's eyes) of painting.[52]

The stand Van Doesburg took on the issue concerning formal means was so radical and uncompromising that in the period 1916–1920 it caused a protracted controversy with other critics and the professors of the Academies, as well as other artists and the architectural profession. In January 1919 he launched an ambitious offensive against the professors in a series of articles called 'Modern Trends in the Teaching of Art'. There he discussed the theoretical positions of four newly appointed academics: J. G. Wattjes as Professor of Architecture in the Delft University of Technology; Professor R. N. Roland Holst to the State Academy of Art; H. C. Verkruysen as Director of the School of Architecture, Decorative Arts, and Crafts, in Haarlem; and Dr Elizabeth Neurdenburg as Reader in the History of Modern Art in the State University, Groningen. With the exception of Neurdenburg, the main point at issue with each concerned the analysis and use of the elementary means of art.

Of the remaining three, Wattjes was the only one whom Van Doesburg did not condemn as being the declared enemy of the new in art. The title of Wattjes's inaugural address at the Technical University, Delft, was 'The Relationship of Architecture to Science, Technical Studies, and Art'. In discussing this lecture, Van Doesburg paid Wattjes a rare compliment: 'Insofar as this lecture contains a programme of principles, it is much more important than Professor Verkruysen's lecture because it at least contains *sections* which give an indication that Professor Wattjes, consciously or unconsciously, has an inner contact with the new ideas of the day.'[53] The line of development which Wattjes followed, though incompatible in parts with Van Doesburg's theory, in some areas provided what is perhaps a more succinct and clearer statement of Van Doesburg's ideas than he himself had so far achieved. Take, for example, a passage which Van Doesburg also quoted:

Without rupturing the lawful state of nature, it is also possible for man's will to influence events; it is possible for the exercise of his will to determine the course of events in conjunction with the laws of nature.

Don't you see now that this possibility is precisely the possibility opened up by technical processes? What else is technology than the deliberate interference by man in a natural state of affairs in order to realise his own ends with the available means.

Wattjes's text continued:

Man's spirit frees itself from the natural course of causal developments through technology. It does that not by breaking, but by using, natural laws. . . . Our roads, man-made waterways and harbours, canals, polders, and irrigation systems, all free us from complete dependence on geographical givens. . . . Ocean-going vessels untether us from the land, and aeroplanes and airships free us from the gravity which binds us to the surface of the earth.[54]

The same general attitude to nature was already evident in Van Doesburg's writings, but it would not be stated definitively until his publication of 'The Will to Style'.

Continuing his discussion of this point in the earlier article, Van Doesburg was anxious to demonstrate that the same principle had been at work in the world of art, for example in the splintering of visual phenomena in the painting of the Cubists and Futurists, and that it had long been recognised by philosophers such as Hegel. Essentially Van Doesburg was demanding for art the same liberation from the chains of nature in visual matters as technology was demanding and achieving in practical matters. Nature was to be conquered (as opposed to Wijdeveld's idea that it was the machine that had to be conquered) not imitated; this victory of the human spirit, as preached by Hegel and Georg Simmel (particularly in his essay 'The Ruin'), is found as a recurring theme in the rhetoric of De Stijl, reaching a crucial statement in 'The Will to Style'. There the intersecting lines in the accompanying diagram represent art and technology converging and synthesising in the work of the De Stijl group (see fig. 49).

Van Doesburg's main objection to the lecture given by Wattjes was that the professor was unwilling to allow the pure technical means of construction alone to provide the aesthetic solution, and continued to advocate the use of applied decoration in works of architecture as opposed to works of engineering. On the one hand Wattjes condemned Ruskin and Morris for their reactionary struggle against machine technology (p. 17), and in good Rationalist tradition he discussed architecture as the integration of functional elements within a mathematically determined construction. Further he decried the excesses and 'constructional nonsense' of the Amsterdam School, particularly Van der Mey, De Klerk, and Kramer. On the other hand, he considered that a purely rational approach was a far too minimal conception of architecture:

While in such a way the construction ought to lay certain limitations on the aesthetic solution, in the sense that the building should be well constructed right down to its component parts, it does not, however, have to go as far as the rationalistic conception of architecture suggests. The rationalists put forward as an aesthetic principle the idea that beautiful architectural form must be the rational consequence of the construction. However, art cannot be absolutely rational any more than it can be absolutely naturalistic. A work is a work of art precisely insofar as it gives more than is rationally necessary and more than truth to nature requires.[55]

Wattjes had actually rejected the 'rationalism' of 'the cold theoreticians of Rotterdam', while embracing the traditional Rationalism of Viollet-le-Duc, Cuypers, and Berlage. Wattjes recognised that a *utilitarian* building had its own beauty arising from the relationship amongst its parts, and that the application of decorative motifs would be inappropriate, but he insisted that in works of architecture the use of some applied decoration was necessary. He stuck to this position when replying in an open letter in *De Stijl* to Van Doesburg's attack. The editorial comment he received can be summed up in this extract from Van Doesburg's retort:

Art that has a certain unity, absorbs [into a balanced relationship] all other qualities as its means.

In good painting, for instance, the higher unity absorbs the idea, the technical means (in the widest possible sense, including the scientific, manual skills, etc.), and the material. Well then, is it not possible that architecture can master the use of all its means of construction, walls, floors, beams, roofs, gutters, stairs, doors, windows, columns, porches, balconies, etc., as plastic means in order to realise the artistic developmental stage in an inseparable unity? That must be possible.[56]

Why is it necessary to apply decoration to works of architecture? The only reason Van Doesburg could find was that they had been poorly designed in the first place and then had to be disguised with decorative blancmange.

Van Doesburg contended that architecture still had a great deal to learn from the art of painting in the use of its own technical means towards the creation of a balanced unity, the synthesis of the aesthetic idea. On a more literal level, the interface between painting and architecture, the wall plane and its treatment, had become a major source of disagreement with Professor Roland Holst, one of the chief practitioners of monumental (that is to say mural) painting in Holland at that period. He had worked on the Amsterdam Exchange for Berlage, and his career reached its zenith with his appointment to the State Academy where he was able to follow in the footsteps of his former and much respected old teacher, A. J. Derkinderen. At the climax of Roland Holst's inaugural lecture when taking over his old master's post, he singled out the 'a-formalists' (clearly a reference to Van Doesburg and De Stijl) for attack, declaring that:

They deem the religious or social idea and nature's blossoming forms to be worthless as subjects for architectonic painting. They try to extract the abstract form as far as possible, but they are never satisfied. Finally, from this abstract form they wish to produce an icon, an idol of their god, that in reality is the industrialisation and mechanisation of the spirit. Indeed, no divinity that has ever reigned on earth is so antipathetic to all human feeling.

   The a-formalists wish to conquer the architectural plane, but don't see that they have already become its slaves. They who wish to conquer have already been overwhelmed and mechanised, and that is precisely their tragic mistake.[57]

Van Doesburg, relishing controversy, eagerly took up the challenge. His reply in the pages of *De Stijl* was addressed not directly to Roland Holst's original text, but to the lecture as reported in the *Handelsblad*. However, the only practical effect this had was that the rhetoric and rambling poesy of the formal address were pared away, leaving the central ideas to stand on their own. Roland Holst had attempted to destroy his opponents with their own weapons. The use of geometry for its own sake was dismissed as a purely intellectual and narrow-minded exercise, a consequence of not being able to see that number and measure are to be found throughout the natural world. The expressive, supple line of the natural object, the lyricism of decorative art, the tried and true principles of tradition, and the lessons of the past formed the basis of his art. Yet he genuinely expected to repudiate the 'a-formalists' with the claim that 'the monumental painter is no realist or naturalist. He does not produce an image of the surface appearance of nature, but its spiritual synthesis. His work springs forth from the idea, in order to rise by the laws of geometry and construction to an exalted recognition of the essential in nature.'[58] His argument was thus attempting to show that, while he accepted some of the premises of De Stijl's formulation, other premises and the resulting conclusions were entirely unaccept-able. Van Doesburg found Roland Holst's borrowing of De Stijl terminology and ideas for the defence of his reactionary artistic concep-tion to be simply laughable. In turn, the De Stijl leader's reply attempted to summarise his own demands on the monumental painter:

Theoretically then, it should be possible for competent persons who are in touch with the times to draw essential distinctions between the ethical and the aes-thetic (the disposition to morality and the disposition to art), between monumen-tality and decoration, between these two and picturesque painterliness, between art measured against nature as a standard and art measured according to its own standards, etc., etc. . . . Practically speaking, experiments with painting in an interior, that is, painting in three dimensions, monumental painting, should be carried out. By this one would have to learn *to see the four walls as one plane*. Further, the question of the meaning of colour on its own, and of the meaning of colour-in-relationship for painting both the interior and the exterior, would have to be explored. In short, the aesthetic, mathematical, chemical, physiological, and psychological effects of colours would have to be handled in practice. All this would be of use to bring the real possibility of monumental art to realisation under the guidance of the modern understanding of Relationship.[59]

When the areas of dispute have been clearly identified, it will be interesting to see just how far Van Doesburg was able to realise these stated intentions in his co-operative work with Oud.

The quarrel with Verkruysen, newly appointed director of the architectural school in Haarlem, had in fact begun long before Van Doesburg's all-out offensive of 1919; it began on the same day and at the same meeting of Architectura et Amicitia as he fell out with C. J. Blaauw (see page 35). There Verkruysen objected to Van Doesburg's analysis of the roles of Rembrandt and Rodin in the drive towards the purification of the means of art. To use the great masters as examples to prove the existence of a drive towards abstraction running through the history of art was sacrilege and 'meaningless rubbish'.[60] It is unnecessary to follow the development of the argument concerning elementary means in painting and architecture yet again. However, it is worthwhile quoting Verkruysen to give an idea of the 'clubbiness' of the opposition squared against Van Doesburg and the close contact and exchange of ideas which they 'enjoyed':

It seems to me that in a Society such as Architectura, where most usually the same people are to be found in the audience attending these lectures, that people are able to get to know one another out of common interest, and that after an address some ideas on those interests are exchanged – for instance the results of study and work are discussed in congenial groups. . . . However, the behaviour of Mr Van Doesburg on that night, with the churlishness to hold a lecture with a cigar in his mouth, and the brutishness with which he denigrated the great masters Rembrandt, Van Gogh, Rodin, and others by his unintelligible use of words . . .[61]

Needless to say, Van Doesburg had little time for the niceties of the gentleman's club while fomenting revolution.

Van Doesburg had distilled a self-consistent theory from the 'independent advances' made by international figures in a variety of disciplines to provide the basis for a new and totally abstract compositional treatment of the means of art, whether in the art of painting or of architecture. The small group which had gathered round in support of common principles was now a force to be reckoned with in the Dutch artistic and architectural community, partly as a result of Van Doesburg's forceful personality and the initial publicity he had generated, but primarily because the principles on which *De Stijl* was founded placed it in the mainstream of international development, rather than in the pursuit of very personal or essentially regionalist artistic visions. He was emphasising the common goals which they shared, in order to give a show of strength, to 'concentrate their power', and to ride to prominence with his ideals on a wave of brilliantly managed publicity.

2

◇◇ ◇◇◇◇◇◇

Elementary means and the development of the painterly conception of architecture

The elaboration and defence of the ideas relating to 'elementary means' were Van Doesburg's main theoretical concerns between 1916 and 1919. In 1917 it set him at loggerheads with Bernard Canter, in 1918 with Edith Pijpers, and in 1919 he was again attacking Verkruysen.[1] Before the end of the first year of *De Stijl*'s publication, a public confrontation took place within the De Stijl circle itself. Huib Hoste, a Belgian architect living in exile in the Netherlands during the war, had close associations with *De Stijl*, publishing 'The Call of Modern Architecture' in the June 1918 issue. In that article he spoke of the use of modern materials, iron and glass, and their most logical use in pure right-angled masses (p. 87). In Van Doesburg's eyes this constituted an acceptance of the De Stijl position concerning the use of elementary means. At the end of the month when Hoste turned around and published an article in *De Nieuwe Amsterdammer*, complimenting Willebeek le Mair's use of supple curving lines in her reliefs, Van Doesburg accused him of hypocritically trying to serve two masters at the same time. A private and public correspondence (the latter running through no less than three journals and newspapers) grew up around the quarrel. Van Doesburg, in the September issue of *De Stijl*, finally published an edited version of Hoste's reply to the accusations. In the editorial comment accompanying the reply, Van Doesburg summed up the central point at issue by asking:

Mr Hoste says: 'If I write about architecture in *De Stijl*, that is not to say that I share the other members' ideas on architecture, to say nothing of their ideas on painting.' We ask: '*Why do you borrow them then?*' (One need only compare, for example, Oud's article on Wright, pages 40 and 87, with the final conclusion drawn by Hoste concerning the call of modern architecture, where the interpenetration and origin of the play of masses etc. come under discussion.) It can be added, and mark this well, that these ideas in architecture are *secondary* in the sense that they have have been borrowed from the art of painting.[2]

Hoste obviously did not feel duty-bound to support only the strivings of De Stijl. He was not convinced, as was Van Doesburg, that De Stijl had an historical mission to fulfil as *the* style of the age. In fact, his answer as published in *De Stijl* made the remark that 'it has never happened that a single ideology was completely convincing for all the masses. Therefore all good attempts are to be valued, and I am not alone amongst

58

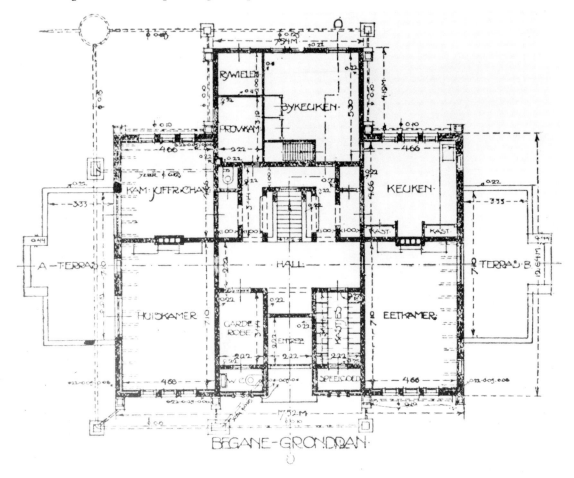

9 J. J. P. Oud, Ground plan for the house 'De Vonk', 1917–18; reproduced in *De Stijl*, II, no 2 (December 1918), p. 20

the co-workers of De Stijl to do this.'[3] The last phrase holds the clue to Van Doesburg's rather extreme reaction to the affair. Hoste, and some of the other members as well, were showing ideological weakness and their willingness to adopt a liberal view, in Van Doesburg's eyes tantamount to eclecticism, was threatening the existence of De Stijl as a revolutionary force. Hoste can then be seen as a marginal member of the group, whose excommunication was intended as an example to the others.

Hoste's direct association with De Stijl was finished, but the quarrel continued into March of the following year. He had in the meantime accepted Van Doesburg's invitation 'to look around and see what Oud and I have accomplished in the holiday centre "Buiten Bedrijf" in Noordwijkerhout. The newly created image *itself* can now, through our step into the future, achieve what previously the Church was able to do through the medium of art, namely create a direct relationship with God.'[4] As a result, Hoste wrote a critique of the house comparing the theory with the practical accomplishment. On the whole he found the ground plan (fig. 9) quite serviceable except around the main staircase,

10 J. J. P. Oud and Theo van
Doesburg, Hall and staircase
of De Vonk, archive
photograph; reproduced in *De
Stijl*, II, no 1 (November
1918), plate I

which unfortunately was the core of the whole design (fig. 10). He complained that here, although a form of staircase that is quite uncommonly
wasteful of space had been used, Oud had still not succeeded in filling
the entire width of the hall. To remain consistent with his principles
of *zakelijkheid*, Hoste contended, Oud was forced to contrive built-in benches and extremely small, somewhat puzzling ante-rooms for the director and for the kitchen. On the other hand, another reviewer, Jan
Gratama, thought that the layout was very good and logical. He
accepted Oud's explanation that the benches provided the possibility for
the children and the group leaders to sit while busy with their handicraft,
and that the small enclosed spaces in front of the doors to the kitchen
and the director's room prevented unwanted overlooking while providing a space for the kitchen's hot water-tank and, on the other side of
the house, a WC for the director. The problem with this explanation
is that the benches face straight into the respective rooms, reducing the
effectiveness of the ante-rooms against prying eyes.[5] These spaces left
and right of the stairs do call attention to themselves as being dark,
rather cramped corners. If we are willing to admit Oud's case for the
organisation of the spaces, then we have to admit Hoste's next objection,
that natural light, admitted through the splendid (though, as Van
Doesburg commented, too darkly coloured[6]) stained-glass windows, is
spread very unevenly through the space. Oud had tried to circumvent
the problem by separating the double-stepped walls of the staircase from
the independent walls of the side passageways. This allowed light from
the stained-glass windows onto the benches, penetrating into the passages to some extent, but the solution was inadequate. Hoste accused

11 J. J. P. Oud, De Vonk,
archive photograph;
reproduced in *De Stijl*, II, no 2
(December 1918), plate II

them of allowing the aesthetic solution to stand in the way of the practical solution, in direct opposition to their stated principles.

Having disproved, at least to his own satisfaction, Van Doesburg's claim that 'the rising stairs, the walls and their openings, the benches at the sides and above in the upper hall . . . have a logical, functional meaning which is expressed plastically when all are moulded together into one organic form', and quoting from the same text, Hoste moved on to uncover further inconsistencies:

'By sacrificing any decoration or decorative detailing [*détailplastiek*] (bits of sculpture, moulded frames, etc.) which are purely cosmetic and not an integral part of the answer to the architectural question, the plastic rhythm of the architecture achieves complete *independent* expression. This expression is independent and free because it is not bound to a decorative mannerism, and thus does not appear to be anything other than it really is, that is to say architectural and not sculptural expression. The understanding expresses itself in the form and the form expresses itself in the material. In this way the observer is forced to see in an architecturally "plastic" manner.' That note on the building by Oud is the opinion of De Stijl. Let us see if this has been realised.[7]

To begin with, the piers which separate the windows were passed off as 'just a search for form', applied, not at all a direct consequence of constructional necessity. In short it was an example of precisely the kind of *détailplastiek* which Van Doesburg so strongly condemned. Hoste pointed out other small details, such as the glazed-brick inset murals above and on either side of the main entrance (see figs. 11, 12 and 13) which breached the same principle. Then, of course, there were the sloping roofs, introducing diagonals which had been so consciously avoided in the stepped walls of the staircase. Some of these aspects of the design were indeed odd and unresolved within the declared programme, but as yet they hardly constituted a serious indictment of the attempt. Hoste, however, had one last objection: that as a free-standing building the

12 Theo van Doesburg,
Glazed-brick panel at the
entrance to De Vonk, 1918;
photograph 1981

massing left a great deal to be desired. The square ground plan with its symmetrical displacement of rooms resulted in an equally box-like exterior. Whereas there was at least some relief on the front elevation, the side elevations were entirely flat. On this count it could not be rated very highly by Oud's own criterion that

the aesthetic value of a building is determined by the purity of its relationships: the clarity of the expression of space by masses, planes, and lines; and eventually by the tension arising from its constructive plasticism and not from decoration. The aesthetic value of painting on the interior and exterior arises from the relationship between the placement and size of the coloured surfaces and results in the painterly conception of architecture (including all its surfaces: ceiling, wall, and floor) . . .[8]

Clearly Oud formulated this position under the influence of Van Doesburg. Gratama, like so many other architects and critics, doubted that this formulation provided an adequate assessment of architecture. In his critique of the house 'Buiten Bedrijf', or, as it is better known, 'De Vonk', he quoted the same paragraph from Oud, adding:

Indeed there is a lot of truth to this view. The forms of geometry, the parts of a building and their relationships, make up one of the chief elements of the beauty of a building. These parts are vested with profound value if they arise purely from the essence of the building, its use and construction. However, is that also to say that they form the unique beauty of a work of architecture? Would a building composed exclusively of architectural relationships be beautiful in the fullest sense? I think not.[9]

Gratama claimed that if the principle concerning the elementary means of architecture were carried to its logical extreme, as De Stijl intended, then all art would have been killed and only dry intellectual principle would remain. Was evidence of this already to be found in De Vonk? Was architecture being emptied of all expressive force by the architects of De Stijl as Gratama believed?

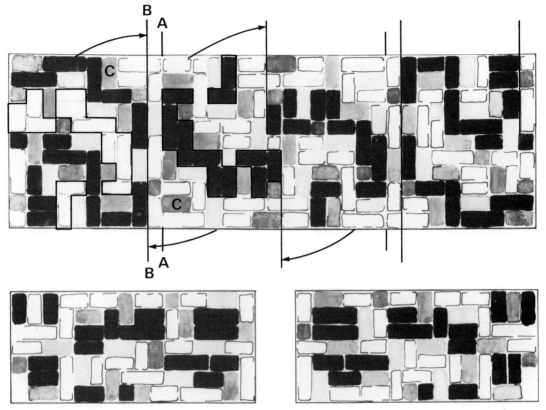

The massing did not live up to Oud's own criteria, but this was more the result of his failure to realise the principle than his execution of it to its logical extreme. The success or failure of the work rested on two interrelated points: 'the clarity of the expression of space by masses, planes, and lines' in the treatment of the interior; and the contribution made by 'the painterly conception of architecture'. A small taste of the latter is allowed the visitor before entering the house. Above and on either side of the main door are Neo-plastic compositions by Van Doesburg in blue, yellow, green, white, and black glazed brick. Hoste had complained that these were simply *détailplastiek* since they did not arise directly from structural or functional needs. It is absurd to apply such Functionalist criteria to Van Doesburg as that was not at all his claim; the claim was rather that the idea expressed itself in form, and form expressed itself in material, basically a Rationalist idea. The ingenious working of the material into a Neo-plastic composition answers the demands extremely well. The ground plan is strongly axial, but allows controlled variation on either side of the axis in response to function. The Neo-plastic compositions above and on either side of the main entrance emphasise the axiality, recognise the variation within the symmetry, and respond to the material by accepting the implied grid of brick construction as the geometric determinant of the composition. In her analysis of the composition, Jane Beckett writes:

13 Theo van Doesburg, Glazed-brick panels above and on either side of the main entrance to De Vonk; schematic explanation of the symmetries

In the decorations Van Doesburg accepts the limiting factors of the media, brick on the exterior (5×5 cm brick end) and interior tiles (10×10 cm), overtly exploiting the module as an elementary constructional unit. A factor which had important repercussions for his contemporary painting (cf. *Composition XIII* – Stedelijk Museum).

Colour as the active element is used to disrupt the geometrical spatial structure of the exterior frieze at De Vonk. The main composition, denoting a symbolic zone between the entrance and the Director's rooms on the first floor, is a triptych, flanked on left and right by two subsidiary friezes. The left- and right-hand panels of the main frieze are of the same compositional format but turned upside down on the right. Van Doesburg repeats the same structure at left and right of the centre panel, turning upside down the left-hand format, yet retaining one white square at the centre point. Left- and right-hand subsidiary panels also have the same compositional format, but in these panels reversed. In all three friezes Van Doesburg uses colour to activate the plane. He employs only three colours, yellow, blue and green, but develops a progressive change in the colour; thus in the large central panel those planes which are green in the left-hand portion become yellow on the right, while in the subsidiary panels yellow changes to green, green to blue and blue to yellow. There is moreover an equal number of green and blue elements which are mirror images of one another, thus the blue is not bound to repetitive form.[10]

The two main points under consideration here are the use of symmetries, and colour variation between symmetrical halves in order to avoid repetitive form. The consideration of the main composition as a triptych may confuse the issue and cause an important point to be overlooked. Presumably the triptych is divided by the lines marked 'A' in fig. 13, since it is defined by the only mortar joint to divide the brick composition vertically without a break. However, if the line of division is moved one brick to the left, marked line 'B', a 'thematic grid' of four interrelated equal parts is revealed within the bi-partite rotational symmetry about the central white glazed brick end. At first the *secondary* rotational symmetry is difficult to locate because there Van Doesburg was playing with the figure/ground relationship. Figure 13 shows the geometrical configurations which are symmetrical, but because one is negative and the other positive (the left-hand figure is white, the right black) the natural tendency to read the composition in terms of figure/ground reduces the symmetry to a subliminal *suggestion* of symmetry. The visual impact of the symmetry is further weakened by the fact that the distribution of colour is in part reversed in the two panels, and at one point the geometrical symmetry is varied slightly (e.g. the green bricks marked 'C' in the diagram).

Van Doesburg had already been experimenting with simple rotational symmetry in an architectural context, as in his 1917 design for the interior of the main room of the De Lange-Woerden house in Alkmaar. In his work with Oud at De Vonk in 1918 he made a highly elaborate game of the use of themes in symmetries of repetition, rotation, and reflection. Sometimes there would also be colour variation, positive/negative alteration, and figure/ground confusions to mask the basic structure of the overall composition. On entering the house, the visitor finds himself progressing down the main axis across a black, white, and

14 Theo van Doesburg,
Ceramic tiling on the floor of
the entrance to De Vonk;
most obvious symmetries

cream tiled floor. If viewed in terms of figure/ground the floor of the
entrance porch divides diagonally into a quadripartite rotational symmetry as in figure 14. If viewed in terms of a 'thematic grid' the composition divides as shown in figure 15. The reason for insisting on the latter
as an alternative, and a much better alternative, is that if the former
approach is continued, it can only elucidate the immediately following
section of floor, leaving the rest of the lower floor as a random distribution of variants of the motif established in the porch. On the other hand,
the thematic grid approach penetrates beyond the figure/ground confusions and reveals the floor to be made up of two themes, established
in the porch and reflected in the immediately following section of floor,
and the second introduced in the main hall. That this thematic grid
approach was indeed Van Doesburg's method of design is confirmed by
the existence of a painting (fig. 16) which corresponds to theme 1 of
the De Vonk floors (fig. 15; very possibly this theme had its origin in
a still life of 1916, see Polano, fig. 43). A variation on the reflected version appears three times, once in a key position at the bottom of the
stairs, and upstairs it will appear once again in the centre of the composition. In the subsidiary halls around the back of the house the treatment
of the thematic grid changes. There it is made up of two paired themes
found in varying relationships with each other. It is interesting to note
that the composition comprising the hall at the very back of the house,
when considered in terms of a triptych, is in many ways comparable
to Beckett's triptych at the front of the house.

In the interior Oud was much more successful in the clarification of
spatial relationships than he had been on the exterior. The architectural
elements of the composition, both plastic and functional (stairs,
balustrade, load-bearing walls, passageways, benches, etc.) are as far

15 (*opposite*) Theo van Doesburg, Original design for tiling, ground floor, De Vonk, 1918
(watercolour on coloured paper mounted on board, 98 cm × 73.5 cm), Van Doesburg
Collection, R.B.K. (AB 5091); symmetries are indicated by an additional network of lines

16 Theo van Doesburg,
Composition, 1917 (oil on
asbestos board,
31 cm × 31 cm including
painted wooden frame);
collection of Mr and Mrs
Armand P. Bartos

as possible kept visually separate as well. The floor is separated from
the walls by a black band of tiles (as are the stairs from the balustrade,
although the tiles had not yet been laid when the photographs were
taken for publication in the November 1918 issue of *De Stijl*). Van
Doesburg had used the same technique when working with Wils on
the De Lange-Woerden house. He described his intention in a letter of
9 September 1917 to Antony Kok:

I have also indicated the use of colour in the whole building . . . In order to
give you some idea of my conception, I'll just say that I started from the principle
that all planes must be *disengaged* by the use of a contrasting light colour. For
example, the door panels of a deep blue are disengaged by white . . . All round

the whole of the house I have drawn a black band which I have broken with white planes so that the house is thereby torn from its stability.[11]

The same attitude pervades the treatment of other elements at De Vonk. The passageways leading from the main hall are functionally subordinate and so are visually differentiated by a lowered ceiling. The encasement of the stair is probably the clearest example. There Oud has isolated the load-bearing and enclosing functions of the wall. An interesting antecedent of the double-stepped balustrade, fulfilling the function of containment, is to be found in the larger of Van 't Hoff's holiday houses at Huis ter Heide, the Villa Henny. There, however, the diagonal has been integrated with horizontals and verticals to correspond more closely with the steps and landings of the winding stair (fig. 17). The functional link may be stronger here, but the visual effect was clearly echoed two years later at De Vonk.

Following the flight of stairs in De Vonk up to the landing, the visitor is confronted with a five-light stained-glass window by H. H. Kamerlingh Onnes, who worked with Oud on the contemporary villa 'Allegonda'. The window, Van Doesburg noted, is too darkly coloured and thus admits less natural light than desired, but it is nonetheless quite a remarkable work. Onnes, Huszar, and Van Doesburg executed stained-glass windows in much the same way as they composed paintings. Beginning with a natural subject, sketches were made dividing the subject into its constituent planes. This was in the manner of the Analytical Cubists, but with a balanced emphasis on form and colour.

Turning for the time being from a study of stained glass, the visitor moves up to the first floor hall. Here the tile floor continues and begs comparison with the floor in the lower hall, but its size and complexity defy any such direct comparison by the unaided memory. The entire floor of the upper hall can be seen from any position, but the search by the curious viewer for a governing principle within the pattern is obstructed by the complexity of the composition. It is necessary then to have recourse to the drawings. Using the same method as in the lower hall, the floor divides into a thematic grid employing the same two main themes as the lower hall with the central position taken up by the second exceptional theme (see fig. 18). The chosen grid does not fit perfectly into the length of the hall, leaving a three-tile width at one end. In preparing his design for the upper hall, Van Doesburg had forgotten, or had chosen to ignore, the extra tiles required within the depth of the door jambs, which caused slight variations around the edges of the executed design. The symmetries of the upper hall were explored on both a smaller and a larger scale. On the smaller scale, all of the three themes employed can be bisected to reveal a sub-theme common to each. Themes 2 and 3 are, then, *different* paired themes in *constant* relationship, as opposed to the two paired themes in the subsidiary corridor at the back of the house which employed *like* paired themes in *different* relationships. The large-scale symmetry in the upper hall, because of the extra tiles at the end of the hall, has had its axis shifted two tile-widths to the left of the main axis of the house. The two halves of the larger symmetry (heavily outlined in fig. 18) spread significantly from the landings at the top of the two flights of stairs to surround the two black and white doors which form a strong positive/negative contrast.[12] The photograph of the upper hall (fig. 19) as published in *De Stijl* indicates a fascinating aspect of this use of symmetry. Light passing through the stained-glass window falls directly on those parts of the floor where the symmetry is strongest. Light is the ordering factor of Van Doesburg's design on the larger scale. Even the axis has moved in the direction of the strongest pool of light.

The same relationship between the natural lighting, the geometry of the space, and symmetry can be demonstrated on the ground floor. The floor of the porch, being on the south-east, is exposed to the strongest natural light and also displays the strongest symmetry, which is at the same time the origin of one of the two dominant patterns. Further into the entrance the light is somewhat less strong and consequently the floor receives a symmetrical treatment, but the symmetry which most readily emerges for the viewer is on the diagonal and has much less visual impact.

Back in the upper hall, colour relationships have been carefully manipulated in painting the doors. The planes of the panelling have been accentuated with various combinations of black, white, and grey. The doors in the corners are painted precisely like their diagonal opposite, while the doors on either side of the axis facing the stairs are given diametrically opposed treatments in black and white.

In his 'painterly conception of architecture', Van Doesburg co-

18 Theo van Doesburg,
Colour-scheme of the upper
hall, De Vonk
(reconstruction); symmetries
are indicated by an additional
network of lines

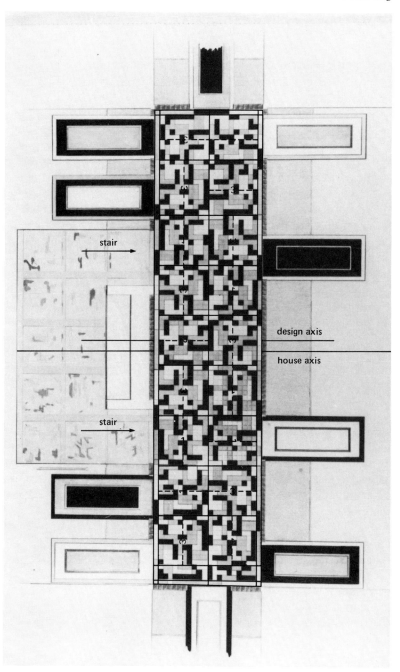

ordinated the whole composition by the use of diagonals, axes, and the
symmetries of rotation, reflection, and repetition. The symmetries were
sometimes so visually weakened by transformations within the thematic
grid that they were reduced to vague remembrances in the experience
of the viewer. The inventiveness and complexity of the various combina-

19 J. J. P. Oud and Theo van Doesburg, Upper hall of De Vonk, archive photograph; reproduced in *De Stijl*, II, no 1 (November 1918), plate I

tions of these regulating principles indicate that he already had a good deal of experience in their use. That experience was gained in the design of glass mosaics and stained-glass windows. During 1917, the year before his work on De Vonk, he designed a glass mosaic based on a theme which was rotated, reflected, or repeated twelve times within the composition. Beginning with the top three squares of the three by four chequerboard, the pattern was set in the first, rotated 180° in the second, and the original reflected in the third. Moving down one row, the procedure was reversed and half the composition was completed. Which of the three possible options to use in the squares in the lower half was determined by drawing lines from each of the outside squares of the upper half through the central point of the whole composition to its corresponding square on the lower half. These were lines of repetition, meaning simply that the corresponding squares in the two halves of the composition were treated in exactly the same way. One square, i.e. the middle square of the third row, was left for a repetition of the original pattern. While this procedure does not lend itself to verbal description, graphically it is very simple (fig. 20).

The simplest version of this sort of treatment is found in Van Doesburg's composition *Pastorale* which was fixed in place in the Agricultural School in Drachten in 1922. The window itself was produced at the beginning of the year from definitive designs produced in the win-

20 Theo van Doesburg, Glass
mosaic, *Composition VI*, 1917
(design reproduced as a silk-
screen print,
65.5 cm × 50.5 cm) Van
Doesburg Collection, R.B.K.
(AB 5047); with schematic
description of symmetries

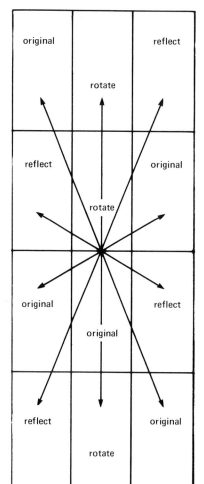

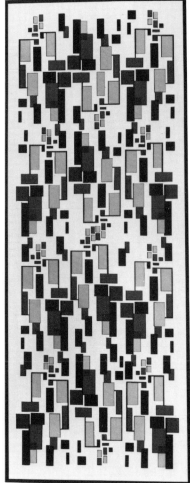

ter of 1921/22. Sketch designs dated 1916 exist and although the idea
has been advanced that some drawings were signed and dated years
later by Van Doesburg, the designs belong organisationally at the beginning of this series of geometrical compositions. An undated sketch shows
a vertical two-panel by four-panel composition using lines of reflection
which are not controlled by the centre of the composition (fig. 21). A
composition signed and dated 1916 used the same four themes of the
'Digger', 'Planter', 'Sower', and 'Harvester', but used them with the
reflected symmetries controlled by the centre point of the composition
in the same way as the glass mosaic. This second version was to be
one of the two carried out in 1922 for the school. The second is shown
in a coloured sketch signed and dated 1919 where the red-blue-yellow
colour scheme is changed to red-blue-green. The structural organisation
of the design is the same but it has been given a horizontal format
because it was designed to fill the window-light above the main entrance.
    Van Doesburg used the same underlying compositional principle for

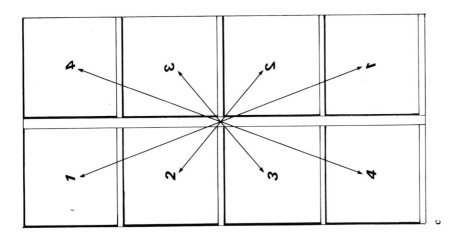

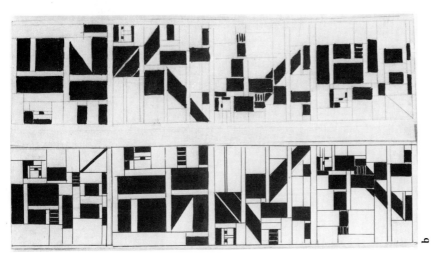

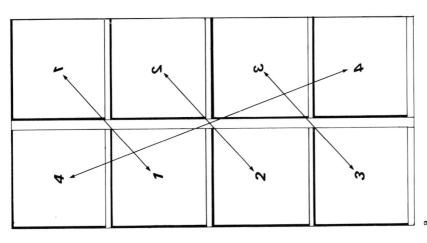

21 Theo van Doesburg. Sketch design for the stained-glass window *Pastorale* (pencil and ink on tracing paper mounted on card, 30 cm × 17 cm) Van Doesburg Collection, R.B.K. (AB 5072); with schematic descriptions of this and a later version

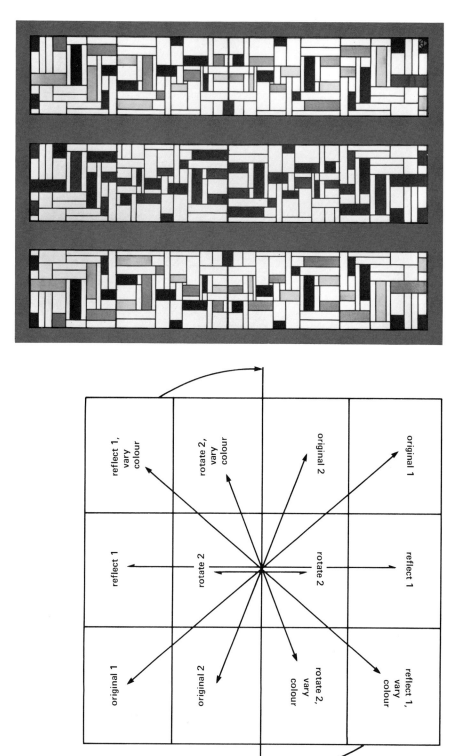

22 Theo van Doesburg, Stained-glass window, *Composition IV*, published as '*Three small windows in a school in Winschoten*' in W. F. Gouwe's *Glas-in-lood*, p. 50, but carried out on a larger scale and placed in a gentleman's residence in Alkmaar as in fig. 23

In the diagram:

original 1

original 2

rotate 2, vary colour

reflect 1, vary colour

rotate 2

reflect 1

rotate 2

reflect 1

reflect 1, vary colour

rotate 2, vary colour

original 2

original 1

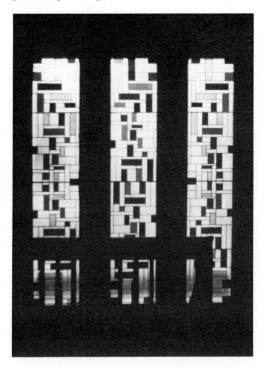

23 Theo van Doesburg, Stained-glass window, *Composition IV – in situ*; 1979 photograph, gentleman's residence in Alkmaar. Window now in the Van Doesburg Collection, R.B.K. (AB 5054)

a three-light window in a school in Winschoten (*Composition IV*, 1917, (fig. 22) which he repeated on a larger scale and apparently with some colour variation (fig. 23) for the De Lange-Woerden house where the glass mosaic was also placed. In *Composition IV* the second row introduced a second theme, and reflections and rotations sometimes displayed a variation in colouring. The lines of repetition, which governed the composition of the glass mosaic, became lines of rotation in *Composition IV*. This had the further result that the composition as a whole had a rotational symmetry about a horizontal axis.

The stained-glass window was an important point of contact between painting and architecture, particularly in these early days. At the time Oud was enthusiastic about the results and wrote an article entitled 'The Leaded Glass of Theo van Doesburg', where he described three windows of 1917 and 1918, that is, contemporary with De Vonk:

In *Composition II* the motif as such is turned and reflected [*door- en omgebeeld*] and orientated in space. White light is manipulated so that the aesthetic idea which forms the basis of the work, the 'rhythmical upward movement of the waves', is formed by relationships alone, without undermining the idea of the window as a translucent closing plane.

Composition III is to be seen as the logical development of the given idea, *concentric* and *eccentric* movement, by which the plastic given, 'figure-skating', is expressed. If the rhythm of *Compositions II* and *III* is still in the manner of opposed repetitions (the continuous melodic element), then in *Composition V* the rhythm has been encapsulated and spiritually intensified by overcoming the *set* harmonic element.[13]

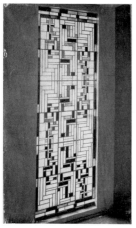

24 J. J. P. Oud and Theo van Doesburg, Villa Allegonda, 1917, and the stained-glass windows *Composition II*, 1917, and *Composition V*, 1918, contemporary photographs on original mount (28 cm × 50.5 cm); Van Doesburg Collection, R.B.K. (AB 5055)

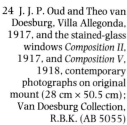

Compositions II and *V* constituted part of Van Doesburg's contribution to the villa Allegonda (fig. 24). *Compositions II, III, IV* and *VI* were produced all but simultaneously in a burst of creative work between about March and the beginning of September 1917. The designs evolved side by side, sometimes with motifs or their variants migrating from one composition to the other. Seen in this way, *Composition II* is curiously enough the logical successor to the window at Winschoten. It is an expanded version of the compositional structure on a larger scale and using the two geometrical themes of its predecessor and adding a third. Here the lines of rotation are again controlled by the centre of the composition and of course produce the same overall rotation about the central horizontal axis (fig.25).

As Oud commented, presumably paraphrasing Van Doesburg, its rhythm is as regular as 'the upward movement of the waves'. Oud's comment on *Composition V* (fig. 24) is also very applicable to this kind of compositional analysis. Leaving aside the 'spiritual intensification' for a moment, the 'dominant' pattern is by no means as dominant and *set* as is the case with the designs previously discussed. The central point and connecting lines are no longer in control, and the patterns, when eventually discovered, are often seen to be in a variant or weakened form. Providing a graph, then, might prove to be more misleading than constructive.

The third window mentioned in the quotation from Oud, *Composition III* (fig. 26), was designed for a house by Jan Wils on the Sint Anthoniepolder (fig. 27). In direct opposition to *Composition V*, its symmetries are strong, regular, and immediately come to the attention of the viewer. There is only one governing pattern, which never varies as it is rotated four times within and four times outside a lozenge within the square format. The underlying compositional principles used in this window were also drawn upon by Van Doesburg in the laying out of the tile floor in the porch of De Vonk. In an extensive tile floor, however, the governing pattern can be taken through an evolutionary process

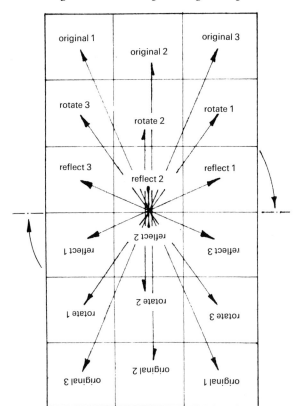

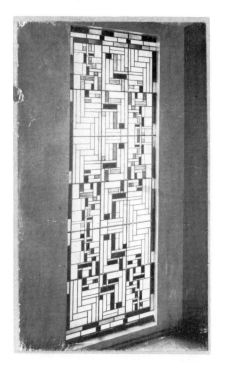

25 Theo van Doesburg,
Stained-glass window,
Composition II, 1917; with
schematic description of
symmetries

26 Theo van Doesburg,
Stained-glass window,
Composition III, 1917 (printed
version of design), Van
Doesburg Collection, R.B.K.
(AB 5052)

27 Jan Wils, Entrance to a
house in the Sint
Anthoniepolder with the
stained-glass window
Composition III by Van
Doesburg, repeated five times
in the facade, archive
photograph; Van Doesburg
Collection, R.B.K. (AB 5052)

along the path of the visitor, and therefore can control his experience of the development of architectural space in its changing relationships.

The general attitude which allowed Van Doesburg to transfer the lessons learned in his work in stained glass to the larger architectural context, was recognised by Oud when he wrote that 'in a certain sense Van Doesburg has gone to work on the solution of this problem [the integration of the practical and aesthetic demands of the window] as the rationalistic architect goes to work in building a house, that is to say, his conception is connected intimately with the functional end and the construction'.[14] The idea of 'elementary means' provided the touchstone for the group's co-operative artistic endeavours in this period. When preparing his contribution to De Vonk, Van Doesburg used symmetries to produce rhythmical effects on a much larger scale embracing a wide range of architectural elements. He used colour, the lessons of painting, and the compositional principles developed in the art of stained glass to separate, and accentuate, the elements of the architecture in terms of his 'aesthetic idea'. In 1916, before this ideal had been accomplished on any significant scale, Oud had written confidently:

In this struggle [towards the purification of the elementary means of their respective arts] they [the modern painter and the modern architect] meet and complete each other's work! Everywhere the need is now felt for a closer bond amongst the arts. Presently, architects might see this symptom in the proper light, and by their active interest they can then lead us further on the road towards the unification of the arts, where the emotional content will at the same time be reproduced in the rhythmical relationship between stone and space, in form and colour, and in sound and measure.[15]

Van Doesburg summarised his approach, confirming that it retained its important position throughout his career, in correspondence of 1930 (he died before it could be worked into a complete article), when he wrote that:

Painting, still in consistent and regular development without diversions, indicated some new possibilities (via Cubism) based on a new aesthetic in a return to the original *cloisonné* technique. Unfettered by the fossilisation of the 'moment-in-time', of the object and of movement, the window was able to develop as an *orchestrated image of coloured light* in organic integration with the new architecture. . . .

It is possible for the truly modern artist to work in complete agreement with truly modern architecture and to realise the composition of coloured light as the perfecting accent of that architecture, at the same time conserving the idea 'window', arising out of all the constructive elements (connections, metal supports, bridging, etc.), with regard to the pure painterly demands such as intensity of light, colour contrasts, measure and number, composition, etc.[16]

Having traced the application, origins, and the progression of the compositional principles used by Van Doesburg in his work in De Vonk, one large question remains. In his invitation to Huib Hoste to look around the house, he made the mysterious claim that just as the Church had used art to produce an icon, so had he and Oud created 'a direct relationship with God' in the architecture of the house. To what kind of icon, indeed what kind of God, was he referring?

In the correspondence surrounding the quarrel between Van Doesburg and Hoste, the latter made it clear that he thought that his expulsion from the group was a result of his being a Catholic, while he described the members of De Stijl as 'the men of pure reason'.[17] This was no loose description. The members of De Stijl, Van Doesburg, Oud, and Mondrian in particular, had shown considerable interest in the writings of Bolland, whose *magnum opus* appeared under the title *The Pure Reason*. Their own artistic endeavours indicated a struggle towards the objectivity of reason as opposed to the arbitrariness of sentiment, towards the logical execution of a systematic development as opposed to romanticisation and the picturesque, towards the embodiment of the universal idea behind natural phenomena as opposed to the reproduction of the face of nature itself. In view of this, the 'pure reason' of Bolland holds the key to the explanation of De Vonk as an icon.

Van Doesburg summarised his work in terms of a 'monumental art of space':

In the composition of the tile floor as well as in the painting of the doors etc., an aesthetic manipulation of space is accomplished by destruction in the manner of painting-within-architecture. The floor is the most closed plane of the house, and therefore from an aesthetic point of view it demands a treatment which, as it were, counteracts gravity. Here this has been carried out logically from the entrance throughout the entire ground-floor and first-floor halls and the corridors.[18]

By means of colour he had dissolved the closed nature of architecture. The different planes of the panelled doors were visually separated from each other; black tiling functioned similarly in the case of the walls and floors; and the floor itself was 'dissolved' in a tile mosaic. Space and the relationships it embraced were clarified by the special treatment of the architectural elements which formed its boundaries, moulded it, punctured it, and constituted the vessel through which it flowed. His use of geometry and colour was intended to perfect the architectural definition of space.

Bolland's explanation of what space, light, and colour meant to a 'man of pure reason' contained striking parallels. Beginning with space, he declared that 'the idea of space is the idea of nature in all its purity and emptiness . . . it is a quantitively endless graphic abstraction. Space is nature in abstraction, freed from all determinants.' The next link in this mystic chain is that 'theologically speaking, Nature is the organ of God; scientifically speaking, God is the never-ending function of Nature'. The revelation of nature and its attendant spirit was the function of light and colour: 'the light of nature . . . is a reflection of the spirit'; and lastly 'What does the reason tell us of colours? It calls them the diversity of visible conception of natural function [*zakelijkheid*]. Colour is the visible ideality of natural reality.'[19] For Van Doesburg, colour provided a revelation of architectural space on one level, visible ideality on another. Spirit as 'reflected' by the light of nature was the controlling factor in the design. In the entrance and upper hall, the symmetries most visible to the viewer, which underpin the whole design, are strongest where the natural light is strongest. Geometric symmetry, light, and colour were to bring the architecture to perfection as a revelation of the universal idea which lay veiled behind the phenomena of nature, in other words as a revelation of Bolland's pantheistic God who was the driving force in nature. Nature, like his art, was based on simple fundamental principles, but the endless transformations within the system of Nature contributed an apparent complexity, veiling the true nature of the Ideality.

Van Doesburg's interest in such Theosophical concepts is well established. As far back as 3 May 1902 he had written that 'now I have a god. Harmony. I want to reveal him in form and colour. Colour is God. God is colour' (Van Straaten, p. 26). Van Doesburg's diary entries continued this theme through 1904 when he wrote that 'Oh, colour! . . . thou art in the high heaven, thou art the air itself and the light. Thou art all-encompassing, in everything, and everything is in thee. Everything that is seen, is seen through thee, Oh colour!' (14 November 1904, Van Straaten, p. 28). In 1914 he opened his 'letters to Bertha' saying 'for me the Light of Goodness, the High, and the Beautiful was the only light that I, for years, recognised as Reality. So also, for years, did I imagine God.'

In De Vonk Van Doesburg attempted to translate theory into form. The arts were finding a unified expression in the chief of all the arts. Ideas had been drawn from contemporary philosophy, various international movements in painting and architecture, most particularly Cubism and Rationalism, and with their combined strength in the 'painterly conception of architecture', the last step into the new cultural epoch appeared to be at hand.

3

◇◇◇

Work with De Boer:
colour, mathematics, and music

At De Vonk Van Doesburg used the 'open' nature of painting against the 'closed' nature of architecture in order to articulate the constituent planes and elements. Further, the resulting more perfect definition of space was intended to be a revelation of the universal idea, or Bolland's pantheistic God. The means used to this end were the elementary means of painting: geometry and colour. Van Doesburg's most basic definition of what was involved in the struggle towards a universal style, that is 'the mathematical definition of plane and colour',[1] retained its pivotal position throughout the most active years of *De Stijl*. An indication of this and its consequences for painting and architecture is to be found in 'Principles of Neo-Plastic Art' ('Grondbegrippen der nieuwe beeldende kunst') of 1919 which appeared as Bauhaus Book 6 *(Grundbegriffe der neuen gestaltenden Kunst)* in 1925. Although a considerable number of years intervened, and the text had to be translated into German, giving a perfect opportunity for complete revision, the 1925 text does not differ significantly from the 1919 version. The later text reaffirms Van Doesburg's position:

The artist, and particularly the modern artist, sees nature creatively in that he gives form to his experience through pure artistic means, not arbitrarily, but according to the logical laws of his branch of art (these laws are the means of controlling creative intuition). . . .

When the aesthetic experience is expressed directly through the creative means of the branch of art in question, the mode of expression will be exact. The artist is, of course, entirely free to make use of any science (e.g. mathematics), any technique (printing-press, machine, etc.) and any material whatever, to achieve this exactitude.

Later in the text the consequences of the position are discussed:

It is unnecessary to record every stage in the development of [the] importance [of the purely expressional means] in the evolution towards an exact artistic expression. We may summarise all these various currents, whether or not they belong to systems as: the conquest of an exact expressional form of the aesthetic experience of reality.

The essence of the formative idea (of aesthetics) is expressed by the term *cancellation*.

One element cancels out another.

This cancelling out of one element by another is expressed in nature as well as in art. In nature, more or less concealed by the accidents of the particular case, in art (at least in the exact, formative kind), clearly revealed.

Although we cannot grasp the perfect harmony, the absolute equilibrium of the universe, each and everything in the universe (every motif) is nevertheless subordinated to the laws of this harmony, this equilibrium. It is the artist's business to discover and give form to this concealed harmony, this universal equilibrium of things, to demonstrate its conformity with its own laws, etc.

The (truly exact) work of art is a metaphor of the universe obtained with artistic means.[2]

This stated intention to create a metaphor of the universe is essentially the same as his claim to Hoste that the architecture of De Vonk produced a 'direct link with God', except that it is no longer couched in such mystical terms. The creation of this metaphor is to be achieved by the application of the 'logical laws of his branch of art' and by the 'cancellation' of one element by another; to put it more clearly, by the laws of vision and the use of elements in a kind of 'visual dialectic'.

In the exact, formative work of art the formative idea is given direct and actual expression by continual cancelling out of the expressional means: thus a horizontal position is cancelled out by a vertical one, similarly dimension (large by small) and proportion (broad by narrow). One plane is cancelled out by another which circumscribes it or one which is related to it, etc., the same applies to colour: one colour is cancelled out by another (e.g., yellow by blue, white by black), one group of colours by another group of colours and all coloured planes are cancelled out by non-coloured planes and vice versa.[3]

The 'logical laws' of vision are determined by the sciences of geometry and colour. Van Doesburg developed his attitude to mathematics from his understanding of Cubism. His debt to Cubism has already been noted in connection with his series of paintings *Three Creative Moments of a Composition* (figs. 1, 2 and 3) where the compositional development is related to that of Analytical Cubism but taken to its logical extreme: it is a geometrical analysis of a natural subject abstracted to such a degree that all natural references have been removed. Van Doesburg also considered his early stained-glass windows to be Cubist compositions as is made perfectly clear by the title of one of his earliest windows, *Cubist Composition with Swan*, of 1916. However, he was obviously using the term in a broader, more fundamental way than those who reserve the title for works of the classical phase of the movement. In *The New Movement in Painting* (*De nieuwe beweging in de schilderkunst*), written in 1916 and published in 1917, he explained his use of the word as follows:

The Cubist (a name that is in fact meaningless and was applied in a derisory manner) extracts the mathematical from the natural form and in so doing retains the pure artistic form. This artistic form comes from within; this is the spiritual form; the spiritual form is the plastic; and the plastic, the pure. The Cubist is fully conscious of the plastic value which an object possesses, but for him the object is the logical clarification of Space and therefore has a deeper, more philosophical meaning for him than for the Impressionist. [p. 24]

The Cubist does not value 'space' above 'the plane', but rather has a different conception of space from that of the naturalistic painter. The plane is for the

28 Theo van Doesburg,
Stained-glass window, *Dance
I*, 1917 (glass in primary
colours with green at the
edges, 47 cm × 27 cm); Van
Doesburg Collection, R.B.K.
(AB 5049)

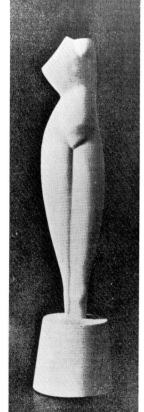

29 Alexander Archipenko,
Torse, 1914; as reproduced in
De Stijl, III, no 3 (January
1920), plate IV

former the symbol of Space, and each thing in this field of perception becomes
the representation of this conception of Space. The point is therefore not to
imitate or copy a section of actual Space, as it was with the painters who used
linear and atmospheric perspective, the point is to express the concept 'Space'.
To this end, the Cubist concerns himself with mathematical forms. [p. 26]

According to his definition of Cubism, then, his stained-glass window
Dance I (fig. 28) formed a Cubist composition by virtue of its expression
of space in its mathematical analysis of form. The direct inspiration of
this composition was Alexander Archipenko's sculpture *Torse* of 1914
(fig. 29). The link in the compositional development is a painting entitled

30 Theo van Doesburg, *Dance I and II* (oil on asbestos panel, 51 cm × 65.5 cm including frame); Van Doesburg Collection, R.B.K. (AB 4096)

Dance Figures I and II of 1916 (fig. 30). The window variation in primary colours uses the right-hand panel of the diptych, repeats the figure and rotates it through 180°. The two figures are pressed together, integrating their geometries to de-emphasise completely any surviving naturalistic references. The final result is a bi-partite geometrical composition rotationally symmetrical about the diagonal. Returning to the left-hand panel of the diptych (which was used similarly for a window in secondary colours), it is easy to see the derivation from Archipenko's *Torse*, and Van Doesburg's editorial comment on the sculpture in *De Stijl* (III, no. 3 (January 1920), p. 32) confirms the comparison:

The emphatically straight vertical line in the middle of the sculpture, as a counterpart to the upper plane of the truncated cone, holds the upper section in rest and balance. On this line the two halves appear to rotate, a movement reinforced by the conical plinth. Though in its subject still a classically conceived sculpture, the mathematically determined form and pronounced posture endow this with a thoroughly modern spirit.

Here Van Doesburg turned his attention specifically to the mathematical build-up of the form and its visual dialectic, using the same sort of terms as previously used by Vantongerloo in his analysis of Archipenko's sculpture *The Gondolier* (*De Stijl*, I, no. 11 (September 1918), pp. 134–35). An early sketch for *Dance I* (fig. 31) shows that in about mid-1916 Van Doesburg was using precisely the same analysis of form as used by Vantongerloo in the illustration accompanying his article (fig. 32). This method included a visual dialectic of forms, planes, and lines of movement placed in 'cancelling' opposition. Van Doesburg was, then, using such a method at least one, and in all probability two years prior

31 Theo van Doesburg,
Sketch sheet for *Dance I* and
for *Cubist Composition with
Swan*, 1916 (pencil and ink on
tracing paper, 19 cm × 17 cm
unevenly cut); Van Doesburg
Collection, R.B.K. (AB 4665)

to the publication of Vantongerloo's article. It is also interesting to note
that a sketch for *Cubist Composition with Swan* appears in the lower left-
hand corner of the same sheet as the sketch for *Dance I*. In 1922 Vilmos
Huszar looked back over Van Doesburg's work to his *Still Life* of 1916
(fig. 4) and approvingly drew the following conclusion:

In this work of Theo van Doesburg (1916) naturalism has already been largely
overcome and geometrical form has taken over from natural form, allowing
us to see planes of colour in 'planar space' instead of in perspectival space.

It is not a visionary conception, but rather a return from the experiential form
(the particular) to the essential form (the general).

The form is in all essential respects the geometrical form. An apple is not
observed in detail, that is to say with its small characteristic bumps and nuanced
colour, but returns to [its essential] round (form) and red (colour). In this way
a shadow also receives a positive value, in other words one proceeds from analys-
ing observation to a synthetic abstraction.[4]

An interest in the mathematics of form led to an interest in the mathematics of colour. Wilhelm Ostwald was a scientist who developed a colour theory on precisely this basis. His work was brought under scrutiny
by Huszar in the August 1918 issue of *De Stijl* where his book *Die Farbenfibel* was reviewed. After an extensive quotation from the introduction
to *Die Farbenfibel*, Huszar praised the clarity, simplicity, and precision
with which Ostwald laid out his argument. Huszar then turned to establish the relationship between this kind of scientific study and the plastic
arts. For the scientist the study of colour was an end in itself, while for
the artist it was simply a means to a creative end. It could be used as
a guide and control over the creative intuition, but if used as a strict

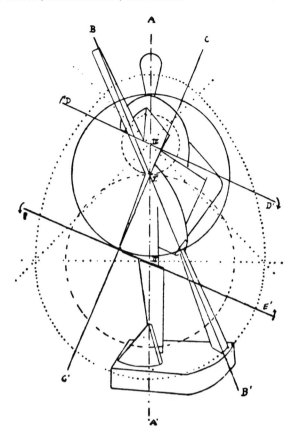

32 Georges Vantongerloo, *Analysis of the sculpture 'The Gondolier' by Alexander Archipenko*, as reproduced in *De Stijl*, I, no 11 (September 1918), plate XVI

formula for the production of 'art', the results would be banal, dry, and academic.

Ostwald was an extremely prolific writer, and in such books as *Die Farbenfibel*; *Die Farbenlehre*; *Der Farbenatlas*; *Goethe, Schopenhauer und die Farbenlehre*; and *Die Harmonie der Farben*, he evolved a system whereby all known colours could be located in a colour solid by means of co-ordinates. Most simply described, the colour solid had the pure chromatic colours arranged on the circumference of a circle while the grey series formed a central axis perpendicular to the plane of the circle. Colour harmonics could be objectively determined using 'lawful relationships':

Harmony = Order
   To find all possible harmonies one must study all the possible orders (arrangements) of the color solid. The simpler the order, the more illuminating or convincing is the harmony. Of such orders we have . . .
   Gray Harmonies. The simplest application of the principle is present in the standardized achromatic colors, as they are arranged by equal intervals . . . from the standard series . . . For example, a, c, e or g, i, l (simple intervals), and also a, e, i or g, l, p (double intervals), and a, g, n or c, i, p (triple intervals) . . . To such gray harmonies will fit chromatic colors whose color symbols contain the same letters [that is, have the same amount of grey], thus to gray harmony

33 Wilhelm Ostwald, *Die Farbenfibel*, p. 19. Van Doesburg's own copy signed and dated *Theo v Doesburg 1918*; Van Doesburg Archive, R.B.K. The colours in the circle range from yellow at 00, red at 33 and blue at 67, through green at 83 to yellow again.

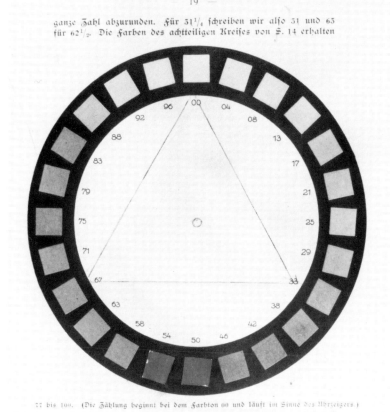

in g, l, p one may take chromatic colors, the color symbols of which end in lg, pg or pl . . .⁵ [See fig. 33]

This passage is from chapter 6, 'The Harmony of Colors' in *Die Farbenfibel* of 1917. In 1918 Huszar experimented with the grey series in a painting, *Composition in Grey*. In the February 1919 issue of *De Stijl*, Van Doesburg juxtaposed Huszar's painting with a related, but 'non-composed' design (fig. 34). The accompanying critique betrays both the influence of Ostwald and an attitude to the place of science in art very similar to that outlined by Huszar. Most importantly, geometry and colour are related within an integrated proportional system:

While in B a few planes are just distributed rather haphazardly, in A each plane has had its shade and position determined by the creative intuition of the artist. This creative intuition, which determines the content of the work of art (aesthetically balanced relationship), is itself controlled in the act of painting by the awareness of mathematics. In this mathematical build-up, the constituent planes are related to each other and the composition as a whole, with the result

A   B

that the proportion of the overall plane is to be rediscovered in the proportion of each constituent plane. In this way unity in diversity arises.

The same is true of the colour or shade. Each shade is given the same relative value in a regular progression from light to dark in the proportion 1–2–4. That again has the closest possible relationship with the proportional dimensions of the planes. Therefore, the geometrical division of the plane is the same as the geometrical division of the colours. In this way a unity, a reasoned harmony, arises through the geometrical relationship of plane to colour.[6]

34 Vilmos Huszar, *Composition in Grey*, 1918 and the comparative example (by Van Doesburg?), *Non-composed planes*; as reproduced in *De Stijl*, II, no 4 (February 1919), plate VII

Unfortunately Van Doesburg, unlike Ostwald, does not have the virtue of clarity, simplicity, and precision in his use of language, so it is not immediately clear what the precise relationship is between the proportional systems governing the geometry of the plane and division of the colours. Perhaps the geometry of the division of colours can be partly explained by a return to Huszar's 1918 article on Ostwald. In that article it was pointed out that colours could be exactly defined in Ostwald's system by number. Combinations of colours, like combinations of sound, were harmonious or dissonant according to their intervals and 'an interval [*samenklank*] of saturated colours is correct if the constituent colours together form a neutral grey'.[7] Huszar reproduced Ostwald's colour circle in the article and described how to determine these intervals:

00 is pure yellow, that is yellow which contains neither red nor blue. One can arbitrarily begin with *any colour* in order to create a chord of 3, 4, or 6 tones, provided that one determines the other colours geometrically, that is to say at equal distances from each other, in the form of a triangle, square, etc. In the same way one can also form dissonances by eliminating one, or two, or more of the tones.[8]

Huszar's definition of pure yellow implies that he believed the classical notion that the primary colours are red, blue, and yellow, as opposed to Ostwald's postulation of four primaries including green with the traditional three. Certainly Mondrian agreed with Huszar, and in Van Doesburg's own copy of Ostwald's 'Einführung' in *Die Farbenlehre* he has written 'Rubbish' next to Ostwald's comments on the '4 Urfarben mit die 25 Punten Abstand'. Van Doesburg continued below: 'In gestaltende Farbenlehre unterscheiden wir 3 Primäre Farbenergien 3 Secundaire also in ganzen 6 und 3 nicht farben.'[9] Despite their inclination towards objective criteria and controlling principles, they refused to be constrained by law or formulae; the principles were meant only as an aid and Huszar warned in his article against their use as hard and fast formulae. The final test for the rightness of a combination and/or proportion remained the artist's eye.

In the design of the stained-glass window for Jan Wils's Residence in Alkmaar (figs. 22 and 23), Van Doesburg used colours which in his terms were complementary primary and secondary triads of colour. Primary colours were used in the two outer lights of the triptych, and secondary colours in the centre light. Years later in 1930 he gave the key to his play with colour variations and geometrical themes in his stained-glass windows:

The decorative method is always based on the repetition of a motif. This motif, consisting of a number of coloured forms or planes, constitutes the actual foundation upon which the composition as a whole is built. This motif (or pattern) is repeated, once to the left, once to the right, reversed, or strung out horizontally or rising vertically . . . and it will not be difficult for the musically trained ear to discover the same decorative development of the musical 'pattern' in the work of no less a personage than Bach . . .

In many of the windows designed and architecturally applied by me between 1916 and 1918, I was influenced by the preludes and fugues of Bach. I followed the same method, however always taking care by a free use of the motif that the unity of the composition of the whole was broken neither by repetition, nor by the lead or bridges. I incorporated these into the motif or the composition itself, and as far as the proportions are concerned I began with the necessary subdivision of the window . . . Taking this method a great deal further we arrive at an indivisible compositional whole which on the one hand answers the undeniable demands of painterly harmony, and on the other fulfils the demands of the new architecture.[10]

In the years 1919–21 when working with the temporary District Architect Cornelis Rienks de Boer in Drachten, Friesland (in the north of the Netherlands), Van Doesburg produced a more radical development of this approach in an all-encompassing painterly conception of architecture than he had previously accomplished in schemes for buildings by Oud or Wils. The most important of the projects with De Boer consisted of a row of middle-class housing and opposite this an Agricultural School. Again Van Doesburg used triads of primaries and secondaries in counterpoint: the primaries on the middle-class housing, and the secondaries across the street on the Agricultural School. Both buildings are really very ordinary in themselves, being in traditional brick construction. Van Doesburg had encouraged De Boer from the very beginning to render the brick white and paint the woodwork in bright colours. In an early letter written to De Boer from Leiden, Van Doesburg cited Oud in support of the idea:

Oud, just as I am, was very much *for* plastering the whole [block of housing] white, picking out the doors and woodwork in strong colours, and contrasting this all the way along with black bands [of the window-boxes above the doors]:

In this way a certain rhythm is introduced . . . Colour against white will contribute a great deal to the long string of houses and will give strength to the whole design.[11]

Van Doesburg's work for De Boer was, as this passage indicates, primarily concerned with the creation of rhythm by the programmatic use of colour. At this stage Oud agreed in principle at least with Van Doesburg's ideas on colour, but from the letter it is evident that Van Doesburg's direct contribution was primarily restricted to 'the grouping of windows, doors, bow-windows, etc.' and how changes in the grouping would affect the ground plan. The changes advocated by Oud and Van Doesburg were suggested not as the result of closer consideration of the 'windows, doors, bow-windows, etc.' as functional elements, but rather as visual elements – again in order to achieve a certain rhythm. 'Most important', wrote Van Doesburg, 'is that you understand our intention, namely to bind all details into a unified whole within certain lines.'[12] Willem Brouwer, a friend of Oud, lived in Leiderdorp not far from Van Doesburg in Leiden. In a letter of 15 January 1920, Brouwer described a visit to Van Doesburg's the previous day when the two had discussed precisely the above-outlined approach to design:

I know only too well that you cannot get a word in edgeways during his crushing propagandising . . . ; I must review my ideas [according to him]. That's easy to say, and perhaps tenable. Brick doesn't count any more. You design (or rather 'construct') a house on *white* paper, *therefore* . . . (do you really want to hear more?) . . . the house must also be in material rendered white; a house designed on purple paper would have to be purple. The windows on the elevations, which are essential to the utility of the interior, can *not* have their size and location determined by an architect; *that* he reserves for 'painters'. If I didn't know that the man really means it, then I would think that he was slowly going mad! The beauty of the colour of brick *is no colour at all*. Everything is *nothing*; only . . . *nothing* is . . . everything. He puts words in your mouth which you've never said, and then proceeds to argue against 'your position' . . . We even turned to *music* for a while. He totally denies *feeling*. Bach . . . is therefore only beautiful because his music is technically perfect . . . And . . . if I understand right, *you* . . . you are letting yourself be hoodwinked to the point that you're of the same opinion, then . . . I denounce you, because all joy is gone from your work. '*Joy* . . . *Foolishness*, sir, that's all subjective.'[13]

The next year, in 1921, Van Doesburg was working on designs for colour-schemes, both interior and exterior, for Oud's public housing at Spangen VIII and IX as well as being in an advanced stage of his co-

35 Theo van Doesburg (C. R.
de Boer, architect), Colour-
scheme for middle-class
housing, Drachten,
Netherlands, 1921 (pencil,
ink and watercolour,
14 cm × 43 cm); in the
collection of It Bleekerhûs
Museum, Drachten, Friesland
(dwg no 581)

operative work with De Boer. Van Doesburg used the same
mathematical/musical approach to both designs. Notwithstanding the
implications of the above-quoted letters that Oud was, for the time being
at least, in basic agreement with Van Doesburg's ideas, it was Oud who
in the event rejected the colour-schemes prepared for him by Van
Doesburg.[14] Oud had himself imagined his seaside promenade of 1917
to be rendered white, with doors picked out in bright colours. He was
also quite prepared to have Van Doesburg add colour to certain elements
of a building, as at De Vonk, or to produce interior colour-schemes, as
for Spangen I and V. Oud even continued a restricted use of colour in
such projects as his submission for a Berlin competition for a private
house, and for his 'Café De Unie' in Rotterdam. However, when Van
Doesburg developed his radically painterly approach to architecture
between 1919 and 1921, Oud shied away from an 'aestheticism' which
threatened to interfere with functionality, and for the same functional
considerations he rejected the 'sentimentalism' of Brouwer.

  Although De Boer was a provincial and formally speaking a rather
conventional architect, Van Doesburg's close friend Evert Rinsema was
able to write at the completion of the projects in Drachten that 'De Boer
is, I think I am safe in saying, over the moon with your work.'[15] The
drawings which he received from Van Doesburg, who was then in
Weimar, included colour-schemes for interiors, exteriors, and even
planting schemes and painted fences for the gardens of the middle-class
housing. By far the most interesting of all the drawings for the two projects are the elevations with their explanatory texts. Van Doesburg's
drawing for the elevations of the middle-class housing (fig. 35) was
copied from the drawing submitted by De Boer to the local council for
planning permission in May 1921. The colour-scheme uses primary colours and distributes them in such a way as to generate a movement
down the length of the block as described by the diagonal lines. Van
Doesburg wrote on the drawing of the front elevation that 'the coloured
lines indicate the movement of the colours and the logical proportion
relating to the essence of the building'.[16] Colouristically these lines of
movement (also to be seen on figure 37) correspond to the form-lines,
or 'lines of force', used by Van Doesburg and Vantongerloo in their
geometrical analyses of Archipenko's sculpture. It would seem, then,

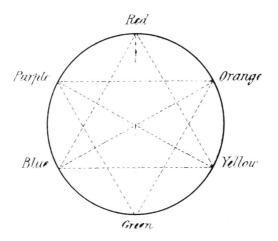

36 J. W. von Goethe, Colour circle with primary and secondary colours; as reproduced in *The Theory of Colours*, plate I, fig. 3

that Van Doesburg was attempting to develop a visual dialectic in the realm of colour. As has already been quoted, but cannot be over-emphasised in this connection:

In the exact, formative work of art the formative idea is given direct and actual expression by continual cancelling out of the expressional means . . . one plane is cancelled out by another which circumscribes it or one which is related to it, etc., the same applies to colour: one colour is cancelled out by another (e.g. yellow by blue, white by black), one group of colours by another group of colours and all coloured planes are cancelled out by non-coloured planes and vice versa.[17]

The colours were to be applied to the window sashes and the door-panels only, leaving the frames and the stiles and rails of the doors painted white. Van Doesburg had originally encouraged De Boer to render the building white and paint the window-boxes above the doors black, thus produc-ing a rhythmical series of black lines 'cancelled' by, or rather in an oppositional contrast to, the white planes of the rendered elevation. Because he was unsuccessful in convincing De Boer to render the brick, it became necessary to isolate the areas of colour from the coloured brick by painting the frames to form a white plane circumscribing the coloured 'plane'. By the same token the window-boxes could no longer be painted black without having a white planar surface to 'cancel' them, and they were therefore integrated into the *colour*-scheme as opposed to the *non-colour*-scheme.

Opposite the middle-class housing was the Agricultural School, designed to be painted in the complementary triad, purple, orange and green. Using the method outlined by Huszar for determining colour harmonies according to Ostwald's theory, but remembering that while the artists of De Stijl were fascinated by the methodology of Ostwald they preferred the traditional three primaries of Goethe, a colour circle showing two interlocking triangles can be constructed as in figure 36. The triangle had particular significance for Van Doesburg in this project for relating geometrical proportion to colour proportion. The gloss on a drawing entitled 'a schematic representation explaining the movement

of colour across the elevation of the Agricultural School in Drachten'
outlines the relationship as follows:

By their opposition the different movements bring each other to rest. In the front
elevation [fig. 37, centre section] green (A) ⌒ is opposed by ⌄ violet (B).
Orange puts these movements at odds and yet at the same time binds them
together (c ⨯ c). In the side elevations [fig. 37, left- and right-hand sections]
the architectural grouping [of elements] with their stepped roofs is accentuated
by the rhythmical use of colour. Purple and green each work against the other
ᵇ⁄ᴬ′ ⨯⨯⨯⨯ while orange works eccentrically in agreement with the architecture. Black, white, and grey work as non-colours or *rests*. The starting-
point for the main scheme for the architecture as a whole is namely the △.
Because the one colour movement works so hard against the other, rest will
be the overall result. The same is true of the colour proportion (± 3·5·8/
o[range]·v[iolet]·g[reen].) and the relationship of the colours to each other (A′)
for which see the accompanying colour chart.[18]

As is often the case with Van Doesburg's writing, his meaning is not
immediately clear. He does not elaborate on how the triangle forms 'the
starting-point for the main scheme of the architecture', but on analysis
the front elevation of the school divides into two Golden Sections (see
fig. 38). The colour proportion 3·5·8 is made up of three consecutive
numbers in the Fibonacci series, and a drawing from a 1925 sketchbook[19] shows Van Doesburg constructing a series of interlocking Golden
Sections using the Fibonacci series as a basis for compositional studies
(fig. 39). The accompanying diagram (fig. 38) shows how the diagonals
of the two major Golden Sections form the triangle on which both the
rest of the architectural design and the colour-scheme are based. The
rest of the diagonals shown in the diagram define other Golden Sections.
Although this explanation may sound contrived, there is another better-
known example of the use of the Golden Section in architectural design.
De Boer submitted his completed design for the Agricultural School to
the town council on 30 May 1921. Perhaps not so coincidentally Van
Doesburg announced the receipt of *L'Esprit nouveau*, no 5, in the March
1921 issue of *De Stijl*.[20] In that issue of *L'Esprit nouveau*, Le Corbusier
had published 'Les Tracés régulateurs', in which he used his own villa
of 1916 as an illustration (fig. 40), commenting that the facade 'est
réglée sur le même angle A qui détermine une diagonale dont les
multiples parallèles et leurs perpendiculaires fourniront les mesures cor-
rectives des éléments secondaires, portes, fenêtres, panneaux, etc.,

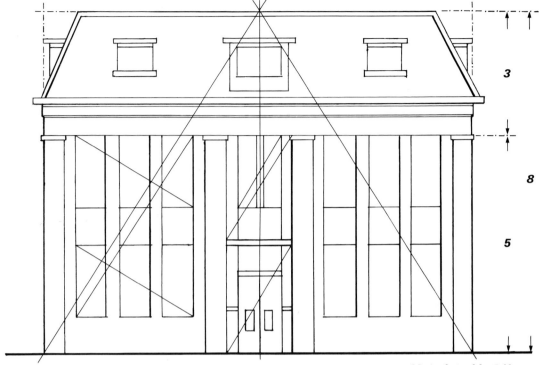

38 Analysis of the Golden
Sections in the facade of the
Landbouwwinterschool,
Drachten

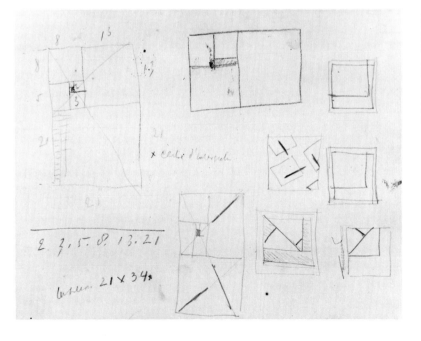

39 Theo van Doesburg,
Sketch study using Golden
Sections and the Fibonacci
series, 1925 (pencil,
27.1 cm × 20.6 cm); from
Sketchbook 2, *Holland en
Duitsland en Belle-Ile 1925 en
Caprie*, MS p. 10r, Van
Doesburg Collection, R.B.K.
(AB 4150 N)

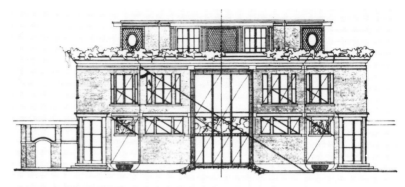

LE CORBUSIER, 1916.   A VILLA

jusque dans les moindres détails'.[21] These 'tracés régulateurs' are again
the diagonals of Golden Sections, and the applicability of the rest of the
quotation to the layout of the facade of the Agricultural School is
obvious.

Considering that in each case where the colour proportion is specified
it is 3·5·8, it seems that Van Doesburg was attempting to develop a
'Golden Section' for colour and 'therefore the geometrical division of the
plane is the same as the geometrical division of the colours'.[22] Comparing
the schematic representation of the division of the plane (fig. 38) with
the schematic division of the colours (fig. 37), the diagonals of the two
major Golden Sections coincide exactly with line A describing the movement of the colour green across the facade. Line B (violet) only approximates to the opposite diagnonals of those Golden Sections, and in the
side-elevations where the control of the geometry of the Golden Section
breaks down on the whole, so does the movement of the colour diagonals
become less uniform, giving way to the influence of the stepped profile
of the roofs. As far as can be determined from the drawings, the proportions of the colours refer very approximately to the area covered by the
colours in question. The dominance of the triangle in the distribution
of colour is demonstrated by a drawing entitled 'a schematic representation of the operation of the three colours on the rear elevation'. Here
also there is a gloss which gives the proportion of the colours as orange
3, violet 5, and green 8 (fig. 41).[23]

The extent of the application of a musical analogy has still not been
established within this analysis of the colour-schemes. Van Doesburg
did state categorically that he used 'the same method' as Bach in the
design of his early windows, so it is interesting to pursue the analogy
by comparing the fugue form with the Alkmaar window to see how
far the analogy can be taken, and how useful it is for an understanding
of Van Doesburg's work for De Boer. In the reproduction of the Alkmaar
window and its related diagram (fig. 22), two themes or subjects can
be identified. The left-hand panel of the triptych (or vertical row of
motifs), then, constitutes the 'exposition' where the four 'voices' have
each been introduced in this 'Double Fugue' or 'Fugue on Two Subjects'.
Also, in the smaller version of the Alkmaar window, designed for a

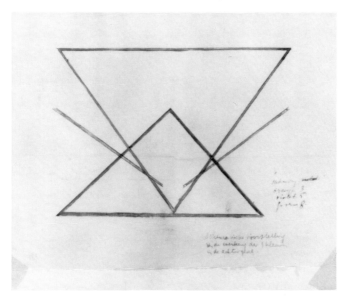

41 Theo van Doesburg, *Schematic representation of the operation of the three colours on the rear elevation*, Landbouwwinterschool, Drachten, 1921 (ink and gouache, 25.5 cm × 25.5 cm); in the collection of It Bleekerhûs Museum, Drachten (dwg no 1973–345–h). Top triangle, green; bottom triangle, violet; diagonals, yellow

school in Winschoten, the colour variation in the two lower panels constitutes in Van Doesburg's terms a change in key, thus 'voices three and four' (the two lower panels) are the 'answer' in a 'two-part fugue'. The centre panel of the triptych is made up of 'counter-subjects one and two' which are developments of the same 'melodic line' found in the corresponding motifs of the left-hand panel. The centre has 'changed keys' from the triad of primary colours to the triad of secondary colours, and in so doing functions as a fugal 'episode' which also has the function of changing the key found in the 'exposition' section of the fugue. Finally, at the end of the piece (that is, in the right-hand panel), there is a return to 'the original key', the triad of primary colours.

The diagrams and illustrations of the windows discussed in the last chapter can now be seen in terms of different 'species of counterpoint' and the glass mosaic of 1917 (fig. 20) is so strict that it resembles Canon. The earlier windows of 1917 are a kind of Strict, or Student's Counterpoint, but as has already been remarked,[24] by late 1917/early 1918 and *Composition V* the compositional method has been much less strictly applied in a sort of Free or Composer's Counterpoint. The same can be said of the colour-schemes for De Boer – the compositional method has not been as dogmatically applied as in the window designs, but it is nevertheless valuable to look at the schemes in terms of music. Van Doesburg himself conceived of the two colour-schemes as a single musical composition. In a letter dated 8 January 1921, but presumably of the same day 1922, Van Doesburg described an altercation over the colour-scheme for the school:

My dear comrade-in-arms,
   Your letter of 4 January was sent to me here [in Weimar]. I was pretty shocked. It really would be too bad if the colour-scheme for the Agricultural School could not be applied! . . . If absolutely necessary the col-

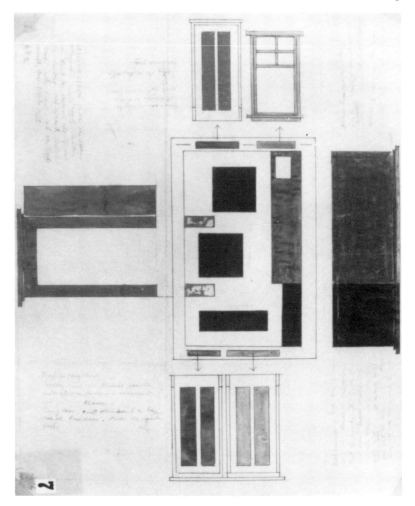

42 Theo van Doesburg, *Colour-scheme for the Kitchens* of the middle-class housing, Drachten, 1921 (pencil, ink and gouache, 26.5 cm × 31 cm); in the collection of It Bleekerhûs Museum, Drachten (dwg no 578)

ours could be tuned to a darker scale [*gamma*], but then they would no longer be balanced with the colours of the middle-class housing. As a last resort the same triad [*drie-klank*] could be given in a lower key . . . As far as the classroom goes, why shouldn't the students be allowed to look at the 3 secondary colours, orange, violet, and green, instead of brown or some other muddy colour? I am convinced that it will make their time spent at the school much more agreeable. Moreover the colours fit in such a public institution, seeing that they symbolise nature (although I do not create symbols, I create plasticism!).[25]

The colours for the two projects had been carefully tuned to each other, although in different keys. The primary and secondary colour-schemes were placed on opposite sides of the street as 'subject' and 'answer' of the overall composition, and the 'voices' of the coloured lines created rhythmical counterpoint moving across the facades, while the primary non-colours, black, white, and grey, acted as rests. This was intended to be visual Free Counterpoint on a monumental scale: 'I used the same

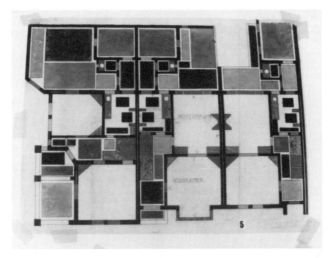

43 Theo van Doesburg,
*Colour-scheme II/Middle-class
Housing*, Drachten, 1921
(pencil, ink and gouache,
33.5 cm × 43 cm); in the
collection of It Bleekerhûs
Museum, Drachten (dwg
no 576)

method [as the preludes and fugues of Bach], however always taking care that by a free use of the motif that the unity of the composition of the whole was unbroken by repetition.' Although written specifically about his stained-glass windows, Van Doesburg's statement is also applicable to his architectural colour-schemes.

It was also Van Doesburg's aim to relate interior and exterior space by integrating their colour-schemes into a single composition. He can be seen making a very similar attempt in the contemporary designs for Oud's Spangen blocks VIII and IX.[26] In the designs for the middle-class housing and the school in Drachten, Van Doesburg integrated interior and exterior colour-schemes in two very different ways. By the simple device of painting the window-frames one colour both inside and out in the middle-class housing (the first scheme to be finished for Drachten), the colour-schemes of the interiors pierced the external wall at the window and were held in the three-dimensional spatial grid by the diagonal 'lines of force' of the facade. In the rooms the walls were papered in one of ten different grey wallpapers forming the ground to which the primary triad was 'tuned' (sometimes being varied slightly, as in the blue for the rooms at the back of the house). Colour was applied to architectural elements or their constituent planes as illustrated in the drawing of the kitchen (fig. 42) and occasionally, as in one of the entrance-halls, an isolated rectangle of colour was carefully positioned on a wall. The kitchen (centre-left) will help in the interpretation of the ground-plan shown in figure 43. Proceeding from the door, bottom centre: the step outside the door is red with white surround; the door has yellow panels on the interior but grey on the exterior; the floor on the hallway contains a blue square, changing to red passing the staircase, and a smaller yellow square faced by yellow doors to the kitchen (centre-left) and the back room. The back of the house is treated similarly but with a single colour for each of the back room, store-room, and WC. To the right of the extension is a terrace paved with a Neo-plastic composition. The main rooms, as the kitchen, have only had the main elements of the furnishing picked

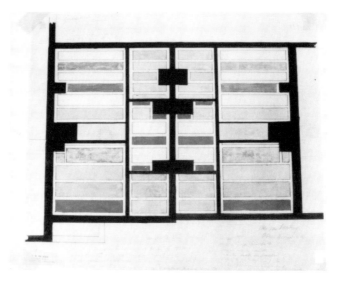

44 Theo van Doesburg,
*Colour-scheme III for First-floor
Ceilings*, middle-class housing,
Drachten, 1921 (ink and
gouache, 30.5 cm × 27 cm);
in the collection of It
Bleekerhûs Museum,
Drachten (dwg no 579)

out in the primaries. Upstairs the emphasis is switched from the floor
to the ceiling where Van Doesburg can be seen using the beams of the
ceiling to separate the coloured planes, but 'in order to create planes
between the beams it is necessary to apply battens of the same width
(that is visually) around the edges [of the room]. Like the beams these
are also to be white.' In this way he is investing structural elements
with visual meaning, but 'if the beams are other than as indicated, this
composition must be kept to as far as possible', runs the text on the
drawing (fig. 44).

In the Agricultural School, interior and exterior were bridged not by
the use of one colour at their points of contact (windows), but by the
use of dissonant pairs, one colour internally and one externally. Both
the middle-class housing and the Agricultural School were, for the most
part, being worked on at the same time, but the correspondence between
De Boer and Van Doesburg makes it clear that the school was begun
and finished last. Not surprisingly, then, Van Doesburg had developed
a much more complex manner for composing an interior and relating
it to the compositional net of the exterior. The one surviving ground-plan
for the colour-scheme (fig. 45) shows how he has used orange to 'bind
together the architecture' as he had in the elevations. Different elements
(a door, windows, and a cupboard) are connected by the use of orange,
while purple and green are set in opposition. This was no random
arrangement as can be deduced from a letter to De Boer:

'Vellinga [the new District Architect] will do the painting', you wrote about the
colours for the Agricultural School, but I am afraid that it will end in disaster.
'V[ellinga] is beginning to muddle through' etc. If Mr Vellinga does not stick
to my design all my work has been for nothing. Surely you can check to see
that he carries out the design according to *my* designs. If it is carried out *differently* from the way I have indicated on the coloured ground-plans, naturally
I can no longer accept responsibility. First he has to understand the *system*,
then there won't be any problems – and above all keep to the correct colours.[27]

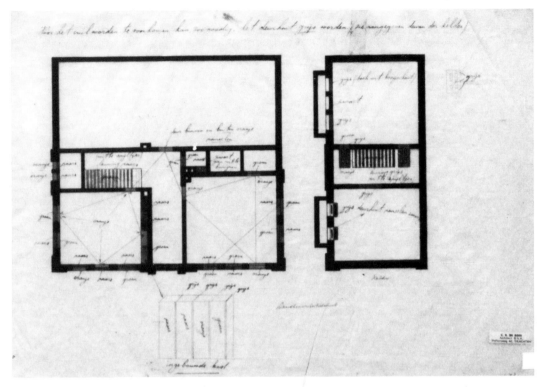

Van Doesburg often found working with De Boer a trying experience. In a letter of 23 June 1921, before the colour-schemes were fully under way, Van Doesburg wrote to a mutual friend, Evert Rinsema, in Drachten, that 'it really is too bad that work with De Boer has not achieved a real co-operative effort'. By the 1st of September, though, when De Boer had received a number of the drawings, Rinsema was able to write that De Boer was 'over the moon with your work . . . For me the main consideration is that you two can really work together.'[28] As usual Rinsema was very efficiently playing the middleman and peace-maker.

The public reaction to these designs was quite different from the enthusiastic reception by De Boer. The middle-class housing was painted according to plan and generally to Van Doesburg's satisfaction, but the result was brutally criticised by one Herman Martin in an article entitled 'Ugly Drachten'.[29] Both De Boer and Rinsema leapt to the defence. The latter, with a more fundamental understanding of Van Doesburg's intentions, wrote that:

Mr Martin sees pictorially, demanding mood. The new art is arising, and moulds spatially. A pillar in yellow and red (to which he refers) is no longer a pillar, and here Mr Martin is entirely correct. His interpretation of what that means is equally wrong. The new conception is not concerned with the pillar, as such; it builds spatially. The new conception aims to dissolve the weight and volume of the pillar.[30]

Van Doesburg had an ambivalent attitude to structural elements. Most often he invested them with an individual visual role and meaning con-

45 Theo van Doesburg, Colour-scheme for the Landbouwwinterschool, Drachten, 1921 (pencil, ink and watercolour, 35 cm × 44.5 cm); in the collection of It Bleekerhûs Museum, Drachten (dwg no 573)

sonant with their structural role, but occasionally their visual treatment contradicted their structural role, as here. He was trying to overcome the limitations of the then available technology of structures, while at the same time clarifying the architecture in terms of a programmatic use of elements.

When Van Doesburg read the defences by De Boer and Rinsema he immediately sent a congratulatory telegram (17 October 1921), followed two days later by an approving letter. He proposed coming to Drachten via Belgium and Amsterdam from Weimar to give an explanatory lecture in defence of his colour theory.

I also think that it will cause an enormous sensation if it appears in the Dragster Courant that Van Doesburg is coming (*from Weimar*) to defend the colour-scheme of the middle-class housing, eh? Colour in our Homes! you could call the lecture. [coll. Mercuur]

Even though there was so much opposition to the colour-scheme for the housing he pressed on with the work on the school. On 2 November he announced that the designs for the exterior were complete and that he was returning to the rest of the designs for the interior.[31] His lecture in Drachten did indeed cause a sensation but did not have entirely the right effect. In his letter of 17 February 1922 sent from Weimar, he explained to De Boer that he had hoped to make it easier for him to introduce the new in art. At the beginning of January it had still appeared that the mayor and town council were lending their support, but now the 'Director, Mayor, and the Minister himself are working against us after my lecture'.

This opposition makes me very nervous. It would be best to convince the lot of them that they're just afraid, but perhaps Martin is behind all this. You should send a message to all modern-thinking architects such as Berlage, Gratama, Wils, Oud, Pauw and Hardeveld, etc., and the foreign architects Peter Behrens, Adolf Behne, Adolf Meyer, Walter Gropius, Bruno Taut, who *all* work with painters and are introducing a coloured architecture.[32]

There was nothing for it, they had lost this battle, but not the war. Schippers claims that the colour had been removed from the housing in about 1922.[33] If so it was certainly not before April of that year because Van Doesburg wrote to De Boer on the 24th of that month, again hopefully inquiring if he had had the red doors painted a slightly different shade since they were too 'bloody' a red.[34] In the end all that survived of the whole two-part scheme was the two stained-glass windows for the Agricultural School (fig. 21). Owing to complications in their production Van Doesburg estimated that he had earned a miserable 40 cents per hour for their design.

Notwithstanding the setbacks and disagreement over payment for the windows, the co-operative work between De Boer and Van Doesburg did not end there. In mid-1922 Evert Rinsema, acting as middleman again, was trying to make a more permanent arrangement between the two:

As far as I can see Mr C[ornelis de Boer] still has bits and bobs in hand. I suggested to him that he have an arrangement with you *at so much per year*. Don't you think that was better? He can't do without your help.[35]

Their association did indeed survive for a short while. On 4 September 1922 Van Doesburg wrote that 'I am most impressed that you are soldiering on with the new idea, in spite of all the trouble', but his sincerity is brought into question when he continues that De Boer's work 'is increasingly valued by the *cognoscenti* here [in Weimar]', particularly considering that the statement is followed closely by a suggestion that the yearly honorarium be quite high, in the region of fl 1500–2000. This same letter was accompanied by the drawings for the colour-scheme for De Boer's own house:

Actually the whole door must be yellow. The yellow must hold the yellow of the balcony in balance:

balcony   yellow door

Besides the design itself I have made a sketch in order to let you see how I have solved the question of colour in the plane of the elevation. The blue of the sitting-room window counterbalances the blue of the dormer window. The red of the office window counterbalances the red of the balcony door. The jambs in this design are also coloured (not white).

I'm interested to see the result! A sample of the correct colours (absolute triad) is enclosed.[36]

The quotation may mean one of two things: either the position and size of the area of a given colour balanced another area of the same colour on the facade; or there may have been two differently tuned primary triads working counter to each other. In the absence of the drawings this remains speculative. Note also that the white surrounds have disappeared. For some reason he has found it unnecessary to isolate the colours of the elements from the colour of the brick. As in his other projects for De Boer, Van Doesburg worked from the exterior inwards. Having finished the exterior design, he was requesting further details in order to continue with the interior design. At the same time Van Doesburg was nearing completion of yet another project for De Boer. It was another colour-scheme, this time for a shop.

One of the last projects for De Boer was for the stained-glass windows for a primary school. Unlike the windows for the Agricultural School, these were Neo-plastic compositions without subjects.[37] Van Doesburg's mathematical/musical system for the statement of theme and variation of geometry and colour was far better suited to stained glass than to architecture. Van Doesburg had said to De Boer that 'I am pleased that my window *Pastorale* for the Agricultural School suits you and also the director. Yes, the new style is still accepted best in stained-glass.'[38] Up until that time his work in glass was his great success. He had made a very interesting programmatic use of colour in architecture, and had made important advances in terms of his later work concerning the spatial use of colour and possibilities of colour for the delineation, clarification, and definition of space. However, a more fundamental change in the application of his painterly conception of architecture was needed in order to fulfil its full potential. Van Doesburg did not have a sufficient architectural skill at this point to make the advance on his own; De Boer simply did not have the talent and imagination; and Oud, who most assuredly had the talent, was unwilling to rein in on his own ideas to give Van Doesburg the scope he needed. Oud did not need a public uproar to convince him not to carry out Van Doesburg's colour-schemes. Oud had suggested changes to the colour-schemes for Spangen VIII and IX and when Van Doesburg refused, the designs were rejected *in toto*.

A related incident is illuminating for an understanding of Van Doesburg's participation in 'collective work'. Jan Gratama had dismissed Oud's work:

The architect Oud is the precursor of the Cubists in architecture. He propagandises on their behalf in the periodical *De Stijl*. Oud, who is not a great talent, still has not managed to avoid all decoration . . . but just take a look at a block of flats by him. It is forbidding in its deadly monotony. It is, however, strict and impersonal. A villa by him is even worse; here one sees the anxious, the bloodless decadence of a dying society.[39]

Van Doesburg, still bitter about the rejection of his designs for Spangen, replied that in practice Oud had failed to realise a Cubist architecture except at the villa De Vonk. The work at Spangen was denied the title – and what if Van Doesburg's colour-scheme had been applied? Would it have qualified as a Cubist work in that case? Oud's definition of a Cubist architecture was in agreement with Van Doesburg's, namely that it was 'the process of separation [into constituent elements] and reconstruction, which our architecture needs'. However, Oud continued that 'I believe that "Cubism" is therefore not the "coming style", but consider that once completely superseded, will give way to the "new" style'. Van Doesburg's rejoinder was that he never intended to posit a 'permanent Cubism'.[40] Cubism was simply a prelude to the new conception of art. Essentially they agreed about Cubism and architecture; they disagreed about the essence of the 'new conception' (*de nieuwe beelding*). In September 1922, Van Doesburg wrote that 'In order to create an image [*beelden*] certain means are necessary. In the modern sense (as opposed to simply the constructively pure sense) *beelden* is therefore *the organisation of means in a simple* (that is to say only with a single explanation) *and real unity*'.[41] These means included space and materials, and colour for Van Doesburg was a material, the *basic* material. Painting led the way towards a new style for architecture in Van Doesburg's conception. The following month, Oud published an article in the same periodical complaining 'that the historical imperialism of architecture (against which a degree of resistance is directed at the same time and to a certain extent rightly so) is now being threatened by a no less imperialistic dictatorship of painting. It is an aesthetic aberration against which only a well-established architectural conviction can raise the necessary reagents.'[42] He did not object to the use of colour as such, but he did object to painting overwhelming or destroying architectural qualities.

Oud's old friend Brouwer, representing a great number of his own contemporaries, levelled a fundamental attack against both approaches. He complained that both had forgotten human feeling and happiness. They, he contended, were the naïve ones, searching for the '*oervorm* [primary form] in all its sobriety':

And that today's men (I mean THOSE few men like you and v. D. and Van 't Hoff et al.) from the strength of their position wish to divest themselves of all stylishness, and want to find the original source BY A REASONED PATH, and by ARITHMETICAL CALCULATIONS (rhythm in numbers and numerical progressions etc.) and therefore by similar scientific means . . . can also be explained . . . That is also what I have against your work which I recently saw in [the journal] *Klei* [Gratama's article about De Vonk, 15 January 1920]. It is ONLY the (search for) primary form.[43]

Brouwer has raised the question whether both Van Doesburg's mathematical/musical and Oud's functional approaches produced a cold, dispassionate, inhuman art, or whether they adopted their respective approaches not solely for an aesthetic, but also for a moral end. Considering the social and spiritual overtones of Van Doesburg's writings, and Oud's continuous work in the area of mass housing, the answer is obviously affirmative, but the complexity of Van Doesburg's position warrants closer inspection.

4

❖❖

Berlage and the new humanism

In spite of the disagreements between Van Doesburg and Oud, Brouwer was quite justified in saying that they both essentially agreed about the question of a moral end for art. However, they would have denied his charge that their art was cold and inhuman. Van Doesburg would claim that such an art was based on a much more practical and effective humanism than the emotional humanism of Brouwer. Van Doesburg advocated a machine humanism as opposed to the sentimental and purely symbolic humanism (or so he would claim) of an architect like Berlage. The distinction can most easily be drawn by a comparison of Van Doesburg's stand with that of Berlage as put forward in his 1919 book *Beauty in Society* [*Schoonheid in samenleving*]. It provides a good summary of the themes prevalent in the numerous earlier works which had had a profound effect on Van Doesburg, while it also elaborates on the particular ideas which were to draw such strong criticism from him in a series of articles written during the winter of 1920–1.

Van Doesburg, in common with Berlage, justified his artistic bias by an argument which was a variant of historicism: in brief, the analysis of historical developments reveals the 'spirit of the age' and the demands of this spirit call a new style into being. Van Doesburg had used the historicist argument over and over again, from the 1915 lecture 'The Development of Modern Painting', through 'The Aesthetic Principle of Modern Plastic Art' and *The New Movement in Painting* both written in 1916, to 'The Style of the Future' of 1917. *Classic – Baroque – Modern*, a lecture delivered in 1918 and published in book form in 1920, deals exclusively with the subject, developing his own strong argument concerning an inevitable, unidirectional development of art towards abstraction, as opposed to growth and decline with vacillations between abstraction and naturalism. This is epitomised by the following passage:

It is my aim, insofar as possible in a short space, to introduce to you the meaning of the principal periods of development in art in their *nature* and *expression*, with the intention of bringing you nearer to the art of your own time and *its* nature and expression.

The principal periods of development, then (wherein the relationship of mankind to the Universal through the beautiful thus *artistically*), I should think, can be most clearly explained as: the *classic*, the *baroque*, and the *modern*. I ask you not to apply the growth-flourish-and-fall system, because systematisation is neither my intention nor does it apply here; and understand that I have no grouping in mind, but rather the distinction of three clearly evident *moments of creation* of the human spirit, which have had, and still have, both an *inner* and *outer* influence on our whole cultural development.

The conclusion of the study was that:

The development of modern art towards the abstract and universal, and thus *away from* the surface of things and the individual, has made it possible that through communal effort and from communal insight a collective style may be realised, that, above person and beyond nation, reflects the highest and deepest and most universal longings for beauty by all peoples, and brings it to a specific and real expression.[1]

Berlage opens *Beauty in Society* with the obvious intention of developing a very closely related argument based, again, on historicism. Usually, he says, architectural histories seem incomplete because they give no insight into the ideas which give rise to the basic principles of the art of a period. He continues his criticism of this kind of history, saying

In the description of a style, at best the government under which it flourished is named, while in a spiritual sphere a general outlook on life is not demonstrated as the deeper cause of the development of such a style. Finally, a possible social or psychological connection between the architectural form and its origins is not conceived . . .[2]

For both Van Doesburg and Berlage the history of architecture is the history of ideas, the truest reflection of the essential culture.

As Van Doesburg pointed out in his *Three Lectures*,[3] Berlage worked in the Rationalist tradition of Semper and Viollet-le-Duc. Besides frequent references to these two, Berlage quotes liberally from Bergson, Bolland, Plato, Schopenhauer, Hegel, Kant, and even Heraclitus, all of whom had had a formative influence on Van Doesburg's theoretical development. Within this common tradition, Berlage too had centred most of his major writings around the structure of historicism. As early as 1904 he published *Concerning Style in the Art of Architecture and Furniture-making*, which, besides being an introduction to the Netherlands of ideas from Semper's *Der Stil*, formulated on this Semperian foundation the problem to which he would dedicate the rest of his working life: the realisation of a style to manifest the new life in the new age. However, he did not expect an immediate solution. Before a new monumental architectural style could arise, society, which had been split by individualism and capitalism, had to be reunited by a new socialist order. *Concerning the Probable Development of Architecture* followed in 1905. It expanded on an article which had appeared in the periodical *De Beweging* the previous year, and in 1910 it provided the core material (as the third of four chapters) for *Studies Concerning Architecture, Style, and Society*.

In the 1905 pamphlet he was more willing to speculate on the style of the future, saying that the beauty of the materials would be allowed to come forth in the non-ornamented object as a reaction to recent ornamental excesses. A beautiful form would need no extra applied decoration, but he later qualified this idea by stating:

Now I believe in a coming culture, but not in a wholly undecorated tectonic reflection thereof, for the very simple reason that appropriate decoration is a natural impulse for man; so, by the same token, those things which appear to be wholly undecorated, on close consideration still appear as decorated.[4]

Here he has effectively returned to the strictly Rationalist position of Viollet-le-Duc, which he further emphasises in the immediately following pages. From Van Doesburg's point of view this was simply backsliding, leading to eventual retrenchment in traditionalist views. They were in fundamental disagreement as to whether art, and most particularly architecture, ought to be 'a wholly undecorated tectonic reflection' of a culture. Van Doesburg had developed an extreme position based on his concept of 'the elementary means of art' and related to Wölfflin's writings about the tectonics of art. Briefly, Van Doesburg's work was involved in the interplay between the literal structure and the visual tectonic structure in the creation of a new aesthetic, while Berlage 'retreated' into the traditional Rationalist position of 'decorated construction'.

Berlage further elaborated his position in *Architecture, Style, and Society* by exploring the relationship between art and society in an attempt to point out the rift in society between idealism and materialism, the source of the disunity which made it impossible for a great new style to emerge. He saw the art of the time in its many and varied forms as a reflection of a disunified society in a period of search, but thought that it was on the brink of a new Golden Age and the realisation of a new aesthetic. In terms of his view of history, they were in the transition between the period of growth in the nineteenth century and the flourishing of a new style in the twentieth.

This reveals another major difference between the theories of Berlage and Van Doesburg. Berlage had been a direct source of inspiration for the idea that style should be grounded in constructional principles. Further, they were both dedicated to the social basis and end of art. They agreed that art, especially architecture, was the revelation of the spirit of social man and that its history was the history of the development of that spirit. But they disagreed fundamentally on the shape of that history. Berlage cites Van der Pek and Hegel as his mentors,[5] but his system did not require that he go beyond the view of history as cycles of the growth, flourishing, and decline of particular styles, to a universal history governed by a single dominant theme or Idea. Hegel's system and Schopenhauer's concept of 'true history' (which saw past the transitory nature of individual events to the repeated application by mankind of a single theme) provided a place for Van Doesburg's essential theme that art was in constant movement towards abstraction by increasingly eliminating natural references. For him, Art and Nature were two entirely separate realms. He wrote *Classic – Baroque – Modern* in reply to the cyclical view of history championed by Berlage. The separation of the realms of Art and Nature became the basis in that work for the definition of the three 'moments of creation':

Every art, no matter when it develops, is to be called *baroque* whenever the inward, whimsically natural, or strange dominates.

Every art, no matter when it develops, is to be called *classic* whenever these . . . are balanced and expressed naturally.

Every art, no matter when it appears, is to be called *modern* whenever the harmony, the essence of beauty, appears wholly through artistic means.[6]

Berlage's view of history resulted in the idea that the state of society prevented any immediate development of a new style for the new age, but he was a patient man and awaited the coming of the new monumental style as the result of a long and careful development from the researches of the nineteenth-century masters Semper and Viollet-le-Duc. As opposed to this, Van Doesburg's idea of history lent an inevitability to the final realisation or reflection of the spirit in a totally abstract style emancipated from the historical styles and their applied ornament. He was impatient to break from all tradition, rejecting Berlage's notion that man has an essential drive towards decoration. Van Doesburg claimed that Berlage's position simply results in wilfully ornamented, that is to say *styled* works of architecture, not in a monumental architectural style. It thus actually impedes rather than facilitates the purification of the means, or elements, of architecture, or at least in these final stages of the process.

In 1918 Berlage completed *Beauty in Society*, which was published in the following year, and in January 1920 Chapter III, 'The Historical Development of Space', appeared as a separate article in the periodical *Bouwkundig Weekblad*. The titles make it obvious that the text was yet another careful reworking of his previous themes. This year also saw Van Doesburg's impatience become manifest in an increasing commitment to Dadaism. As I. K. Bonset, he began to publish poems entitled 'X-images', an article on poetry, and one on Dadaism – 'The Other Face'. In the last-mentioned, patient search and development is rejected in favour of undogmatic and unfettered experiment. The evolution of society and art through a development from the soul-searching, mimeticism, and stylistic copyism of the nineteenth century is characterised as 'The Ape in man':

The mimetic art of former times is the best evidence for Darwin's theory regarding the descent of man. If one just visits the museums of Europe one is no longer required to search out the fossils of transitional forms.

Nevertheless . . . most 'artists' have not yet been successful in overcoming the ape in themselves.[7]

He even refuses socialism as not being revolutionary enough and points out that 'Even if one has the word "proletarian" painted on one's front teeth . . . that does not make one a revolutionary.' On this basis, and demanding 'Dada Now!', he attacked Berlage in a series of three articles running from December 1920 to January 1921, which were written as a reply to *Beauty in Society*.

It is in this series, under the title of 'The Task of the New Architecture', that Berlage is berated as an 'arty' architect in opposition to the new mechanical aesthetic.[8] Quoting Hegel in *Beauty in Society*, Berlage asserts that the beauty of art is superior to the beauty of nature because it is born in the spirit of man. While fully agreeing with this, Van Doesburg maintained that Berlage's work remained too ornamental, that is to say too individual, wilful, and subjective. Berlage had attempted to avoid this attack by adding on to his idea of the work of art as the revelation of the soul of the artist, the argument that purely utilitarian works produced by mathematical calculation could not be works of art because, as the result of the fulfilment of function alone, they would be the same regardless of the age in which they were produced. Thus they could not reflect the spirit of the age and reach the status of art. This could only be achieved by the application of decoration as a complement to the construction.[9] Van Doesburg objected that functional needs changed, and they were now living in an industrial culture. The machine and the mathematical, objective design techniques of the engineers were therefore the direct reflection of the spirit of the age. 'Dr Berlage is blind to the great spiritual processes of his own time, processes which are consecrated in an aesthetic and social sphere.' It was a great disappointment to Van Doesburg that the important strides Berlage had made threatened to culminate in what he saw as a new facadism, an 'ersatz-Catholic' symbolic architecture. He quoted from *Beauty in Society*:

In that vision I saw the temple built in the middle of Europe, on a high hill on the plain; eight highroads leading from all climes to the entrances. These entrances are between the towers of life and courage, of inspiration and sobriety, of understanding and power, and of freedom and peace; these towers stand as watchmen round the great hall and at night send out their rays of light far into the darkness, giving passage to the temple . . . The galleries of the recognition of exultation and of the all-embracing reach high above the great hall, while the interior space is enclosed by the cupola of the community of the peoples.

    Thus I saw the temple stand as a Pantheon of Mankind . . .

Van Doesburg's reaction:

In what are called in this Biblical/pathetic writing, the 'towers of life and courage, of inspiration and sobriety, of understanding and power, of freedom and peace', is symbolised something which is realised in the modern factory, but in a completely unintentional way.[10]

Van Doesburg agreed that Rationalism had been an appropriate reaction to the facadism of the historical styles, but Berlage had allowed his yearning after an applied natural ornamentation to block the way to the realisation of a new aesthetic by the application of pure geometric and mechanical means. The new 'beauty in society' was to arise from necessity, from the most direct solution of the practical problems by the 'inner necessity' of the independent means, that is from both the means of production and the elementary means of architecture, *not* from the aesthetic intention and contrivance of individuals. 'Rationalism . . . may have been a necessary and refreshing reaction, yet really the spirit created by rationalism was itself too poisoned to call an architecture into being that commanded respect only by the confident fact of its construction.'[11]

Although his argument sounds close to Functionalism, it must be remembered that he treated the 'elementary means of architecture' as both functional and aesthetic elements in the solution of the two-fold nature of the problem of contemporary architecture: a new style for the new functional demands.

As has already been pointed out, Berlage supported his argument with numerous quotations from the philosophers who had also been influential on the development of Neo-plastic theory. However, as would be confirmed in 'The Meaning of the Mechanical Aesthetic for Architecture and the Other Professions' of 1921, Van Doesburg was apparently denying that premeditated stylistic formulae derived from their work had any application in the modern world. In spite of this denial, Schopenhauer still held a special place in Van Doesburg's Dadaistic stance. While Van Doesburg refused to acknowledge the relevance of 'the outdated dialectical systems of Kant, Schopenhauer, Fichte, *et al.*' to the precise mathematics of engineering, Bonset in 'The Other Face' distinguishes between Schopenhauer, Bergson, Nietzsche, on the one hand, and the others:

The philosophy of our time – Parliamentary philosophy (Kant, Hegel, Fichte, *et al.*), constructed and extended in fixed dimensions (thought-forms), is worthless in our time in which Schopenhauer's principle of self-negation is going to be fulfilled. This negation of form comes to expression in the intuitive philosophy of Nietzsche, Bergson, and Dada . . . – formless thought, wherein the object identifies itself with the subject. The individual, or thinking subject, has thrown himself into the universe. In formless thought it is not the 'I' (consciousness), but the 'all' (universal subconsciousness) that thinks.[12]

This 'formless thought' and 'negation of the self' were to be the basis of a 'true revolutionary' collective social reconstruction with architectural means, and the means of production in general, free from the constraints of a tradition to develop towards the solution of practical problems solely within their own terms, not the imposed 'artistic' terms of an individualistic architect.

The power of the human will, and the command of the natural elements and materials by constructive calculation, are becoming the basis of a new logically consistent experience of beauty, and the new aesthetic (we mention for convenience the mechanical) is the immediate consequence. The new style will be mechanical, synthesising all the elements from which previous generations drew their separate art idealism. The new mechanical style will not only make possible the expression of our strongest inherited longings for beauty, but it will realise mechanical socialisation at the same time, because from this style must follow the liberation of the individual and the masses from the servitude of manual production.[13]

As a prelude to his direct attack on Berlage, Van Doesburg had published a photograph of the American factory, Bethlehem Shipbuilding Works, in *De Stijl*, April 1920, and in the following issue he included editorial remarks on the illustration. This new 'paradise of glass, iron, and light' had the power to liberate man both practically and aesthetically. Further, it was morally uplifting, a place where 'the atmosphere for great deeds, in which humanity with and against the material world, forms a contrast with . . . itself as the conqueror of nature'.[14]

This was a new humanism, contrary to what he termed Berlage's 'Roman Catholic commitment'. It was a humanism quite different from the Humanism of the Renaissance which stressed the worth of the individual; it was a broader, social humanism. Van Doesburg considered that he had replaced the symbolic humanism of Berlage with a practical and productive mechanical humanism. As this could fully realise man's needs, it was no longer necessary for architecture to act as a symbol for those longings. He thus accused Berlage of clinging to the picturesque, as in his chapter on 'The Pantheon of Mankind' in *Beauty in Society*.

A central motivating factor in the positions of both Berlage and Van Doesburg was the intimate connection they saw between architecture and society. Architecture not only reflected the daily lives and the aspirations of a people, it could be used as an instrument for social reform – to reshape the material and moral life. As a moral instrument it could deepen experience and set the stage for 'great deeds' (as Van Doesburg said of the factory), creating a world fit for the new man out of the chaos of the war years. The individual was to find his freedom in collective work and, for the younger architects in particular, by harnessing the fantastic power of the machine. Industrial socialism, in an artistic not a political sense, provided a means and an end – a joyous, selfless struggle for the greater good of all in a revitalised Europe.

Berlage had proposed the 'Pantheon of Mankind' as a symbol of the longings of the people for peaceful, collective work. Van Doesburg proposed that the factory was such a 'Pantheon', with the power to bring those longings to a substantial realisation. As a reflection of these aspirations, the course and basic nature of the new architecture was very closely determined by machine production and its revelation of a new beauty – the beauty inherent in the material and the appropriateness of form. As far as this was concerned, Van Doesburg contended, Berlage had not followed through to the logical conclusion of his own work. Like the Cubists in painting, he had been frightened at the prospect of completely abstracted forms and had clung to natural form and decoration.

The respective attitudes to nature continued to be the major point of dissension between the two men. For Berlage the process of design was directly parallel to the natural process of growth – a constant variation and manifold production by the simplest, fewest, and most purified means. For Van Doesburg, man was in a continual struggle against the limitations of the material world, as was the case for Simmel in his article 'The Ruin'. Van Doesburg's social humanism had the power to overcome those limitations, to conquer nature. He attacked Ruskin and Morris for the same reason, even though Ruskin's attitude to abstract qualities in art in many ways showed a surprising resemblance to his own.[15] Ruskin's and Morris's romantic notion of socialism led to a picturesque handling of material (in Van Doesburg's terms), to handicraft, which could not hope to solve social problems and rebuild Europe after the devastation of the war. In support of his argument, Van Doesburg quoted

Lenin: '*If we could only build a great number of electricity stations on the land, we would accomplish a great cultural/historical work . . .*'[16] Berlage's Rationalism was not radical enough, and he had not enlisted the aid of what could be its strongest ally – the dynamism of the machine. Rather than creating the *symbol* of social unity and fulfilment, which eventually became a symbol of tragic longing and non-fulfilment, Van Doesburg was proposing that society harness the enormous sources of power for *the accomplishment* of those ends.

Each of the three instalments of 'The Task of the New Architecture' carried quotations as epigraphs. The core of Van Doesburg's argument can be found in the second:

Ne poursuivant pas une idée architecturale, mais simplement guidés par les lois que donnent les calculs (dérivés des principes qui gèrent notre univers) et la conception d'un ORGANE VIABLE, *les* INGENIEURS *d'aujourd'hui font emploi des éléments primaires et les coordonnant suivant des règles, atteignent au grand art faisant résonner ainsi l'oeuvre humaine avec l'ordre universel.*

Voici des silos et des usines américaines, magnifiques PREMICES *du nouveau temps, les* INGENIEURS AMERICAINS ECRASENT DE LEURS CALCULS L'ARCHITECTURE AGONISANTE.[17]

'L'idée architecturale' is the '*a priori* system' in Van Doesburg's parlance; there is a similar humanistic basis, construction of a new beauty with elementary means, and finally, the liberation from dead tradition in a mechanical aesthetic in architecture. Although the point of departure for the final two articles was taken from texts by Le Corbusier, this is not to say that the ideas themselves had been borrowed from him. Since the beginning of De Stijl, the machine had been considered to be an embodiment of the spirit of the age. It appeared in that role in Oud's 'Art and Machine' and Van 't Hoff's 'Architecture and its Development', of late 1917 and early 1918 respectively, and in Van Doesburg's own writings as early as 'The Style of the Future' written in November 1917, the month after the founding of *De Stijl*.

The relationship between Neo-plastic architecture and the Rationalism of Berlage is very much the same as the relationship between Neo-plastic painting and Cubism. Just as the painters of De Stijl found inspiration in Cubism, but considered that the Cubists had not followed their own principles to their logical conclusion, Van Doesburg had rooted his attitude to the purification of the means of architecture and the social basis and end of art in the writings of Berlage, but considered that his love of ornament had blocked the way to an objective mechanical aesthetic:

Forasmuch as Dr Berlage oriented himself towards the formulation of a rationalistic architecture and against the architecture of the styles, that is to say against the imitation of old styles, his admiration for decorative architecture was too great for him to re-establish his architectonic conception on a purely constructive basis and to crush the archaism in himself. It is from here that the contradictions, which I shall explore more fully, arise in his evaluation of modern architecture. These contradictions, to be found on nearly every page, must have their origin in an inner doubt which the writer attempts to abolish by submitting himself to one or another artificial logic. The great admiration for the 'architecture' of the past, with the 'house of God' as its centre, is incompatible with the geometric, strong, and real art of building, of number and measure, of volumetric and planar relationships which arise from the industrial culture.[18]

Van Doesburg recognised, and would continue to pay tribute to, Berlage's pioneering accomplishments (for example in 'The Will to Style' published in 1922, and in 'The New Architecture and its Consequences' written in 1930), but he registers strong disappointment in Berlage's 'fear of drawing what I should like to call the architectural consequence'.[19]

For all Van Doesburg's criticism, his own architecture found an essential basis in the work of Berlage. But Berlage could by no means see Van Doesburg as his successor. Regally, he made no reply to Van Doesburg's criticism. In fact, when *Beauty in Society* went through a second printing in 1924, he simply reiterated the short explanatory note which prefaced the first edition, adding that although the occasion had arisen he had no intention of making changes to or extending the argument, that it could be clearly evaluated as it stood.

Van Doesburg's evaluation, as demonstrated, was very severe indeed: the machine aesthetic had made decoration (in any case a very individualistic pursuit) an unnecessary self-indulgence. In his alternative the new materials, especially reinforced concrete, revealed the beauty of the smooth plane. Colour gained a special place through its emphasis of planar qualities and its ability to create relationships amongst the structural and functional elements. The elementary means of architecture (the plane, colour, and mass) controlled by the objective means of the mechanical aesthetic (proportion, measure, and function) were brought to bear on the problem of creating the new society.

For Van Doesburg, Rationalism perished along with the rest of a dead culture in the flames of Dada, but it was to arise phoenix-like in a more beautiful and complete form. The flames, however, continued and the phoenix of the new humanism remained somewhat insubstantial. Much had been accomplished, but the historical process and the fulfilment of the ultimate consequences of the work begun by Berlage were not moving as inevitably and swiftly as Van Doesburg had hoped. Shortly after the inauguration of *De Stijl* Van 't Hoff ceased to make an active contribution, Wils faded from the scene, and following quarrels with Van Doesburg, Oud withdrew from the group in late 1921 or early 1922 during the preparatory stages of the De Stijl exhibition for the Rosenberg Gallery. Wils continued to work patiently on the basis established by Berlage, and Oud, as city architect in Rotterdam, struggled with the problems of a large modern city. Van Doesburg's endless enthusiasm and dedication to his ideals, however, attracted a bright young architect, Cornelis van Eesteren, enabling De Stijl to rejoin the battle with even greater vigour.

Part II

The Hague 29/12 1922

Dear de Boer! – Thank you very much for your nice letter! To be sure my position is the same as yours: de Stijl ideas will carry the day against all others. Just look at how similar aspirations are to be found every-where. For example, look at the last issue of *Bouwkundig Weekblad*: that house by Dudok and the Sculptures by Csaky. Compare earlier works by Dudok (previously a great enemy of DE STIJL (the movement)) with the Villa Sevensteyn. The earlier works were vague and romantic affairs, sport with all possible decorative details, but now much more planar, stricter, more conscious, and more monumental. He worked for some time with Wils and that has left its mark! The article by Boeken is also a witness to the same spirit![1] So you can't pick up a journal any more without noticing the same sort of influence throughout! As long as it is honest work it's good to see. However, I know only too well that there are also dishonest workers. I saw, for example, a cheap imitation right here in the neighbourhood, in which the means of Neo-plasticism have been applied 'à la Biedermeyer', stained glass for example, with □, but apart from that ordinary *bourgeois* decorative ornament. To consider that it is just a matter of right angles is *the* big mistake. Squareness *began* with the need to draw the logical consequence with the maximum expression. The right angle is the simplest and at the same time the most expressive means of closure for a space, or drawing the boundary of a plane (colour-plane). It approximates 'formlessness' closely, because one can think the [outermost] boundary-points through to the infinite. As opposed to this the circle produces the strongest sense of enclosure:boundary, and is also the expression of intro-version (in its literal sense) and individualism.

When I cycle round The Hague I can see how much has already been achieved. Everywhere whole streets plunge past me in right-angled apparitions. On the Frankenslag, I saw a magnificent corner building by Bijvoet and Duiker, whom I would like to visit in Zandvoort. Further, there is also a whole series of concrete housing along the railway tracks.[2] Admittedly they are not *so* terribly good, but still to be admired. Here in the neighbourhood of Houtrust it is simply a miracle! The best in The Hague, however, remains Daal en Berg.[3] The house in which I am myself living has already been inspected and admired by all architects of note. It is delightful to live in a space that is so fresh and clean! There is a lot to see here, in spite of the fact that the use of colour is still deficient. Most architects just spread a bit of colour loosely about, and thereby still achieve no unity; painting requires a completely different attitude from building. –

Still it's delightful to see that the ideal which drove me to found De Stijl all of six years ago is now turning into a reality – yes and will presently be seen on the streets. That gives me the courage to continue my reform work with the same energy as before. –

Today Rietveld came past. He brought me a few very beautiful photographs of good interiors with completely new lighting solutions and with very beautiful furniture etc. We talked for a long time about our plans for the future and I think that the new year will begin with a substantial amount of work. We have, namely, plans to appear at the exhibitions in Germany with some exceptional work.[4]

I will also exhibit the photos of the shop and the drawings of the Middle-class housing (which you still *haven't sent* to me!). Perhaps there is something else of ours from that period that would be good for exhibition. –

Now I would like to answer your questions:

In order to achieve a monumental play of forms in architecture in my opinion it is necessary that any idea of separation must be eschewed. As long as we still recognise *separation* (that is things on their own: mantel-piece, window, door, window-frame, wood) then there is no *Unity*. Often that is the result of trifles. For instance, I have a mantel-piece in this room that could have been very beautiful, but which stands *completely* on its own because of the wooden laths and little things which completely isolate the mantel:

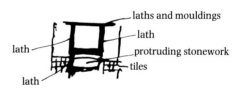

As far as I can see, it is much better to get rid of this kind of lath-work, which in any case serves no purpose. The protruding stonework is broad enough to sit a clock on, while it would have been sufficient to have used granite or marble facing stone. This is just *one* example. The same applies to the subdivision of windows. In a case where it is not the result of Constructional necessity, it's better to avoid subdivision. The division of the whole *window* must be in proportion with the wall-plane and thereby . . . a *non*-conventional form arises that is therefore not just *affected*. Moreover, I very much advocate an a-symmetrical grouping of doors and windows. For example, one can have a grouping thus, and so there come to be two different doors, a broad and a narrow, whereby the possibility arises in which to work counter to symmetry in a very practical way. At present symmetry is generally retained far too much,

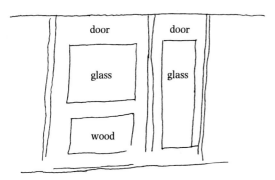

whereby a monotonous grouping arises. An a-symmetrical grouping is much livelier. As far as the subdivision of the wall (by the use of colour) is concerned, I believe that it seems restless sooner if the walls are not subdivided. As you also quite rightly remark, a feeling of oppression arises. This happens because the Constructive and closed character of architecture makes itself felt *too* strongly. Colour can be used instead to introduce a feeling of *liberation*. Therefore painting is an opener and *liberator* [of form]. Colour is sometimes destructive, but it is so *to the advantage* and not disadvantage (as Oud believes!) of the constructive character of Architecture! Colour *completes* the architecture, and with that is a moral influence as far as the user is concerned. Naturally that does not rest on the amount of colour, but only on the *relationship* between colour and space and the architectonic plane. It is certainly a characteristic of the new art that it always has two *polar elements* to bring into balance. That is what gives the new art a paradoxical char- acter. This causes confusion for those who only half understand. For example, Oud argued this way too: 'well, if colour is destructive, and destroys my arch[itectural] construction, then I want nothing to do with colour, etc.' But naturally it's not meant like that. What is meant is that colour generally is a loosening and freeing agent as far as closed form is concerned. However, what it really amounts to (and this is how one recognises the true artist) is that when the artist divides the closed walls and thereby loosens them from the Construction, he controls his *material*, that is colour, in such a way that he still achieves a unified, harmonised *whole* as a result. –

I find it very good indeed to note in your writing that you take *every- thing* into account and have thought things over. –

Yes, the Lissitzkies are very good,[5] and are all the more so because they have unbounded possibilities. I think that architects must surround themselves much more with these kinds of works (which are, however, rare), and through them begin to sense the endless spatial possibilities at the same time as coming to realise these possibilites in practice. Such works are the best nourishment for modern man. It's nice that you can find a few good things round at Rins's place, eh?[6]

In a few days I'll send you papers concerning the colouring for the Christian School. I'm already moving right along with the stained-glass compositions. It's great not to be bound by a figurative theme.[7] I'm sure that you'll like these comps. I'll put them straight into production, but can't send an accurate price until the glazier has seen the designs. [However, I] think that it will be quite favourable: all inclusive about fl 225. – to fl 250. – Too bad that it never comes to *complete* solutions. I would find it so nice if I could do up an interior *completely*, even if it was just one room. I mean where *everything*, furniture and all, worked together, and in which I did not remain restricted to little door-panels and applied strips. –

Let's hope that it will come to that yet.

I'm staying about another fortnight in Holland. Provided that it's possible to give another lecture in Friesland or Groningen, I will certainly come up to see you people in order to celebrate my departure. Couldn't I hold one at 'de Ploeg'?[8] I'll send them a card or something. I enclose one of my cards, perhaps you know another club in Friesland to whom I could speak. Most likely I'll have to speak in Konigsberg and could then come back again via Groningen. But that has *not* been confirmed yet! Couldn't you come down to The Hague some time? On 10 January in the Haagsche Kunstkring[9] there is going to be a Dada soirée for which Kurt Schwitters is coming over (from Hanover). Can't you drop in then too? For me there's always the question of the journey which is quite expensive, but still if I have a lecture up in that direction everything will fall into place.

We'll just hope for the best!

Tell Thijs[10] that I have the design for the clock ready in sketch form. I'm sending him the drawings at the first opportunity. I've also been considering the lamp. I haven't received anything, typographical design or text, from Buysse yet.[11]

In the meantime, I wish you all a plastic New Year [*beeldend nieuw jaar*], with ☐ greetings.

Doesburg

P.S.: How is your wife? Say hello to her for me.

P.P.S.: Were you still able to get the article about my lecture in Groningen?? –

[Letter in the collection of Thom Mercuur, Franeker, Friesland]

Introduction to Part II

Van Doesburg's attack on Berlage, his quarrel with Oud, splits in the fabric of De Stijl, and the uncomfortable relationship with De Boer, to say nothing of the hostility of the artistic and architectural communities in general, combined to render his position in the Netherlands if not untenable then at the very least ineffectual. That, along with the excitement of new ideas and contacts made during his stay in Weimar, made inevitable a shift in the centre of his operations and a renewed emphasis on the international character of the new architecture. During the last days of 1922 while temporarily staying in The Hague in preparation for the Dada tour, he wrote the foregoing letter to De Boer which casts a critical eye over the situation in the Netherlands, assesses the need for change, the salutary influence of De Stijl, and finally turns to the broader international contacts and his hopes for the future.

The letter begins by singling out Dudok and Boeken, both former critics of *De Stijl*, as examples of the growing influence of the publication. 'You can't pick up a journal any more without noticing the same sort of influence throughout!' Although Van Doesburg saw cheap imitations of De Stijl work being produced, he was confident that some architects had recognised the essence of the teachings of De Stijl and, most exciting, they were realising works based on De Stijl principles. He placed Bijvoet and Duiker in this category, citing their houses on the Oldenbarneveldlaan and Doornstraat. Jan Wils's 'Daal en Berg', however, was singled out as the best in The Hague. At the time, Van Doesburg was staying at number 18 Klimopstraat on the 'Daal en Berg' estate.

The house in which I am myself living has already been inspected and admired by all architects of note. It is delightful to live in a space that is so fresh and clean! There is a lot to see here, in spite of the fact that the use of colour is still deficient. Most architects just spread a bit of colour loosely about, and thereby still achieve no unity; painting requires a completely different attitude from building.

This quotation is a summary of the painterly conception of architecture developed in the early years of De Stijl, but in the letter he also elaborates on the emergence of a 'formless' architecture from the destructive properties of colour. This will provide the basis of the Elementarist conception of architecture developed in collaboration with Cor van Eesteren.

121

46 Theo van Doesburg,
Sketch designs for two
stained-glass windows for the
Christian Primary School,
Drachten, Netherlands (pencil
and gouache,
100 cm × 33 cm each); Van
Doesburg Collection, R.B.K.
(AB 5075 and AB 5076)

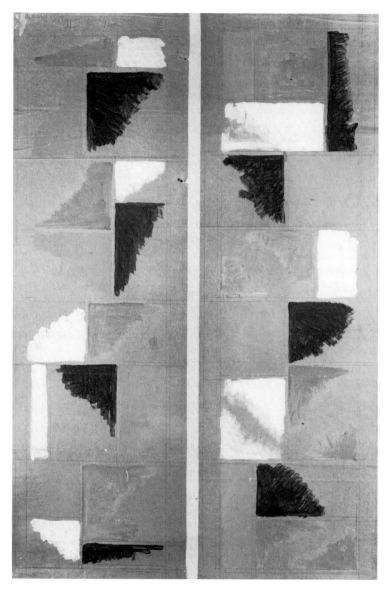

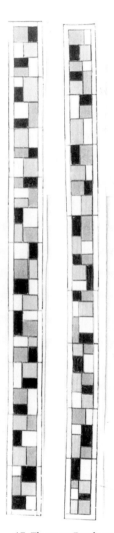

46 Theo van Doesburg,
Sketch designs for two
stained-glass windows for the
Christian Primary School,
Drachten, Netherlands (pencil
and gouache,
100 cm × 33 cm each); Van
Doesburg Collection, R.B.K.
(AB 5075 and AB 5076)

47 Theo van Doesburg,
Working drawings for
stained-glass windows for the
front door surround, Christian
Primary School, Drachten
(pencil and gouache,
136 cm × 11 cm); Van
Doesburg Collection, R.B.K.
(AB 5074 A and B)

Squareness *began* with the need to draw the logical consequence with a maximum expression. The right angle is the simplest and at the same time the most expressive means of closure for a space, or drawing the boundary of a plane (colour-plane). It approximates 'formlessness' closely, because one can think the [outermost] boundary-points through to the infinite. As opposed to this the circle produces the strongest sense of enclosure: boundary, and is also the expression of intro-version (in its literal sense) and individualism.

Here he prefigures an architecture of coloured planes which defines a place for man within infinite, universal space, and decries the closure produced by the curved line such as will be used by Oud in his housing at the Hook of Holland. Van Doesburg is advocating an architecture which will place man in a unified relationship with the universal, not in an egocentric opposition to it. His idea of the Universe has changed and so, of course, has his metaphor of the Universe. Some time between mid-1918 and mid-1919, Van Doesburg abandoned the idea that the painterly conception of architecture produced a 'direct link with God' and replaced it with the notion of giving 'form to this concealed harmony, this universal equilibrium of things, to demonstrate its conformity with its own laws, etc.'.[1] At the time of writing this letter to De Boer at the end of 1922, he had reached the point where, quite unsolicited, he added in a marginal note that 'The ☐ will conquer the +!' The pantheism of Bolland had been expunged from Van Doesburg's idea of the Universal.

The passage in Van Doesburg's letter beginning with the remarks about the subdivision of the wall (see p. 119) indicates that he had spent a considerable amount of time re-inspecting those aspects of the painterly conception of architecture which brought him into conflict with Oud. The passage has far-reaching consequences for the development of Van Doesburg's architectural theory. The 'destruction' of architectural form works at two levels. First, it loosens and separates the constituent elements of the architecture, clarifying the architecture as a synthesis of functional/aesthetic elements, and investing them with meaning. This aspect of architectural 'destruction' was at work in De Vonk, where separately functioning elements were for instance kept visually separate by a dark band of tiles, or by the treatment of the door panels as integral colour planes. Secondly, if the element or plane was considered to be too closed, such as the floor in De Vonk, it was divided and 'dissolved' with its integrity denied visually. These polar opposites give a paradoxical character to the new art and architecture, which in the Elementarist models of 1923 denied the actual construction while emphasising the visual structure. At the Aubette the paradox would be carried even further with the ambivalence to constituent elements emphasising the aesthetic/functional dichotomy by alternate integration or disintegration. (Compare the treatment of the Ciné and the large Party Room (figs. 100 and 102).) This will become the greatest distinguishing factor between Van Doesburg's treatment of architecture and Rietveld's approach. The Schröder house (fig. 48), for instance, demonstrates a complete integration of structural and visual elements. All of the structural or functional elements, from wall-planes to hand-rails to downpipes, all work within the visual composition as integral aesthetic elements. Rietveld's, or for that matter Oud's, work leaves no implied paradox. However, while Van Doesburg's idea of architectural composition was always based on proportion and relationship, the relationship was often a contrast. Even the contrasts had to be tuned and balanced to create a pervasive unity. A closer examination of his later architectural projects will serve to clarify the detailed application of these ideas.

At the end of 1922 the influence Van Doesburg saw being exercised by De Stijl on the modern architecture of the Netherlands, and the fresh

48 Gerrit Rietveld, Schröder
house, Utrecht, 1924

ideas being injected into *De Stijl* by the new international contacts he
was making, gave him fresh energy to carry on. He records in his letter
that Rietveld had been to visit him that very day (29 December 1922)
and that they had discussed future plans, which included exhibitions.
In December 1920 Van Doesburg had

been commissioned [by Léonce Rosenberg] to design an ideal house along with
all the other De Stijl people according to our theories. Now I don't know if
it will proceed because it demands a great deal of work and Oud will not take
the risk upon himself, because it naturally requires a considerable amount of
drawing. Still, I hope it will all come in order. Isn't it too bad that it has not
come to a real collective effort with De Boer![2]

On 29 December, presumably, he also discussed the possibility that
Rietveld would make the model of the design for Rosenberg, since Van
Eesteren already had his design for the first model under way by this
time.[3]

Van Doesburg's short stay in Weimar during the preceding months gave him a much more direct contact with the artists of Eastern Europe. He had, of course, shown a strong interest in Archipenko's work and had already had personal contact with him,[4] but the exchange of ideas in Paris, Berlin, and at the Düsseldorf and Weimar Conferences gave him renewed vigour and much-needed impetus for continuing his struggle. The issue of *De Stijl*, published a month before this letter to De Boer, featured El Lissitzky's Constructivist fairy-tale, 'Suprematist Development of Two Squares, in Six Constructions'. From the letter it appears that De Boer had seen a copy of the Lissitzky issue while visiting Evert Rinsema, and had written approvingly to Van Doesburg. Van Doesburg replied 'that architects must surround themselves much more with these kinds of works (which are, however, rare), and through them begin to sense the endless spatial possibilities at the same time as coming to realise these possibilities in practice. Such works are the best nourishment for modern man.' Lissitzky has clearly exercised a powerful influence both on the concepts and on the graphics of Elementarism. Since 1919 Van Doesburg had followed reviews of Russian artistic activities. In 1922 Van Doesburg attempted to arrange a tour of Russia and again in 1925 he and Kurt Schwitters were working vainly to arrange a trip to see the Russian experiment first hand.[5]

Van Doesburg's sojourn in Germany in 1922 had convinced him that while many positive radical steps were being taken by foreign artists, Dutch artists on their narrow nationalistic stage were indulging in a kind of artistic protectionism. As I. K. Bonset, he wrote in the 'Chronique scandaleuse des Pays-Plats':

Berlagé	arabesque romantique – maison avec closet hégelien sentimentalisme infantile.
van Deyssel:	Bas-bleu de la litérature catholique.
Bolland:	Diarrhée de monsieur Hégel
van Eeden:	Clown. Poire pourrie de 1880. Traître de la barbe de Jésus Christ.
Havelaar:	Chemise malpropre de Tolstoï.
de Meester:	Domestique de la littérature de laine. A.K.O.
Roland Holst:	Dilettante en édition de luxe. (Je hais la peinture sans sexe!)[6]

In Holland, he contended, they were still struggling with the move away from naturalism which had already been realised in other countries, often by Dutchmen who had been driven to go abroad for the sake of their artistic development. He wrote in contorted English:

Holland is a country of pretensions and rigorous conservatism. Any new blooming, no matter what its nature is systematically opposed by the journalists. They are satisfied only when they succeeded in exiling the representative personalities of the advance have guard. In this way we lost our outstanding artists (Jongkind, Maris, Israëls, van Gogh, Thorn Prikker, Van Dongen, Mondriaan). They were forced to develop their talent and win respect for their art elsewhere before Holland took them seriously.[7]

He saw a move from the Netherlands as necessary for his own development, but he was not one to slink away unnoticed. What Holland needed
was to be shaken from its self-satisfied sleep. Dada's aggressive questioning of the 'logical' basis of society and its art was negative, but its positive
contribution was that it left in its destructive wake an attitude of mind
amenable to the new logically Constructive art. Van Doesburg's parting
gift to the Dutch would be the Dada tour. When he wrote to De Boer
at the end of 1922, he was just about to embark on the Dada tour with
Kurt Schwitters. Van Doesburg asked De Boer, 'Couldn't you come down
to The Hague some time? On 10 January in the Haagsche Kunstkring
there is going to be a Dada soirée for which Kurt Schwitters is coming
over (from Hanover). Can't you drop in then too?' He had headed
the letter with 'Vive DE STIJL, Vive le NEO-PLASTICISME, VIVE DADA!',
and closed with wishes for 'a plastic New Year [*beeldend nieuw jaar*],
with □ greetings'.

Dada was to be the great purgative, a crazy satire of a crazy world,
scripted by Bonset and delivered by Van Doesburg. According to Aldo
Camini (Van Doesburg's deceased alter-ego), what is 'favoured with the
name "dada" is nothing other than a quick-action purgative (recom-
mended as a People's diet), which will purify the stinking cellars of
taste'.[8] Schwitters insisted that only one Dutchman was Dada, Bonset,
and only one Dutch woman was Dada, Petro van Doesburg. In introducing the cast of the Dada soirées in a mixture of Dutch and German
Schwitters declared:

Wir wecken den schlafenden Dadaismus der Masse. Wir sind Propheten. . . . Ein
Lächeln zittert über seine beamteten Gesichter, als ich sage: 'DADA ist der sittliche
Ernst unserer Zeit!' Wie Hörner ohne Propheten. Nur einen Augenblick lächelt
er, aber wir haben es bemerkt, wir, die Träger der dadaistischen Bewegung in
den Niederlanden.

Darf ich uns vorstellen? Kijk eens, wij sijn Kurt Schwitters, nicht dada,
sondern MERZ; Theo van Doesburg, nicht dada, sondern Stijl; Petro van
Doesburg, Sie glauben es nicht, aber sie nennt sich dada; und Huszar, nicht
dada, sondern Stijl. Sie werden erstaunt fragen: 'Warum kommen nicht
Dadaisten uns dada vorzumachen?' Kijk eens, das gerade ist das Geraffineerde
van onze Kultuur, dass ein Dadaist, weil er eben Dadaist ist, nicht den im
Publikum schlummernden Dadaismus wecken und künstlerisch läutern kann.
Begrijpt u dat?[9]

Dada was the mirror held up by non-Dadaists to the public to show them
their own Dadaism. There was a blurring of roles in the Dada play with
its audience participation. According to Van Doesburg the most successful evening was in Utrecht when fights broke out in the audience and
the 'performers' sat down on the stage to watch the ensuing chaos. Dada
might be mad, but then the world was mad.

The ploy was a qualified success and Van Doesburg gleefully reported
in *Mécano*, 4/5, that 'the Dutch bourgeoisie has confessed its sins in
journalistic form', and he triumphantly quoted from the newspapers:

Yesterday in 'Diligentia' we had another Dada evening. Again we roared and
screeched, not caring whether Heine was being recited or Mendelssohn played,
or whether meaningless rubbish was being knocked about. . . . We howled and

whined, bawled and made stupid remarks . . . and we did all this to prove that *we* are *not* dada. We made such a hellish and completely ridiculous spectacle of ourselves that it is now proven with absolute clarity that we are all of sound mind; that everything is thus in order. [*Het Vaderland*, 4 February 1923]

Even in the *Christelijke Amsterdammer* he found the very satisfactory conclusion that '*there is an ugly dadaist incipient in the heart of each of us!*' In the same issue of *Mécano* Van Doesburg published 'The Characteristics of Dadaism', where he confirmed Schwitters's description of him in his Constructivist persona as a non-Dadaist. In a footnote he described the article as 'a talk by Theo van Doesburg the anti-Dadaist, used as an introduction for the non-Dada soirées held in the Netherlands in the winter of 1923'. Oud disapproved of Van Doesburg's increasing involvement in Dada because he considered that the necessary destructive work had already been accomplished and that eventually constructive work must be embarked upon. Van Doesburg agreed, but because of his more radical conception of the new architecture he disagreed about the completeness and effectiveness of the destruction.

The reconciliation of the negative, destructive character of Dada, and the positive, Constructive character of Elementarism, has always posed a difficult problem. In an article entitled 'Dada Conquers Itself'[10] in the *Haagsche Post* of 20 January 1923, Kurt Schwitters addressed the problem. The stock-in-trade of Dada is nonsense, but the exposition of that nonsense is not art. Dada showed the public the absurdities which formed the premises of their daily lives and the absurdities which were the foundation of traditional art and taste. These *a priori*, fossilised conventions were the greatest obstacles to the realisations of the new Constructive art. The new art was to be style-less, that is, independent of any stylistic *a priori*. The style, as Van Doesburg had been insisting since 1915 in his *Three Lectures* (p. 15), would arise directly from the elementary means of the particular art in question, or, in other terms, from the inner necessity of the material. As Schwitters wrote elsewhere in 'Dada complet':

Wollen Sie aber sehen, wie gute und sachliche Architektur aussieht, fahren Sie mit lijn drie bis Endstation und sehen Sie sich den Papaverhof und die Kliemopstraat [*sic*] an. Eine Oase in einer Wüste von missverstandener Architektur. Das sind Häuser, die mit dem Bewusstsein ihrer Bestimmung aus ihrem Material und ihrer Zeit wachsen, wie eine Blume wächst and blüht.[11]

The article 'Dada Conquers Itself' is even more specific, bringing the ideas to bear more directly on Van Doesburg and *De Stijl*:

The dadaistic artist [which is not to say the Dadaist as artist] shows our own time the way for the future. He unifies in himself the contrasts: Dada and Construction. Only logically consequent severity is the means to free us from chaos. In this way the dadaistic artist conquers himself through Dada. He is elevated by an inner consequentiality above the compromising nonsense that he consciously perpetrates. Only the strictest construction frees us from chaotic lawlessness. Abstraction was only a precondition to this process. Abstraction is still somewhat playful and misses the seriousness of Dada and of construction. We are living at the end of an old and the beginning of a new age. The transition is Dada. If we want to take part in the Construction of a new age, then we

are obliged to proceed with the simplest of means. We must unify within ourselves simplicity, and consequentiality, and create a grammatical, constructive
discipline for art. *De Stijl* has already begun with profound pioneering work.[12]

Here again are the polar elements construction/destruction which the
new art must bring into balance, as Van Doesburg had contended in
his letter to De Boer. At the time this provided the basis of Van Doesburg's
essays in poetry, painting, and later his Elementarist vision of architecture. Schwitters's article was published in Dutch which is so standard
(as opposed to his short and inexpert letters in Dutch to Thijs Rinsema
as late as 1926[13]) that it is reasonable to infer that Van Doesburg himself
had translated, if not reworked, the article.

In the work of many Dadaists it can be difficult to determine exactly
how ironic the machine images, or collages with machines, were meant
to be. Van Doesburg and Schwitters, on the other hand, were committed
to a machine aesthetic. This was not a recent introduction into De Stijl
theory; it had been in evidence since the second issue, where Gino
Severini wrote of the parallel between art, science, and mechanisation.
For all three artists the implications of the machine for art were the
simplest of means, a constructive grammar, and an inner logic; the
result was an aesthetic determinism based on material qualities and the
somewhat nebulous idea of 'the requirements of modern life'. For Van
Doesburg a mechanical, deterministic aesthetic was by no means a blind,
lifeless, spiritually bankrupt aesthetic. It presented a new humanistic
view of the Universe: 'a shining reality of a mechanical universe, with
our spirit as its motor'. In the guise of Aldo Camini, Van Doesburg wrote
of a work by Carlo Carra that 'from an industrial mechanical point of
view this painting is more valuable than many technical mechanical
drawings, and I believe that the mechanical aspirations of the Latin
race . . . will begin to put forward the quality of such paintings as examples for their modern constructions'.[14] The machine was the icon of logical order, discipline, and economy; it made sense of man's life and his
universe without recourse to God. Far from being lifeless, the machine
was the most succinct description of life, as Bonset wrote: 'every mechanism is the spiritualisation of an organism. The will is the activity which
the power of the universal mechanism vests in the individual
mechanism.'[15]

The collages by Van Doesburg and Schwitters from this period had
strongly mechanical overtones. They were made of the waste products
of mechanical production, and they were produced by an aesthetically
deterministic procedure analogous to machine production, culminating
in a mechanical icon of the universe:

Einstweilen schafft MERZ Vorstudien zur kollektiven Weltgestaltung, zum all-
gemeinen Stil. Diese Vorstudien sind die Merzbilder.
  Das einzig Wichtige im Gemälde ist der Ton, die Couleur. Das einzige Material
dafür ist die Farbe. Alles im Bilde entsteht durch die Farbe. Hell und dunkel sind
Werte der Couleur. Linien sind Grenzen von verschiedenen Couleuren. Also ist
beim Bilde nichts wichtig ausser dem Werten der Farbe. Alles Unwichtige stört

die Konsequenz des Wichtigen. Daher muss ein konsequentes Bild abstrakt sein.[16]

The collages were experiments and it is easy to see that working with Schwitters, whose ideas closely paralleled his own, would give him much-needed reinforcement on the Dutch stage. Experimentation had its place, but Van Doesburg was becoming impatient with his half-realised architectural ambitions. He had complained to De Boer that he had never been allowed to realise a complete interior, 'I mean where *everything*, furniture and all, worked together, and in which I did not remain restricted to little door-panels and applied strips'. The project commissioned by Rosenberg represented Van Doesburg's real hope for the future.

5

◇◇◇◇◇ ◇◇◇◇◇ ◇ ◇◇◇

Towards an elementary architecture

In the early 1920s the machine was a potent image at the centre of a wide-ranging debate. Attitudes to the machine had split the Werkbund and had spilled over into the Dutch controversy over the founding of a Nederlandsche Werkbond. In the aftermath of the war, the dehumanising potential of the machine and machine production was all too clear. Ironically, it was also clear that the capabilities of the machine, and at the very least machine-aided production, were the only viable means for rebuilding Europe. For Van Doesburg this rebuilding of Europe was not just a material necessity which could be provided for by machine production, the machine played an operative role in the spiritual revitalisation of Europe and provided the foundation for Van Doesburg's new humanism.

The most important documentation of Van Doesburg's position in the debate on the mechanical aesthetic is his 1921 series of articles 'The Significance of the Mechanical Aesthetic for Architecture and the other Professions'.[1] Here he describes the mechanical aesthetic in terms of unpremeditated beauty resulting from the logical consequences of the means of production, the means of art, and the characteristics of the materials used. Just as the engineer calculates the relationship between load and support, the modern architect must calculate light as the revelation of space to produce the new beauty, 'which would be impossible without a totally new conception of time and space (the most important elements of music and plastic form)' (no 25, p. 164). Already it can be seen that this mechanical aesthetic went beyond simple functional appropriateness: 'the purely functional division of space is mathematically controlled by number and measure and is made subject to the creative will, and becomes a calculation for a monumental beauty' (no 25, p. 165). As in his earlier theoretical writings, he had set up the creative will as the controlling principle over the forces of nature in opposition to the Romantic admiration of the sublime force of nature. The straight line and the right angle, being the most characteristic result of the machine and mechanical calculation, acquired profound significance in terms of his mechanical aesthetic as an outward sign of the new spirit of the age. Unfortunately, in support of his position concerning the right angle, he quoted Le Corbusier on the use of reinforced concrete. The seeds of dispute sown here would yield bitter fruit after only a short

130

space of time.[2] Continuing his reference to Le Corbusier, Van Doesburg spoke of the house in terms of a machine: 'the house will in the first place be understood as a practical and beautiful apparatus of the function of living'. In case the architects should fear the loss of architectural beauty, he reminded them that 'there is no better architecture than one which calculates the whole of the function of human life in terms of mechanically transformed materials, in the division of light, space, volume, and colour'. Creative control over these materials and natural elements, through calculation and the machine, would not only yield a higher beauty appropriate to the new life, but the mechanical process would also liberate the worker from 'the servitude of handicraft'.[3]

In the second article of the series Van Doesburg continued the theme of 'mechanical socialisation', quoting Lenin as saying that '*if we could only build a great number of electricity generating stations across the land, we would accomplish a work of great cultural/historical significance*' (no 28, p. 179). To corroborate this, Van Doesburg cited the example of Chicago which, after the great fire, had been rebuilt as a large industrial city through the application of technology. Architecture could revitalise itself in the same way, by creating an absolute, mechanical aesthetic by the application of technology. In reply to the champions of craftsmanship he proclaimed:

It is a mistake to think that the love of working with materials, which was felt by the medieval craftsman, would be lost in the mechanical production of art. In mechanical production, the spiritual intention of the designer is so inseparably connected with the material that it perfectly realises the spirit in its spotless purity. That is surely the unassailable essence of all art; that it reveals the spirit and not the hand, which is only the primitive tool of the spirit. [no 28, p. 180]

If the technical and the functional aspects continued to be considered separately from the aesthetic, the aesthetic would remain mere decoration 'as camouflage for the construction'. The union of the technical and aesthetic in the mechanical, Van Doesburg contended, provided the means for the solution of the urgent problem of the housing shortage which was the legacy of the war. The technical and aesthetic means were there; what stood in the way were sentimentality, on the artistic side, and private capitalism, on the economic side.

The danger of aesthetic sentimentalism was that architects caught in its web were bound by traditional form and style. In this connection Van Doesburg put forward his conception of 'formless' architecture free of the *a priori*, but arbitrary, compositional strictures of the styles. Tradition had been isolated as the great stumbling-block much earlier in the writings of Sant'Elia, Berlage, and in the first issues of *De Stijl*; later in 1921 Van Doesburg was using its antithesis, the conception of a formless architecture, as a corner-stone in the development towards an Elementarist architecture. The standard-type was, he believed, a survival of traditional stylistic type-forms in an industrial, architectural guise. 'Even form in the sense of a typical product of the character of an age and a people is not the aim of the new art, and the search for a new architectural "form" is just as wrong as copying old aesthetic formulae' (no 28, pp. 182–83). For Van Doesburg, architectural form was properly the result of the internal logic of mathematics, the material itself, the mechanical means of production, and the independent means of architecture. In his terms, an applied style, whether 'new' or traditional, could only produce a symbol or expression of the artistic idea. An applied style could not produce a direct, concrete embodiment of the 'metaphysical content of the modern conception of life' (no 28, p. 183). The ultimate conclusion for architecture is 'formless monumentality':

The coloured planes of a painting which delimit each other and hold each other in strict, right-angled, determinate proportionality, remove once and for all the idea of form. The same applies to architecture in terms of strict, determined, and compositionally balanced bodies in space. In this way architecture acquires a new element: it is *open*, bounded but not organically enclosed (*form-architecture*). If the building achieves a *Gestalt* arising out of the internal constructive divisions, then it also excludes form, the type, once and for all. Every plane that forms the boundary of a space has a continuing spatial extension, while overcoming the closed nature of organic form. This is *formless monumentality*. [no 28, p. 183]

Clearly a 'formless' aesthetic also excluded individual artistic expression; instead it demanded a communal effort. In the same way as he had placed the architecture of form and the 'formless' aesthetic in opposition, Van Doesburg considered the political ideologies of capitalism and even socialism or communism to be 'form-thought'. It was not political ideologies which changed ways of life; 'it is the creative temperament, most particularly the architects and engineers, who dictate culture' (no 33, p. 220).

In this way the modern artists in Russia, in my view some of the leading lights of the modern movement, as I have already indicated, were forced to abandon the spiritual and collective interests of art and to place themselves at the service of the violent rule of the individual. The spiritually liberating influences of communal mechanical labour were considered to be sins against the spirit of society, until eventually it was recognised that no single culture would allow itself to be engulfed without being confronted with electrical power, machines, and radio-magnetism. In that way mechanical control of life and the mechanical aesthetic has by itself and in the name of a higher morality conquered the fixed mentality of Europe. [no 33, p. 220]

The machine was the great liberator from restrictive political and aesthetic constructs.

The central issue in the debate was a definition of the fundamental nature of the machine and its relationship to man. The problem had been addressed in the pages of *De Stijl* since the second issue, which carried Severini's discussion of '*machinisme*' and the analogy between machine construction and the construction of a work of art. Van Doesburg himself had written on the subject under each of his assumed names and, interestingly, the radical position outlined in 'their' collective *oeuvre* resembles in certain important aspects the position of another prominent participant in the debate, Dr M. H. J. Schoenmaekers. In the 1922 yearbook of the Association for Technical and Applied Arts (de

VANK), Schoenmaekers wrote an article entitled 'Concering the Essence of the Prosthetic Device' in which he defines the tool (*werktuig*: tool, implement, or more abstractly a prosthetic device in general) as 'the concrete form of the specifically human capability of overcoming biological limitations'. He continued:

The tool is an ever-present symptom of 'de-individualisation', the human manner of extending the frontiers of biology. It is a kind of spiritual universalisation. *Spiritual* universalisation means a generalisation which does not remain an abstract concept, but which in spite of its isolation in an individual form becomes for the individual a *practically* concrete sign of the abstract concept. . . . Man wishes to control matter in the sense that his life is at its root quite as universal as 'dead' matter which unconditionally obeys universal laws. Thus the practical connection between organic life and 'dead' matter is made concrete in the tool, a trophy of the regality of mankind.[4]

This idea of the mystical significance of the machine as a perfected tool bears a marked resemblance to Bonset's contention that: 'every mechanism is the spiritualisation of an organism. The will is the activity that the power of the universal mechanism vests in the individual mechanism.'[5] Both writers posit a unity amongst the universal life force, machines, and man's will. They differ in that Schoenmaekers used the argument in connection with a pantheistic view of the world, as did Bolland, whereas Van Doesburg employed a kind of 'Occam's razor' to remove God as unnecessary for a complete description of a mechanistic world.

The conception of the tool or simple machine as a symbol of the nobility of man, as opposed to William Morris's position that the machine was a symbol of the degradation of man, had enormous consequences for the arts in general:

No, do not mourn over the loss of 'beauty' through the machine. The machine has its own beauty, which goes beyond the aesthetically pleasant; it is the beauty of the practical, universally valid intellect, the beauty of man's control over matter. It is the beauty of the full and living extension of the frontier. It is the beauty of a metallic human life. . . . It is a beauty which unifies mathematical exactitude with the tangible and concrete.[6]

A number of different strands of development can be traced: one through Schoenmaekers and Berlage, to the pioneering work of J. L. M. Lauweriks concerning the rule of system, logic, and mathematics in the cosmos and hence in art as the sign of the Universe; another strand is evident (although placing less emphasis on the machine, and therefore with different aesthetic consequences) in the mathematically based designs of J. H. de Groot, whose ideas were known to Van Doesburg.[7] The reason for mentioning these strands of development is not to establish direct lines of inheritance, but to indicate the breadth of the discussion within which Van Doesburg shaped his conception of the mechanical aesthetic and its humanistic, but universal, basis. Within this larger discussion, statements which otherwise seem mystical almost to the point of being cranky reveal their fundamental seriousness. For instance, a summary of Van Doesburg's position in relation to his contemporaries can in this light be discovered in an otherwise enigmatic and perhaps even inexcusably esoteric passage in 'The Balance of the New':

Under the term 'the new' is to be understood the experience of the deepest significance of life, which is polarity (differently described as ideality and reality, spirit and nature, abstract and concrete, etc.) as the undivided and indivisible reality; the Synthesis of indivisible contrasts experienced. This appears in art as directly determined creation, that is to say determined without the intermediary aid of nature, image, or symbols, but rather with the means of the particular art used. The various developmental stages, which 'the new' has helped to realise, give us proof that this is the one and indivisible 'new' and that it has its source in a steady development ([a new conception of] tradition) of man from the point of view of his environment. In that development, 'the new' revealed itself in an increasingly determinate way, by degrees in an increasing precision and perfection, and in the mechanical control and application of the elementary forces. ... 'The new' is revealed in the clarity of construction, a construction in terms of the logic of (purified and intensified) feeling.[8]

As for Schoenmaekers, the machine for Van Doesburg was a concrete sign for the abstract universe; at the same time it was an idealisation of the real organism. The machine was the synthesis of these polarities, and the constructive logic of the machine vested its products with precision and perfection, allowing man-the-inventor to conquer both the forms and the forces of material nature.

An appeal to the writings of Schoenmaekers is useful in an explication of Van Doesburg's attitude to the machine, but to be accurate it is essential to draw attention to a major distinction between these two and the Hegelian tradition. Van Doesburg was attempting to escape from the dualistic world-view of Bolland and Hegel by describing the polarities, abstract/concrete etc., as different facets of the same unity 'undivided and indivisible'. Their unity was in the analogues: life, the machine, and art. Van Doesburg contended in 'From the Aesthetic to the Material' that if art was 'directly determined' through its own formal and material characteristics and not determined by the 'externals' of natural references, or by symbolic references to ideas or objects external to itself, then an art would have been created that would be a material realisation of ideality, not simply a symbolic reference to an imaginary, external, ideal world. 'This need for a unity of form, for a single and indivisible real world gives rise to the will *to realise in the materials of architecture* what the ideal aesthetic of the "free" arts has revealed.'[9]

In his article 'From the Aesthetic to the Material', Van Doesburg noted that the Russians, both the Suprematists and Lissitzky with Proun, had been working in parallel with the efforts of De Stijl in their move 'from the aesthetic to the material'.[10] Van Doesburg's first personal contact with the avant-garde of Russia (with the exception of Archipenko) dated from April of 1922 when he was in Berlin to deliver his lecture 'The Will to Style'. Lissitzky was in Berlin in connection with the 'First Russian Art Exhibition' of 1923, at which the 'Proun Room' was to be displayed. In a letter of 24 April 1922, Van Doesburg wrote excitedly to De Boer that after a stay of fourteen days in Berlin, I'm back again in Weimar. . . . In Berlin I got to know all the artists I could, and what was most interesting was that, besides Kandinsky, I also spoke with Lissitzky and other artists who have played such an important role. My expectations concering their work were not proved wrong: the younger ones all work in the *same spirit as ours*, that is to say Neo-plastic.[11]

One reason that he noted for his enthusiasm was that they were well on the road to uniting the polarities of the creative world of the constructive artist and 'the world in which we live, and . . . the duality of God and man, Nature and Spirit'. He announced to De Boer that he had approached Kandinsky for advice concerning a personal visit to Russia (at least partly to be financed by lectures), and that preparatory measures were already in hand.

The tour never materialised, but the contacts were nonetheless fruitful. In the June 1922 issue of *De Stijl* Van Doesburg published Lissitzky's article 'Proun' dated Moscow 1920. The article opened with 'Nicht Weltvisionen, SONDERN – Weltrealität' which Van Doesburg considered to be in support of his argument against dualism. It continued by criticising mimetic artists and saying that at least the painters of pure form were on the right path: 'der Künstler wird vom Nachbilder ein Aufbauer der neuen Welt der Gegenstände'. However, they had as yet failed to unify art and technology. To correct the situation, 'Proun ist die schöpferische Gestaltung (Beherrschung d. Raumes) vermittels der ökonomischen Konstruction des umgewerteten Materials'.[12] Most significant for Van Doesburg's theory at the time was Lissitzky's contribution of the idea of colour as material. Van Doesburg's move towards the position as focused by Lissitzky could be seen in his reference (in 'The Significance of the Mechanical Aesthetic' of 1921) to 'mechanically transformed materials, in the division of light, space, volume, and colour' as 'the natural elements and materials' (see above, p. 131), but whether he was treating colour as a material at this stage is ambiguous. After an exchange of ideas with Lissitzky, however, his references became quite specific, and the clarity of Lissitzky's development of the ideas parallel to Neo-plasticism added impetus and resolution to the development of Elementarism.

Lissitzky submitted that, as the barometer of material, colour was the visual embodiment of the other specific qualities of material form, that 'die materielle Form bewegt sich nach bestimmten Achsen im Raume: über die Diagonalen und Spiralen der Treppen, in der Senkrechten des Aufzuges, auf der Horizontalen der Geleise, in der Geraden oder der Kurven des Äroplanes, entsprechend ihrer Bewegung im Raum muss materielle Form gestaltet sein, *das ist die Konstruktion*' (p. 84). This analysis of form in terms of colour and movement of elements gives a key to Van Doesburg's use of colour in his analyses of Elementarist architecture. Suprematism and Neo-plasticism had reduced painting to an absolute zero, a primary form; Proun and Elementarism were the first steps in rebuilding or reconstruction of the intuitive mathematics of formal space. In Lissitzky's comment on his Proun Room, published in the magazine *G*, he speaks of defining space in terms of axes and controlling man's movement and experience of this space by means of these axes. In this way he intends to bring the living environment into harmony, and that harmony into motion.[13] Van Doesburg's use of colour in Elementarist architecture was to the same end, that is, to complete the space and reveal the harmony-in-movement of the architecture.

Although Lissitzky had in effect introduced 'colour as material' to the Elementarist vocabulary, the other ideas contained in the article 'Proun' as published in *De Stijl* were, in Van Doesburg's eyes, simply a confirmation of his ideas concerning elementary means and 'monumental art'. Van Doesburg's article 'Elemental Formation', published in *Architectura* and later also in *G*, demonstrates this attitude, especially in his use of 'elementary formation', 'monumental formation', and 'construction' as interchangeable terms.[14] This more sophisticated 'construction', in his terms, is quite different from the absolute zero 'construction' of the Suprematists. 'N.B. [*Nieuwe Beelding*: Neo-plasticism] has transcended the construction without underestimating the constructive laws of the relationships between measure and number', he said,[15] but here he is using the term 'construction' in the restrictive sense of the Suprematist construction which, unlike Proun and even Neo-plasticism, had failed to rebuild a greater construction with all the means of art, including colour as a material. The concurrence of Elementarism and Proun continued into 1923 as confirmed by Van Doesburg's publication of 'From the Aesthetic to the Material' in a German translation, 'Von der neuen Ästhetik zur materiellen Verwirklichung' in the March 1923 issue of *De Stijl*. By mid-1924, however, a certain emphasis was being placed on differences between their views. In June 1924 Lissitzky wrote to Oud:

Sie erwähnten Mondrians Standpunkt, den kenn ich nicht, den holländischen verstehe ich nicht, und Doesburg hat mir darüber nichts mitgeteilt, ausser der Gegenüberstellung der Kunst der Natur. Damit bin ich nicht einverstanden. Das Universelle = Gerade + Senkrechte, entspricht nicht dem Universum, das nur Krümmungen, keine Geraden kennt. So ist die Kugel (nicht der Kubus) das Kristall des Universums, aber wir können damit (Kugel) nichts anfangen, denn das ist der vollendete Zustand (Tod), darum konzentrieren wir uns an den Elementen des Kubus, die sich immer neu zusammenlegen und zerstören lassen (Leben). Die moderne Maschine muss Rundes haben, denn die Kreisbewegung ist ihr *Vorteil* gegenüber der geradlinigen hin und her Bewegung der menschlichen Hand/Fuss. Und wenn die Wohnung, das Haus, ein Apparat zum Unterbringen von unserem Körper ist (so wie Kleidung) dann warum soll er nicht das Runde haben?

The first flush of allegiance between Van Doesburg and Lissitzky was giving way under closer inspection of their respective positions, and the final result would be mutual public criticism.[16]

In 1922, however, the emphasis was still very much on the parallels, and the axis of alliance amongst the Constructivists would be demonstrated in Düsseldorf and Weimar. In the 24 April letter to De Boer, Van Doesburg announced that 'in Berlin I have laid the "cornerstone" for an International of Creative Artists. I am coming back in the Autumn and hope that then I can do a lot for the "new".' It is intriguing to speculate on what Van Doesburg meant by saying he had 'laid the "cornerstone" for an International of Creative Artists'. The letter suggests that in Berlin he had already discussed with Lissitzky the position to be taken a month later at the 'International Conference of Progressive Artists' in Düsseldorf. The events of the Congress between 29 and 31 May are well known through the account in *De Stijl* (V, no 4, 1922). From that account it becomes evident that Van Doesburg had indeed come to an agreement with both Lissitzky and Richter under the title of the International Faction of Constructivists (I.F.d.K.). On the first day their main question was whether the International was concerned primarily with art itself or art dealing. The conference had been called for the international encouragement of the arts through a common international periodical, exhibitions, and an international music festival. The Constructivists considered that the directorate of the Congress was dominated by individualistic artists concerned more with the art trade than with a collective effort towards artistic development. The statements made by all the Constructivist groups, 'Synthèsc', by Lissitzky for *Gegenstand-Objet*, by Richter 'representing the Constructivist groups of Roumania, Switzerland, Scandinavia, and Germany', and by Van Doesburg on behalf of *De Stijl*, make it clear that they were willing to see an International founded only on Constructivist terms:

Erklärung der internationalen Fraktion der Konstruktivisten (Konstruktivisten ist hier nur gebraucht, um den Kontrast mit allen 'Impulsivisten' zu charakterisieren. *De Stijl*) des ersten internationalen Kongresses der fortschrittlichen Künstler. Wir sind nach Düsseldorf gekommen mit dem festen Willen eine Internationale zu bilden. Dabei hat sich folgendes herausgestellt . . .

Die Union hat, wie es aus dem Gründungsmanifest hervorgeht, eine Reihe von Unternehmungen vorgesehen, die in der *Hauptsache einen internationalen Betrieb von Bilderkunstausstellungen bezwecken.* Die Union hat demnach den Plan, kaufmännische *Kolonisations-Politik zu treiben.*
Wir verneinen die jetzigen Kunstausstellungen als Magazine, wo mit Dingen, die beziehungslos gegeneinandergestellt sind, Handel getrieben wird. Heute stehen wir noch zwischen einer Gesellschaft, die uns nicht braucht, und einer, die noch nicht existiert; darum kommen für uns nur Ausstellungen in Betracht zur *Demonstration* dessen, was wir realisieren wollen (Entwürfe, Pläne, Modelle) oder was wir realisiert haben . . .

Die Handlungen des Kongresses haben bewiesen, dass durch die Vorherrschaft der individuellen Einstellung eine Internationale fortschrittliche Solidarität aus den Elementen dieses Kongresses nicht aufgebaut werden kann. [17]

The same motivation exists here for the founding of a Constructivist International as existed for the founding of De Stijl itself, when Van Doesburg was already involved in the group 'De Sphinx' and had the opportunity of participating in the formation of a Dutch Werkbond. In the 'International of Progressive Artists' as proposed by the 'Impulsivists', creative power would only be dissipated in the self-seeking economic interests of individualistic artists, as opposed to its being concentrated in a communal effort towards artistic development. This idea was stressed throughout the manifesto of the Constructivist International of the Commune of Creative Artists, translated into French as the

49 Schematic representation
of Van Doesburg's theory of
the development of art (from
'Der Wille zum Stil', *De Stijl*, V,
no 2 (February 1922), 23–32
(p. 26))

(from right to left)
E = Egyptian G = Greek
R = Roman M = Medieval
R = Renaissance B = Baroque
B = Biedermeyer
IR = Idealist–Reformation
NG = The New Plasticism
('Neue Gestaltung, die jetzt
beginnende Epoch')

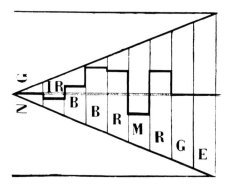

'Union Internationale des Constructeurs néo-plasticistes'. The same idea was stressed in the opening lines of Van Doesburg's lecture 'Der Wille zum Stil' which he had delivered in Berlin on the tour when he met Lissitzky. As Jane Beckett notes: 'Many of the ideas in this lecture re-appeared in the statement of the *De Stijl* artists which was read out at the Düsseldorf Congress of Progressive Artists in late May 1922.'[18] It may be added that Van Doesburg's idea of history was delineated in one of its fullest and clearest forms in this lecture. The diagram which he used to illustrate the lecture shows the swings between art as the revelation of spirit or nature to be getting smaller and finally becoming totally synthesised in the 'neue Gestaltung' (fig. 49). In opposing the individualism of the Expressionists, Van Doesburg evidently considered himself to be acting as the instrument of the historical process. The nature and function of the Berlin 'cornerstone' is becoming much clearer.

This analysis of Van Doesburg's position indicates that even if he had been invited to take up an official position at the Bauhaus, he would have found it impossible to accept because of the diversity of its artistic production. The report of Herta Wescher's interview with Nelly van Doesburg provides further confirmation:

En ce qui concerne leur propre séjour à Weimar, les récits de mon interlocutrice font revivre le climat ambigu qui les y attendait. Elle se souvient d'un dîner chez Gropius, quelques jours après leur arrivée au printemps 1921, auquel parti-cipaient Itten et Muche. Le romantisme de leurs costumes de compagnons du moyen âge et plus encore les exercices matinaux quasi-religieux, voués au culte de 'Mazdaznan', n'étaient pas sans choquer Doesburg profondément. Dans ces conditions, il n'était pas question pour lui d'entrer au Bauhaus, et il organisa dans son propre atelier des cours sur un art d'avant-garde, de l'esprit sobre du néo-plasticisme. Le nombre des étudiants qu'il attirait incita Gropius à apposer un jour une affiche avertissant ceux qui y participaient qu'ils seraient désormais exclus de l'enseignement du Bauhaus. Ce qui n'empêcha pas certains élèves de se ranger hautement du côte de Doesburg, tandis que d'autres venaient com-pléter auprès de lui les instructions reçues à l'institut de Gropius . . . Aux récep-tions du samedi chez les Doesburg, les professeurs ne manquaient pas non plus, tels Feininger, Schlemmer, Adolf Meyer et Moholy-Nagy. Celui-ci se sentait appuyé par Doesburg dans ses idées constructivistes qui devaient modifier l'orientation du Bauhaus.[19]

According to Van Doesburg's article 'Dates and Facts' in the 10-year jubilee issue of *De Stijl*, the Van Doesburgs left for Berlin in December

1920, and visited the Bauhaus in January 1921. Van Doesburg was indeed shocked by what he found and from the first had indulged in subversive activities. As early as 7 January he wrote to Antony Kok that 'I have radically turned everything in Weimer on its head. . . . Every evening I have spoken to the students there, and have spread the poison of the new spirit.'[20] Van Doesburg's aim was to replace the individualism encouraged by the Expressionist elements in the Bauhaus with the single communal goal of the Constructivists. When writing about German art in general and the Bauhaus in particular, Van Doesburg's main theme was, as he phrased it in his review of the 'Grosze Berliner Kunstausstellung' of September 1921: 'What I have already so often tried to demonstrate, once again becomes clear as day in this case: *that freedom in the sense of individual licentiousness stands in the way of the collective realisation of a monumental treatment of form.*' In his article 'The Influence of the De Stijl Movement in Germany' the theme was the same, with only industrial production providing some basis for a counter-development to Expressionist excesses. He claimed that during his short stay he not only introduced a will to collective work, he also gave them an understanding of the elementary means necessary for collective monumental work.

What the Bauhaus in Weimar, because of its internal factions, could not achieve in four years (namely an objective basis for communal 'building'), De Stijl was able to achieve in eight months because here a method was followed which arose directly from reality and *collective recognition.*[21]

Van Doesburg published this article in *Bouwkundig Weekblad*. Reactions published in later issues were either highly sarcastic or highly critical. The critic Boeken wrote in his review of the Bauhaus exhibition of 1923 that although the likeness of some of the exhibited works to works by De Stijl made Van Doesburg's claim of influence quite convincing, there were many other works which were in a different spirit and made his 'conquest' of Weimar seem incomplete. Adolf Behne wrote a review of the exhibition for the *Nieuwe Rotterdammer*, which was again published as part of an editorial in *Klei*. Like Boeken, the editor accepted that the exhibition showed the undeniable influence of De Stijl, but, he said, that influence did not always yield happy results. He referred to these as examples of *Kwadratisme*, the mannerism of the square. His criticism hit at the basis of Van Doesburg's Constructivist position: 'It often appears that the aesthetic formula falls in fairly well with the practical function even though their conflict can still be felt, and the end result is a *compromise between*, and not a *synthesis of*, theory and practice.'[22] In the section of the article given over to Behne's critique, despite a certain amount of wavering, Gropius was praised for founding the Bauhaus on the principle of elementary building, and Behne pointed to his factory at Alfeld as a realisation of that principle.

Van Doesburg agreed about the facts, but interpreted them quite differently. In the articles in the long series 'Attempts at Renewal', which were concerned specifically with developments in Germany,[23] he began with a discussion of the industrial influence. An illustration of the Fagus factory at Alfeld was at the head of the page. Designing for industry, Van Doesburg suggested, forced Behrens and Gropius to lay aside, if only temporarily, their search for a romantic beauty. Their works, although indisputably good and even 'monumental', were only the result of a compromise with industrial necessity, not of fundamentally constructive vision. Van Doesburg wrote of Behrens's work for AEG and Gropius's Fagus factory saying that 'in these works, which *had to* provide for the new demands of industry, ideas concerning constructive necessity, such as economic planning, clear arrangement in plan, and a purer application of architectural means, were already realised to a greater extent than in any other work of architecture of the time'.[24] In other words, the elementary nature of their industrial architecture was not the result of an inner theoretical discipline for architectural design, but was adopted only as a matter of compromise with the demands of industry. They were still working on the purification of old forms as opposed to Van Doesburg's 'formless' architecture arising from the internal logic of the material, independent of tradition. In the last of the series of articles on Germany, Van Doesburg implied that Gropius finally did come round to 'the aim of forming an organic unity between the creative/ constructive, and purely technical/constructive aspects of architectural formation'. The results were a bit disappointing according to Van Doesburg, and

this is not surprising when the teaching went on without a certain principal direction. . . . No one knew where he should begin with the discipline and when I asked the director, during my first visit in 1920, how he thought he would realise the communal Bauhaus idea, I was not just a little surprised to hear that he denied a collective building conception and 'left each individual free to work as he thought fit'. That was naturally bound to lead to excesses.[25]

Van Doesburg considered that the situation had improved somewhat, and as he made perfectly clear on the final page of the last issue of *Mécano*, the change for the better was due to his own influence:

Obviously Van Doesburg's claims were overstated. The objection that the debate concerning the machine was so broadly-based as to transcend a view of the problem in terms of an Itten/Van Doesburg clash of personalities is to a great extent justified. However, in consideration of Van Doesburg's extremely radical position on the debate, and his effectiveness as a polemicist and propagandist, he must surely be considered to be more than just a pawn in a larger game. It is true, however, that to a certain degree he was used by Gropius to break the power of Itten over the first-year students, and this alone was of considerable significance for the development of the wider debate concerning the industrial aesthetic. In view of Van Doesburg's philosophy of history, it is perhaps unlikely that he would have objected strongly, if at all, to being called a 'pawn of history'.

Because there was no question of compromise on Van Doesburg's part, there was no place for him at the Bauhaus. Gropius seemed quite relieved when he wrote to Oud on 28 January 1924 with the news that 'Van Doesburg ist schon wieder weg nach Paris. Er glaubt noch immer, dass er den neuen Geist der Zeit allein erfunden hat.'[26] After Van Doesburg's short stay in Weimar, the Bauhaus came under the Constructivist influence of Moholy-Nagy who, although he differed with Van Doesburg, could still write of him: 'Dass Doesburg wicht in dem Sinne Konstruktivist, wie des ich von uns verstehen, beweisse ich nicht. . . . In einer Zeit dachte ich, dass D[oesburg] nur Sprachrohr von M[ondrian] ist; heute sehe ich, dass in D[oesburg] viel grössere Lebendigkeit und gegenwärtige Erkennungen liegen (ohne es qualitativ zu westen) als in M[ondrian]'.[27]

One young architect who followed Van Doesburg's counter-course at the Bauhaus was to be instrumental in the further development of an Elementarist architecture. In his 4 May 1922 letter to De Boer, Van Doesburg noted that 'in these last few days I met a young architect named Van Eesteren. He won the Prix de Rome in architecture and is on a study tour. He is very enthusiastic about our work, but doesn't understand it all yet.'[28] In Weimar the two became very close, and in his diary Van Eesteren noted long and wide-ranging discussions with Van Doesburg in the weeks following their meeting. Van Eesteren's diary entry for 14 May 1922 states:

Yesterday afternoon I read and took notes from some of Van Doesburg's books and I also received a few from him. Our meeting has been very influential on me, I believe. Should it be the case that I don't finally opt to follow this theory it will still be a great influence on my development. I can feel it: this philosophical assimilation of modern discoveries and scientific theories of physics gives perspectives which are endless. One only senses this once in a while. I have felt it. However, I know too little, even if I can grasp a great deal. My basis is too small.[29]

At the time of their meeting Van Eesteren was at work on a scheme for a University Hall, his final project for the Advanced Architectural Diploma.[30] Blijstra notes in his monograph on Van Eesteren that the project, 'sketched out in the Netherlands, received its definitive form in Weimar and Berlin between May and August 1922' (p. 7). It was not until the summer of 1923 that Van Doesburg became involved directly in the project, that is, after the designs had been rejected by the diploma examiners in March. March 1923 had brought two great disappointments for Van Eesteren. Besides not being granted his diploma, the committee of the Prix de Rome on 16 March refused his next annual grant because they considered that his report had been unsatisfactory for the

50 Cornelis van Eesteren,
Plan for a Hall for Amsterdam
University, 1922–23 ; Van
Eesteren, Fluck en Van
Lohuizen-stichting, N.D.B.
Amsterdam

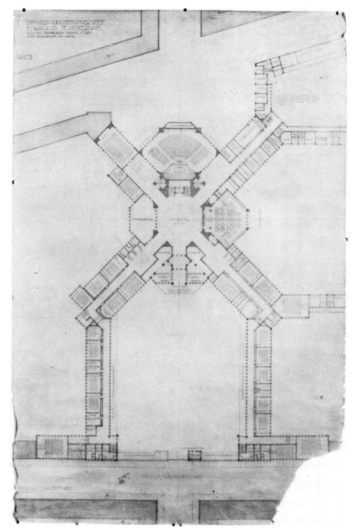

previous year. While he was meant to be studying North German brick architecture, he had in fact spent most of his time studying town planning and contemporary German developments in architecture. In the 31 March issue of *Bouwkundig Weekblad* Van Eesteren complained bitterly about the topic he had been assigned. 'My instructions were, for example, a word-for-word copy of the one which Mr Slothouwer took with him on his fourteen-year journey.' He complained further that the Institute of the Prix de Rome placed too much emphasis on the production of 'so-called superior drawings' for exhibition. He then explained the rationale behind his year's work:

Respect for architecture and for myself has had the consequence that I have reacted to the expressed wishes of the Institute in this way, that I have not wished to display any love either for a superior exhibition or for superior drawing, but have concentrated my work on the elements which I considered to be the points at issue. In this, drawings play a very modest role, as rightly remarked by Mr J. P. M[ieras] in his article.

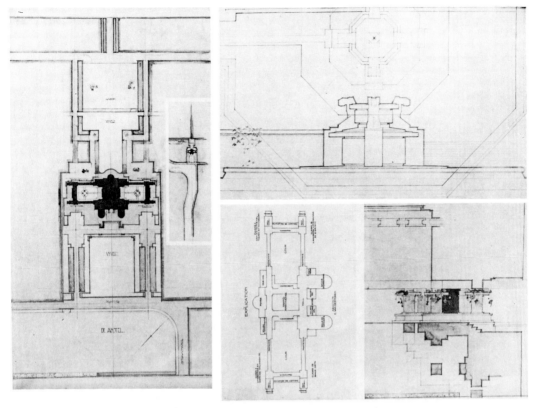

Let me cite as an example the problem of town planning in architecture. One wonders if it makes sense to produce beautiful and sensitive drawings of city planning while on a study tour, when what matters is to help to trace the main ideas of town planning which our own era is looking for.

Let that be the aim of a study tour: to become acquainted with the forms and expressions of modern life. The area of study for the young architect is formed by the burning issues of modern society and not by the piles of rubble left by an ancient civilisation.[31]

51 Cornelis van Eesteren, *Projet pour un Institut Royal Hollandais des Sciences, Lettres et Beaux-Arts*, 1921; as published in *L'Architecture vivante* (Winter 1923), plate 47

The site-plan for the University Hall (see fig. 50) demonstrates Van Eesteren's concern with both the integration of the elements of the university, and the integration of the university complex itself into the city. The site was to be where the Ferdinand Bolstraat crosses the Amstel Kanaal. The main axis of the project is a symbolic continuation of the surrounding street pattern. The principal entry is from the Ferdinand Bolstraat through the main gates and, remaining on the axis, across a *cour d'honneur*, through a vestibule into the University Hall itself. Once there in the centre of the complex a pair of cross axes set at forty-five degrees to the main axis takes over. The octagon of the University Hall is thus the integration of the opposed square geometries of the street layout and the university complex itself. This reconciliation of opposi- tions, long a preoccupation of Van Doesburg's, produced a fascinating transformation of the use of axial planning evident in Van Eesteren's Prix de Rome design for a Royal Academy for Science, Literature, and the Arts, of 1921 (fig. 51).[32]

52 Theo van Doesburg,
Colour-scheme for the floor of
the Hall for Amsterdam
University, 1923 ; this and
fig. 54 as published in
L'Architecture vivante
(Autumn 1925), plate 12

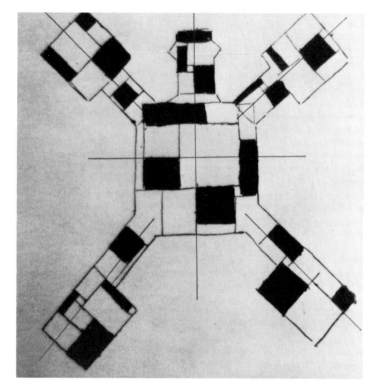

52 Theo van Doesburg, Colour-scheme for the floor of the Hall for Amsterdam University, 1923 ; this and fig. 54 as published in *L'Architecture vivante* (Autumn 1925), plate 12

The controlling principles of Van Eesteren's planning of the university complex provided the basis for Van Doesburg's stunning colour-scheme. Reproductions of the floor and ceiling plans of the colour-scheme appear in *L'Architecture vivante* (Autumn, 1925, pl. 12), titled 'La couleur, fonction de l'architecture'. The plan of the rubber-tiled floor (fig. 52) shows the vestibule and the Hall itself to comprise compositions running orthogonally with the main axis. (Note how the floor composition for the Hall appears to be a square rather than an octagon.)[33] The four subsidiary corridors and foyers comprise compositions orthogonal to the 45-degree cross axes. The treatment of the ceiling is quite different (fig. 53). On entering the vestibule, the influence of the cross axes is already felt through the diagonal setting of the ceiling composition. The treatment reverts quickly to being orthogonal with the main axis and this is continued across the soffit of the balconies. The centre-piece of the whole composition is the 28 m by 28 m stained-glass roof of the octagonal Hall (fig. 54). There the strong black diagonals visually establish the diagonal cross axes as the main lines of circulation (and, of course, of the distribution of rooms as elements of the organisation) within the envelope of the building complex. This composition gives only the faintest nod to the previously established 'main axis' of the project. The ceiling compositions of the corridors and foyers are again orthogonal to the diagonal axes.

In an article entitled 'The Meaning of Colour in the Interior and the Exterior of Architecture', published in the 26 May 1923 issue of *Bouw-*

53 Theo van Doesburg,
Colour-scheme for the ceiling
of the Hall for Amsterdam
University, 1923

kundig Weekblad, and a year later in the May issue of *La Cité* as 'La Signification de la couleur en architecture', Van Doesburg explained his
intention in producing such colour-schemes. In the year between the
two publications, he had completed his work on the University Hall and
the Paris models for Rosenberg. The later publication used the University
Hall and the second model to illustrate his ideas. The article opened with:

Pour l'architecture nouvelle, la couleur a une importance considérable; elle est
un des éléments essentiels de ses moyens d'expression. C'est grâce à la couleur
que les rapports des volumes, recherchés par l'architecte, deviennent *visibles*;
ainsi la couleur *complète* l'architecture et en est un élément *essentiel*. [p. 181]

He continued, saying that in an architecture totally devoid of colour
it is impossible to orientate oneself. It is necessary to use colour intervals
and contrasts to reveal the relationships between the elements of the
architecture. A perspective drawing of the Hall ' "neutre", sans couleurs'
was juxtaposed with a coloured perspective of Van Doesburg's colour-
scheme which 'complète "a" par une construction plastique'. (The same
drawings were used as below in figure 54.) He concluded the article
by attacking the functionalist position which had restricted him to the
treatment of the constructional or 'anatomical' parts of the architecture

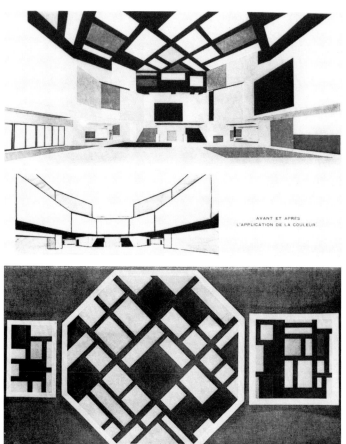

(window-frames, doors, etc.) in his colour compositions for Oud and De Boer:

Dans l'architecture constructive, qui sert exclusivement les besoins matériels, la couleur n'a pas d'autre rôle que d'accentuer davantage encore, par une teinte absolument neutre – gris, vert, brun – l'élément qui relie et unifie l'architecture, et de protéger le bois, le fer, etc., contre l'action de l'humidité. En conséquence, elle conduit à l'accentuation du caractère constructif, anatomique, de l'architecture.

L'architecture utilitaire ne tient compte que du côté pratique de la vie; la mécanique fonctionnelle de la vie, de l'habitat, du travail, etc. Mais il existe encore une autre nécessité que celle purement pratique, à savoir une spirituelle.

Du moment que l'architecte ou l'ingénieur veulent rendre visibles les rapports équilibrés des proportions, c'est-à-dire exprimer comment un mur se comporte en relation avec l'espace, leurs intentions ne sont plus exclusivement constructives, mais également plastiques. Dès que l'on rend visible, que l'on accentue ces rapports, y compris ceux des matériaux, l'esthétique entre en jeu. Exprimer consciemment des rapports équilibrés est faire oeuvre plastique.

***

Arrivée à ce stade, le stade de l'architecture plastique, la couleur devient une *matière d'expression*, de valeur équivalente à tous les autres matériaux, tels que la pierre, le fer, le verre, etc.

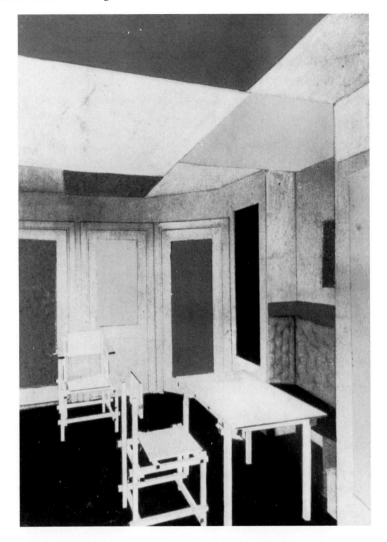

55 Theo van Doesburg,
Interior designed in
collaboration with Rietveld for
Bart de Ligt, 1919 (poster
paint on a photograph,
27 cm × 21 cm), reproduction
from *De Stijl*, III, no 12
(November 1920), plate XIV;
in the Van Doesburg
Collection, R.B.K. (AB 5097)

Alors la couleur ne sert pas seulement à l'orientation, c'est-à-dire pour rendre visible la distance, la position, la direction des volumes et des objets, mais surtout afin de satisfaire le désir de rendre visibles les rapports mutuels entre les espaces et les objets, de direction à la position, de mesure à la direction, etc. C'est dans l'ordonnance de ces proportions que réside le rôle esthétique de l'architecture. Si alors on atteint à l'harmonie, on atteint également au style. Il n'est pas nécessaire d'entrer dans d'autres démonstrations; un équilibre ne peut être atteint que par un partage judicieux entre l'ingénieur, l'architecte et le peintre. Arrivée à ce stade, l'architecture aura dépassé sa période purement constructive, durant laquelle elle s'est épurée. Aussi elle ne se contente plus de montrer son anatomie, elle est devenue un corps indivisible et animé. [pp. 185–87]

Van Doesburg was developing further the ambivalent attitude to the integral element in architecture which had been nascent in his 'destructive' treatment of the floor of 'De Vonk', and more particularly in the composition for the ceiling of the 1919 interior with Rietveld (fig. 55).

In the latter, large planes of colour float on the architectural plane surface much as they do on the bounding surfaces of the Hall, where
enamelled planes of colour are applied to the architectural elements but
retain a distinctive independence from them. Aesthetic elements complement and clarify functional elements without simply providing a direct
diagrammatic definition of them within the constructional programme.
The basic elements of the two arts, painting and architecture, are given
independence within an aesthetic whole, avoiding the merely ornamental or 'baroque', 'in which the different arts destroy each other instead
of reinforcing each other', to use Van Doesburg's words in 'Conditions
for a New Architecture', first published in the 11 August 1923 issue
of *Architectura*.[34]

For Van Doesburg's purposes, drawings had proved to be inadequate
to the task, as Van Eesteren noted in his article complaining about the
Prix de Rome requirements. The drawings could only show two-
dimensional, or at best certain portions of three-dimensional, aspects
of the design. The principles governing the design could not be realised
in their totality through the medium of the drawings. An extended quotation from a 1927 article by Van Doesburg gives a fairly complete idea
of their intentions:

Ich selbst habe während meiner Zusammenarbeit mit dem Architekten C. van
Eesteren (1923) versucht, die Farbe als *Verstärkungsmittel* der architektonischen
Raumgestaltung zu verwenden. Hierbei wurde von jeder 'künstlerisch
kompositorischen Tendenz' abgesehen. Die den Raum gliedernden Flächen
wurden je nach ihrer Lage im Raum durch Farbe betont. Höhe, Tiefe und Breite
wurden durch rot, blau und gelb hervorgehoben, die Massen dagegen wurden
grau, schwarz oder weiss gestrichen. Die Dimensionen des Raumes kamen
lebhaft zur Wirkung. Auf diese Weise war es möglich, die Farbe als Architek-
turelement zu benützen, ohne dass eine ästhetische Wirkung vorausgesetzt war.

Wir kommen damit zur dritten Anwendungsmöglichkeit der Farbe im Raum,
zur 'Gestaltenden'. Seit Beginn der Stijlbewegung haben wir diese Frage prak-
tisch und theoretisch zu lösen versucht. Nachdem uns das Bild in der Malerei
nicht mehr eine in sich abgeschlossene individuelle Austrucksform unserer
Privaterlebnisse war, kam die Malerei mit dem Raum, und was noch wichtiger
war, mit dem Menschen in absolute Berührung. Es enstand eine Beziehung von
Farbe zum Raum und von Farbe zum Menschen. Durch diese Beziehung vom
'Bewegenden Mensch' zum Raum ergab sich eine neue Empfindung in der Architektur: die Empfindung der *Zeit* nämlich.

Die Fährte des Menschen im Raum (von links nach rechts, von oben nach
unten, von vorn nach hinten) wurde für die Malerei in der Architektur von
prinzipieller Bedeutung. Wurde der Mensch durch das statische Bild an einen
bestimmten Punkt gefesselt, hat die dekorative Malerei ihn schon für einen
kinetischen 'linearen' Ablauf im Raum empfindlich gemacht, so will ihm die
gestaltende Raumzeitmalerei ermöglichen, den ganzen *Inhalt* des Raumes zu
empfinden (malerisch, optisch-ästhetisch). Diese Empfindung war ebenso neu
wie die erste Empfindung einer Flugzeugfahrt im freien Raum.

Es handelte such bei dieser Malerei nicht darum, den Menschen um bemalte
Wandflächen herumzuführen, damit er die malerische Entwicklung des Raumes
beobachten könnte, sondern: um eine zusammenwirkende *synoptische Wirkung*
von Malerei und Architektur hervorzurufen. Um das zu erreichen, mussten die
bemalten Flächen sowohl architektonisch als malerisch zueinander in Bezie-

hung stehen, ein einziger Körper werden. Konstruktion und Komposition, Raum und Zeit, Statik und Dynamik in einem Griff gefasst. Die gestaltende Raum-Zeitmalerei des 20. Jahrhunderts ermöglicht dem Künstler, seinen grossen Traum zu verwirklichen: Den Menschen statt vor – in die Malerei zu stellen.[35]

This revolutionary, all-encompassing conception of a monumental architecture for the twentieth century was Van Doesburg's contribution to the collaborative work with Van Eesteren. In 1922 Mondrian had written pessimistically to Van Doesburg about the possibility of creating a new Neo-plastic architecture through the use of colour.[36] Van Doesburg demonstrated in his colour-scheme for the University Hall that it was possible even in 1923. The realisation of this conception in the project required the combined talents of both Van Doesburg and Van Eesteren. Separately it would have been impossible. Van Doesburg did not have the architectural or draughting skills necessary, and Van Eesteren had neither the painterly skills nor had he absorbed the theoretical conception sufficiently to proceed in this direction on his own.

Van Doesburg's fervent wish to present the projects designed for the exhibition at the Rosenberg Gallery as collaborative works has led to a long-standing dispute over the authorship of the projects. As early as the end of September 1926 Van Eesteren wrote bitterly about the published attributions that 'Van Doesburg studied colour in architecture on and in my architectural designs. He had this work which was entirely designed by me, published under his name with the note: "C. van Eesteren, associate".' Van Eesteren continues to maintain the position that Van Doesburg was simply a painter who either coloured original drawings by Van Eesteren himself, or traced directly from his originals. *Prima facie* these sentiments seem to be the antithesis of those Van Eesteren expressed in a letter of 15 August 1924 to Van Doesburg:

that our collaborative work does not result in an addition of ability: *C. v. E. + Does or Does + C. v. E.*, but in *a new unity*, a new existence, that we together have given life.... When *we* collaborate we do not just double our power, our energy, our combined individual power is increased by an order of magnitude ... In such a way our collaborative work has become depersonalised.[37]

However, Van Eesteren's two statements are not necessarily totally contradictory.

In 1969 Jean Leering took the opportunity presented by the retrospective exhibition of Van Doesburg's works to produce not just an outline of the problem of attribution, but what was the first 'precise research on the nature of the contribution of each of the two artists'.[38] By an examination of drawing techniques in the various axonometrics and plans, Leering discovered clear evidence of a difference in hand. From that evidence combined with reported reminiscences of Van Eesteren, Leering concluded that Van Doesburg produced the coloured counter-constructions after the axonometric drawings by Van Eesteren of the completed architectural project. In short, the first project for the Rosenberg house was completely designed by Van Eesteren before he joined Van Doesburg in Paris. The second project for a private house was architecturally the work of Van Eesteren, while coloured analyses in terms of Van Doesburg's new conception of architecture were produced by the latter. Leering does bring up the question whether, and if so to what extent, Van Doesburg had influenced the development of a centrifugal movement on plan and a corresponding de-emphasis of the corners of the building. Leering leaves this as a moot point, saying that it would be difficult to determine the roles more fully. However, he considered the case of the third project, the studio house, to be much clearer. According to Leering, Van Eesteren

is able to remember the direct involvement of Van Doesburg in the third project, which is probably also to be seen in the building programme [the inclusion of a studio and a music room as in the Meudon House] tailored to Van Doesburg's needs, but above all in response to the previously drawn counter-constructions in which Van Doesburg established his vision of architecture and proved the necessity of solving the problem of the unification of colour and plane in a different manner.[39]

Leering has produced a convincing argument, which largely reconciles Van Eesteren's conflicting statements by making the first statement apply primarily to the private house project and the second to their third project, the studio house. However, Leering's findings have been disputed. Baljeu categorically states that the second project 'clearly derives from Van Doesburg's hand since the interpenetration of architectural spaces is an enriched elaboration upon the Weimar models'.[40] For further support he points to the use of an implied 45-degree angle in the layout. These seem to be inadequate grounds for a reattribution to Van Doesburg's hand; in the first place the Weimar models were not actually by Van Doesburg, and secondly Van Eesteren used the 45-degree angle in planning the layout of the University Hall. Van Eesteren's attack takes another form. Whatever he said to Leering about Van Doesburg's contributions to the third project, he had denied in subsequent interviews that Van Doesburg did more than just trace his drawings and add colour.

In the latest study of what has unfortunately become the *cause célèbre* of De Stijl architecture, Troy presents evidence, in the form of a letter of 10 August 1923 from Van Doesburg to Rietveld, that Van Doesburg may have contributed more to the Rosenberg House than previously thought: 'Last night we worked through the entire night; the drawings of the Rosenberg project are ready and have been blueprinted.'[41] Of the second project Troy reasonably argues that

it therefore seems most likely that the development of the Private House involved a continuous dialogue between Van Eesteren and Van Doesburg who worked together on the project in Van Doesburg's Paris atelier. Thus their respective contributions cannot be entirely isolated in terms of colour and form. [p. 110]

As far as the third project is concerned, she agrees generally with Leering about the influence of the counter-constructions for the second project on the more successful integration of colour and the architectural plane in the third project (pp. 112–14).

There are two further studies, Jaffé's seminal *De Stijl 1917–1931: the Dutch Contribution to Modern Art* (1956) and his later work *Theo van Doesburg* (1983). In the former the problem is dismissed, saying that 'it is difficult indeed to get a clear vision of the personal factors of this collaboration and it is perhaps even quite unimportant as the results, by themselves, are so extremely important'.[42] While this is true, the question is not simply one of authorship of the drawings but responsibility for the development of the new ideas which the drawings represent. As Van Eesteren himself wrote regarding his Prix de Rome report: 'I . . . have concentrated my work on the elements which I considered to be the points at issue. In this, drawings play a very modest role . . . One wonders if it makes sense to produce beautiful and sensitive drawings of city planning . . . when what matters is to help to trace the main ideas . . .'[43]

In Jaffé's recent book about Van Doesburg his approach has changed. He takes issue with Leering precisely in terms of the conception of architecture behind the 1923 models and the relative contributions of Van Eesteren and Van Doesburg.

There can hardly be any doubt concerning the outcome of [Leering's] research. The only objection which one could offer (and Leering is aware of this) is that both artists have presented their work as 'collective construction' and they have never departed from this position. . . . Here we are not so much concerned with the distinction between the two spirits, or rather the hands, of the professional who made the axonometrics and the non-professional who gave form to an abstract vision of architecture in the contra-constructions; we are much more concerned to answer the question how much Van Doesburg after the experience of collective construction differs from the Van Doesburg of previous years.[44]

To answer this question Jaffé inspects the contents of three articles: the fifth manifesto of De Stijl signed by both Van Doesburg and Van Eesteren in 1923; secondly, 'Vers une construction collective' by Van Doesburg and Van Eesteren; and third, Van Doesburg's own article, 'Towards a Plastic Architecture'. The strategy is that ideas which seem to differ from earlier writings by the 'old' Van Doesburg can then be attributed to the young Van Eesteren. The result of the analysis is that:

Here, as opposed to a speculative aesthetic (characterised in the article as a 'childhood illness'), scientific research with its criterion of verifiability is demanded – and this is also new for Van Doesburg. This idea, and equally the formula 'we have done the research . . . and we have discovered . . .', must have been Van Eesteren's. But this new demand of verifiability, of the accountability of results, in the coming years will be a decisive influence on all Van Doesburg's work, not just in the realm of architecture.[45]

However, these ideas were neither new at this period, nor were they Van Eesteren's contribution. They had already been developed to a significant extent in connection with Van Doesburg's conception of the mechanical aesthetic. In 1921, before he had met Van Eesteren, Van Doesburg had written in 'The Meaning of the Mechanical Aesthetic for Architecture and the other Professions' that

Art, religion and philosophy develop with or are limited to the scientific discoveries of a given period. Architecture, above all, is unthinkable without a
scientific component. The calculation of load and support, light and space etc.,
comprises the greatest part of architecture.

The distribution of light and the division of space both have a scientific basis.
As soon as the purely functional organisation is controlled by mathematics and
subjected to the creative will, the calculation becomes monumental beauty.[46]

More than a year before he met Van Eesteren, Van Doesburg was demanding objective, scientific criteria for architecture and the other arts.
He may have borrowed many of the ideas concerning calculation, scientific method, etc., but it was obviously not from Van Eesteren. Van
Doesburg had placed an aphorism taken from André Salmon at the head
of his introductory article on the machine aesthetic. It read: 'L'adoration
du machinisme et sa révélation auront eu leurs Jean Jacques, comme
la nature.' For Van Doesburg at this point, the 'Jean Jacques' of the
machine aesthetic was Le Corbusier.

Perhaps the closest there will ever be to a definitive attribution of roles
in the creation of the Rosenberg models is a very simple statement in
a letter of 6 August 1923 from Van Doesburg to Antony Kok: 'Van
Eesteren is working on something new, a private house with a studio.
I have also designed a very modern house which we will work out
together.' (Van Doesburg Archive, R.B.K.) Essentially this confirms Leering's analysis. As yet Van Doesburg was not enough of a professional
to be able to work out the architectural detailing by himself. However,
in a letter of 18 October 1923 to Kok, Van Doesburg claimed of the
model for the 'Maison d'Artiste' that 'I made it in the last week before
the exhibition. [I] worked on it day and night. The fenestration is
executed in copper, the other parts in wood, mica, pasteboard and glass.
Above all the staircase is very beautiful. The colours are splendid.' (Van
Doesburg Archive, R.B.K.) In the same letter he continued his description
of the exhibition in Rosenberg's Galleries: 'In room II there is the whole
development of a House. First, on the walls are the three ground plans,
then the schematic diagrams, then my analyses, then the contra-
construction in colour and the final result is a splendid, perfectly
executed model in colour!' Van Doesburg may have been rather boastful,
but on the whole his letters to his great friend Kok are a reliable source
of information. It would appear, then, that Van Eesteren was primarily
responsible for the 'Maison Particulière', with analyses contributed by
Van Doesburg. The Maison d'Artiste, on the other hand, was originally
Van Doesburg's idea with technical assistance from Van Eesteren.

The question of authorship illuminates only part of the whole conception of architecture behind the designs. The brief, as outlined by
Rosenberg, and the three-fold solution detailed in the projects themselves
will reveal the rest of the conceptual background on close inspection.

The nature of the Rosenberg commission had been fermenting in his
correspondence with Van Doesburg since the early days of *De Stijl*.
Rosenberg was highly sympathetic to Van Doesburg's views and quickly
offered help in the form of a series of articles, 'Parlons peinture'. An

international, collective, and virtually anonymous effort (which is at the root of the problem of authorship) was dear to Rosenberg's heart. On 2 August 1920 he wrote to Van Doesburg:

Nous sommes cependant beaucoup plus près de l'effort collectif que nous ne l'étions depuis la fin de l'époque des cathédrales et je ne désespère pas d'assister au commencement du règne d'un art monumental avant ma mort. Cet art ne sera ni français, ni hollandais, ni anglo-saxon, il sera universel, car de toutes les nations des initiés se dressent pour le grand effort. C'est pourquoi j'ai l'intention de fonder, à partir de l'hiver prochain, un petit périodique, qui sera comme la tribune à laquelle viendront parler toutes les intelligences dont le concours peut être précieux à la cause commune. J'ose espérer que vous voudrez bien nous apporter vos avis éclairés.[47]

Van Doesburg's earlier writings had dealt with the same theme, as for instance in *Classic – Baroque – Modern*. In 1923 and 1924, his own publications and those written in conjunction with Van Eesteren were particularly absorbed with the theme. For example, an extract from *Classic – Baroque – Modern* was republished under the title 'Vers un style collectif' in the April 1924 issue of the *Bulletin de l'effort moderne*, Rosenberg's own 'petit périodique'. Manifesto V, 'Vers une construction collective', followed in the November issue of the same periodical, and was also published that year in *Pasmo*. In *Stavba* (a Czech magazine) and *De Stijl* an article under the same title and with similar content was published under both their names. Van Doesburg reiterated his position as late as 1927 with the publication of 'L'Art collectif et son importance sociale'.[48] The content of these articles will prove to be of great interest when examining the three designs for the Paris models.

The official invitation to produce designs and exhibit them in the Galerie de l'Effort Moderne is to be found in a letter from Rosenberg dated 3 December 1920:

Je vous retourne les photos que vous avez eu l'extrême obligeance de m'envoyer à l'examen et dont l'interêt pour moi, je ne vous le cache pas, a été particulièrement grand. Je les ai montrées à des amateurs, ici, qui ont été stupéfaits de ces heureuses réalisations d'art monumental moderne, alors que chez nous, malheureusement, vous n'en trouviez que l'imitation maladroite d'époques décadents. J'ai mis à part les photos que je préférais. Elles indiquent assez dans quelle direction je me sens porté, ce sont aussi celles susceptibles de plaire à des milieux de culture latine, à cause de leur simplicité, de leur logique, de leur classicisme et de leur *mesure*.

Si vous et Monsieur Oud vouliez exécuter des maquettes représentant vos constructions et vos intérieurs en miniature, je serais disposé à en faire ici l'*exposition à mes frais* l'année prochaine.[49]

Rosenberg had been very optimistic about the date for the exhibition. In fact it was not until 3 January 1922 that he provided Van Doesburg with the brief for his private house:

I hasten to reply to your very kind letter of 1 January last.
a. Basement: kitchen with service room, cellars for wood, coal, and wine, storage-space for cases, furniture for changes, a dayroom for the personnel, different service rooms – such as ironing room, laundryroom, etc., toilet for personnel.

56 Cornelis van Eesteren,
Ground plan for the Hotel
Particulier, 1922; this and
fig. 57 as reproduced in
L'Architecture vivante
(Autumn 1925), plates 8 and
9 respectively

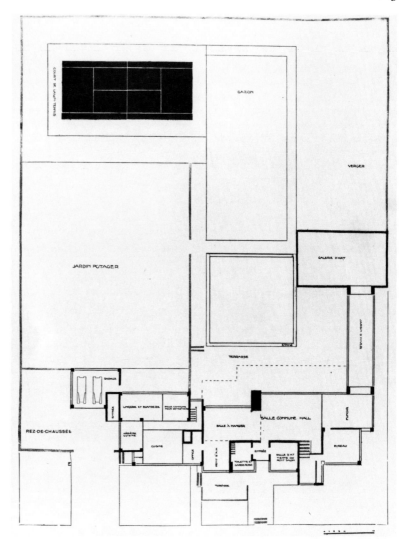

b. Ground floor: entry with an adjoining room, a dining or sitting room opening
  on to the garden, large and small salon, smoking room/library, toilet.
c. 1st floor: five bedrooms, of which 3 should have adjoining toilets, 2 bathrooms
  with toilets, boudoir.
d. 2nd floor: room for the butler, 4 bedrooms for the staff, 2 WCs, exhibition
  room with skylights for collections of paintings and sculptures.
e. garden: small garden in front of the house, large garden behind with a small
  pool, tennis court, vegetable garden and orchard, poultry yard, garage with
  dwelling for the chauffeur.
Above all do not forget the necessary closets and drawers.

As far as the orientation and dimensions of the different rooms go, I'm sure
that your feeling for form and your good taste will secure a good result, and
therefore I won't advise you further.[50]

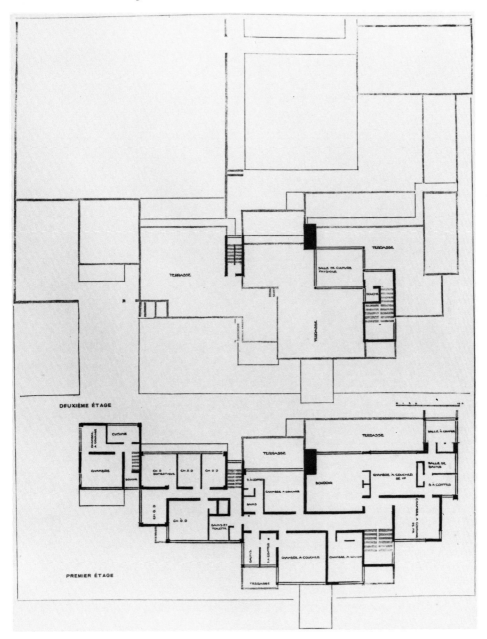

DEUXIÈME ÉTAGE

PREMIER ÉTAGE

An examination of the plans for the 'Hotel Particulier' (figs. 56 and 57) will show that Van Eesteren produced a fairly direct solution to the brief. All of the required rooms are there (with the exception of the cellars), and highly fashionable accoutrements such as roof-terraces and a '*salle de culture physique*' have been added. The 'Hotel' is in fact three houses: one for Rosenberg, one for the staff, and one for the chauffeur. Each has a separate entrance, but there is naturally a connecting door between the former two. The vertical division of Van Eesteren's design

57 Cornelis van Eesteren, First- and second-floor plans of the Hotel Particulier, 1922

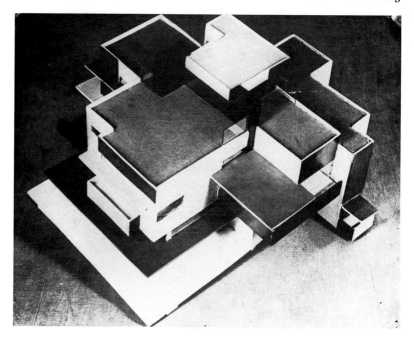

provides for progressively increasing privacy more successfully than
Rosenberg's original commission. The facades are the most direct expression of enclosure and natural lighting. The handling of the eaves over
doors to the gardens and terraces gives both protection from the weather
and, with the high strip-windows above, provides for deep penetration
of light into the related interior. At the same time it also becomes an
important aspect of the aesthetic, in evidence in both the other models.
(See figs. 58 and 59.)

The architectural form as the direct result of the demands was a basic
principle of Van Doesburg's new conception of architecture. It was the
ultimate conclusion of his fight against stylistic historicism. The previous
acceptance by architects of styles as *a priori* formulae prompted Van
Doesburg to call his conception of a new architecture 'a-stylar' and
'formless'. He stressed this point in the articles 'Diagnosis of Architecture: with Reference to the Architectural Exhibition of the De Stijl Group
in the Galerie Rosenberg, Paris', in 'Towards a Plastic Architecture', and
in the many reworded versions of the latter. It appeared as a sixteen-
point (in *L'Architecture vivante* point 10 was separated into two, creating
a seventeen-point) programme for the new architecture. Van Eesteren's
plans for the three houses answered the practical demands of the programme very well. Gradations of privacy determined the division of each
into floors; the directness of the architectural solution produced a formal
economy and an elementary monumentality. In the second model, that
of the Maison Particulière, there remain problems with points 7 to 9,
concerning the relationship of the window to the wall and an unnecessary complexity on plan.

Van Doesburg's contribution to the Maison Particulière project took

59 Theo van Doesburg and Cornelis van Eesteren, Model of the Maison d'Artiste, 1923, contemporary photograph on original mount (37 cm × 28 cm); in the Van Doesburg Collection, R.B.K. (AB 5132)

the form of counter-constructive analyses of the house in terms of the inter-relationships of the constituent planes (fig. 60). The study of this sculptural aspect in axonometric projections was repeated in colour all round the house to build up the *Raumzeitmalerei* described above (pp. 148–49). The work could not be experienced in its entirety all at once, so the space of the painting, of the architecture, became a conceptual space. 'Par cette détermination des plans on peut les étendre à l'infini de tous côtés et sans arrêt. Il en résulte un système coordonné dont les différents points correspondent à une même quantité de points dans l'espace universel' (point 5).[51] Van Doesburg had taken Kandinsky's idea of placing man inside painting and achieved that ideal in his own terms; he had placed man inside Neo-plastic painting. As he stated in 'L'art collectif et son importance sociale':

L'art monumental pur trouve sa base dans *une opposition, dans ce rapport complémentaire d'architecture et de peinture, de formes plastiques et de couleurs plates.*
    . . . Le mouvement n'est pas optique et matériel. Il est esthétique. Il s'exprime en peinture par des rapports de couleurs. Il doit être contrebalancé par un mouvement contraire. Le caractère neutre de la plastique architecturale y contribue.
    Synthèse: Pourra être atteint sur une base purement moderne – par le développement de cette collaboration complémentaire de la peinture et de l'architecture – le but de l'art monumental qui est de placer l'homme *dans (au lieu de vis à vis) l'art plastique et de l'y faire – par ce fait – prendre part.*[52]

60 Theo van Doesburg,
Counter-constructive analysis
of the Maison Particulière,
1923 (lithograph hand-
coloured with gouache,
57 cm × 57 cm); Van
Doesburg Collection, R.B.K.
(AB 5122)

61 Theo van Doesburg,
Counter-constructive analysis
of the Maison d'Artiste, 1923
(pencil, pen and chalk on
tracing paper, 37 cm × 38 cm
unevenly cut); Van Doesburg
Collection, R.B.K. (AB 5130)

The process was not completed, however, by the analytical studies
for the application of colour to architecture. The axonometric and
counter-construction for the Maison d'Artiste (figs. 61 and 62) show
how the experiment with the Maison Particulière, where the colour-
planes and architectural planes were unsatisfactorily resolved in terms
of panels, had influenced the treatment of the architectural elements

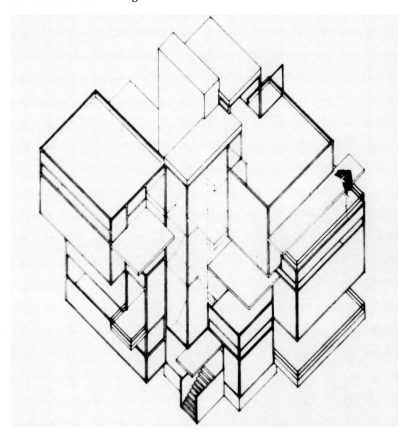

62 Cornelis van Eesteren, Axonometric of the Maison d'Artiste, 1923; Van Eesteren, Fluck en Van Lohuizen-stichting, N.D.B. Amsterdam

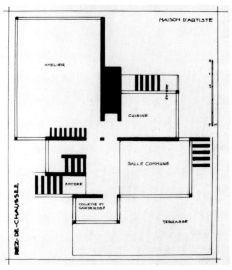

63 Cornelis van Eesteren and Theo van Doesburg, Plan of the *Rez-de-Chaussée*, Maison d'Artiste, 1923 (photographic reproduction, 51.5 cm × 49.5 cm); Van Doesburg Collection, R.B.K. (AB 5126)

themselves in the Maison d'Artiste, the third model. There the unity of colour and architecture was complete. The elements of the architecture are more firmly under control, as can be seen in the clarity of the plans (figs. 63–66). The development of the plans vertically about the

64 Cornelis van Eesteren and Theo van Doesburg, Plan of the *Premier Étage*, Maison d'Artiste, 1923 (pencil, ink and collage, 51.5 cm × 49 cm) Van Doesburg Collection, R.B.K. (AB 5127)

65 Cornelis van Eesteren and Theo van Doesburg, Plan of the *Deuxième Étage*, Maison d'Artiste, 1923 (pencil, ink and collage, 51.5 cm × 49 cm); Van Doesburg Collection, R.B.K. (AB 5128)

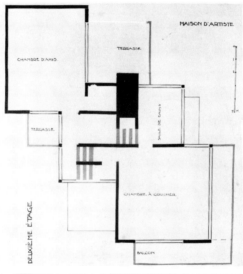

66 Cornelis van Eesteren and Theo van Doesburg, Plan of the *Troisième Étage*, Maison d'Artiste, 1923 (pencil, ink and collage, 51.5 cm × 49 cm); Van Doesburg Collection, R.B.K. (AB 5129)

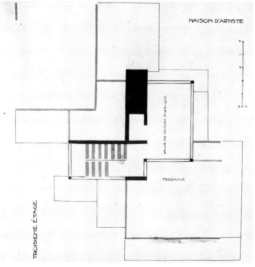

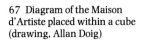

67 Diagram of the Maison d'Artiste placed within a cube (drawing, Allan Doig)

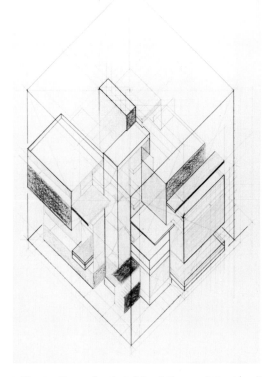

stair is also a more direct illustration of point 12 of the architectural programme (in the *Architecture vivante* version):

12. ASTATIQUE. – La nouvelle architecture est anti-cubique, c'est-à-dire que les différents espaces ne sont pas comprimés dans un cube fermé. Au contraire, les différentes cellules d'espaces (les volumes de balcons, etc., inclus) se développent excentriquement, du centre à la périphérie du cube, par quoi les dimensions de hauteur, de largeur, de profondeur, de temps, reçoivent une nouvelle expression plastique.

Ainsi, la maison moderne donnera l'impression d'être planée, suspendue dans l'air, de s'opposer à la gravitation naturelle.

Figure 67 demonstrates this movement from the staircase outwards towards the faces of the cube. Van Doesburg himself illustrated this movement with his 'tesseracts' (figs. 68 and 69). There is, however, no question of frontality or corners of the house; it is a 'développement plastique polyédrique dans l'espace-temps' (point 14).

The co-operative effort between Van Doesburg and Van Eesteren continued beyond the work for the Paris exhibition. While Van Doesburg was away in November 1924 Van Eesteren kept the business of *De Stijl* turning over in Paris. In a letter in the Van Doesburg Archive, dated 21–23 November 1923, Van Eesteren announced to Van Doesburg that he would be returning to Holland after 15 December to build a house for his parents. In the section dated 23 November he added the exciting news that '*Architecture vivante* wants to publish a special De Stijl num-

68 Theo van Doesburg,
Tesseracts with arrows
indicating centripetal and
centrifugal movement in four-
dimensional space (ink on
tracing paper, both
19.5 cm × 24.9 cm); Van
Doesburg Collection, R.B.K.
(AB 4857 and AB 4858)

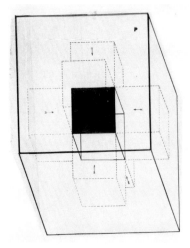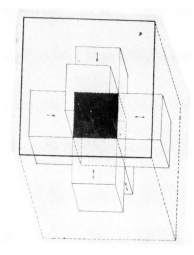

69 Theo van Doesburg,
Tesseract entitled NENOUVELLE
DIMENSION (pencil on tracing
paper, 32.5 cm × 30.3 cm);
Van Doesburg Collection,
R.B.K. (AB 4863)

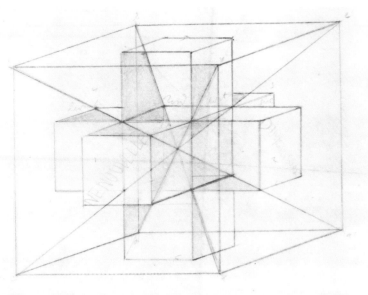

ber'. Van Doesburg's colour-scheme for the house in Ablasserdam for
Van Eesteren's parents was published in that issue of *Architecture vivante*.
The realities of building had taken the painter back from his space-time
architecture, to a further development on the work for Oud and for De
Boer. Colour could only be applied to window-frames, shutters, and
doors in this small brick house. As in the previous drawings, the colour
movements were indicated by diagonal lines of movement.

A few days later, on 27 November, Van Eesteren wrote again,
announcing:

I've begun work on two designs for a house, one on the river, and one in The
Hague. Neither is bad, only very restricted in the choice of materials etc. Finally,
I have a few changes to make in an existing house and the addition of a garage.[53]

The first two buildings were very similar to the Maison Particulière in the handling of the massing, but were left uncoloured. The garage was left extremely simple, but was painted in primary colours.

On 11 August 1924 Van Eesteren wrote inquiring if Van Doesburg would like to help on another project:

> enclosed are a programme-drawing and two projections of an entry for the competition: shopping centre, Laan van Meerdervoort. If you would like to do a colour study, I would be pleased to send it in as a joint entry.[54]

Van Doesburg complied, producing alternative studies for himself with two different solutions in primary colours, sending the preferred scheme to Van Eesteren (figs. 70 and 71). The entry was submitted under the motto *Simultaneïté*, but nothing came of it; there was no mention of it in the report of the jury.[55] Van Eesteren submitted an entry for the Rokin Competition with a colour-scheme which owes a great deal to Van Doesburg.

The co-operative work was not to last. Only ten days after the invitation to work together on the Laan van Meerdervoort project, Van Eesteren wrote again to Van Doesburg:

> All things considered we have problems enough. Therefore, it seems to me better (naturally, that is as long as we trust each other – specifically, it must always remain a divided relationship) not to make things unnecessarily difficult for each other.[56]

70 Theo van Doesburg, Sketch designs for a colour-scheme for a group of flats and shops on the Laan van Meerdervoort, The Hague, 1924 (pencil, ink and gouache, on two separate sheets of tracing paper, 45.5 cm × 64.5 cm irregularly cut); Van Doesburg Collection, R.B.K. (AB 5133)

71 Cornelis van Eesteren and
Theo van Doesburg, Colour-
scheme for Van Eesteren's
competition entry for a group
of flats and shops on the Laan
van Meerdervoort, The
Hague, 1924 (pencil, ink and
gouache, 43 cm × 76.5 cm);
Van Doesburg Collection,
R.B.K. (AB 5134)

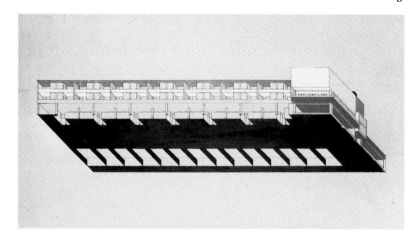

Again Van Doesburg seems to have rebelled at the idea that his colour-
schemes should be restricted to elements of the architecture as
determined by the architect. After this, small difficulties arose over
money and grew through professional rivalry, and again the collective
effort collapsed. In the last-mentioned letter (21 August 1924) Van
Eesteren also complained about the attribution of 'Towards a Plastic
Architecture':

. . . it would have been more proper for the title to be as follows:
   'Towards a Plastic Architecture' (large print)
small: 'Results of the co-operative work of C. Eesteren . Théo van Doesburg',
than 'Théo van Doesburg'.
In the case that it is translated and published in other periodicals . . . I expect
it to be printed in that way.

The two had apparently discussed the ideas contained in the article during the design of the models, and Van Eesteren thought it only just that
his name be included although the final text was Van Doesburg's responsibility, just as the final architectural decision on the models had been
Van Eesteren's responsibility. For the time being Van Eesteren was willing to forget the whole thing, but the issue came to a head at the end
of 1926 when Van Doesburg turned the tables and accused Van Eesteren
of betrayal. The reply to the accusation read:

I have allowed work to be published in Oud's magazine, but I don't really know
very much about the magazine itself. However, it is not against De Stijl. When
you judge the periodical you mustn't forget that *De Stijl* has become a totally
personal expression of Van Doesburg, with all the consequences that entails.
De Stijl is a kind of private correspondence between yourself and your readers.
As such it is important, but it has with that ceased to be the organ of the so-called
Stijl group.
   Concerning the De Stijl special issue of *Architecture vivante*, I should be pleased
to see the mistakes rectified in the next issue of *De Stijl*.[57]

Van Eesteren had had problems with mistakes before. In a letter of
10 December 1924 (R.B.K.) he complained about a mistake in the way
the composition for the University Hall had been put together (see *De*

Stijl, VI, no 8, Series XII (1924), p. 118; the design was correctly published in *Architecture vivante* (Autumn 1925), pl. 11). What Van Eesteren objected to even more was the fact that the dimensions were given as 50 m × 50 m.

The dimensions of the hall are not 50 m × 50 m, they are *28 m × 28 m*. Be so good as to announce in the following issue of *De Stijl*, that 50 m × 50 m is a mistake. It is, namely, impossible to span 50 m in that way. The way it has been published *I* am the laughing-stock.[58]

On 11 January 1925 Van Eesteren asked Van Doesburg again, but still no correction was made. As far as the mistakes in *Architecture vivante* were concerned, Van Doesburg simply printed a disclaimer in two issues of *De Stijl*,[59] saying that 'Theo van Doesburg ne prend aucune responsabilité pour le numéro de l'*Architecture vivante*, consacré au groupe *De Stijl* (Edition Albert Morancé). Ce numéro plein d'erreurs typographiques, est composé hors de sa Rédaction'. There the matter rested, which was obviously unsatisfactory to Van Eesteren. Van Doesburg did not even answer Van Eesteren's last letter. The Dutch contingent of De Stijl had all but disappeared. Of the magazine itself, only another half dozen numbers would appear under Van Doesburg's editorship.

6

The Aubette and related work

In 1924 Van Doesburg saw a chance to obtain official recognition for De Stijl and at the same time confirm his idea of collective work in the minds of his rather reticent co-workers. This opportunity presented itself in the form of 'L'Exposition des Arts Décoratifs', which was to take place in Paris in 1925. Van Doesburg wrote to the Exhibition Commissioners for Architecture and the Related Arts, Dutch Section, asking for official sanction and, more important, official subsidy for the group participation of De Stijl. After having gone into debt to pay his half of the expenses for the Rosenberg exhibition, Van Doesburg could not hope to finance yet another, this time virtually alone. He received an extensive answer from the engineer J. de Bie Leuveling Tjeenk, Commissioner General for the Dutch section, outlining the history of the organisation.[1] The commission had been formed from thirteen members chosen by the main artistic and architectural organisations in the Netherlands: BNA, Architectura et Amicitia, de VANK, the Dutch Circle of Sculptors, and 'De Opbouw'. In the spring of 1924 the government had been very negative about providing a subsidy for Dutch participation in Paris, but when the Exhibition Commissioners appealed to the French exhibition organisers and the Dutch cabinet, a subsidy was agreed and three government commissions were formed. The membership of these commissions included many well-known figures, amongst them men with whom Van Doesburg had had previous contact, for instance, C. J. Blaauw, Berlage, Jan Gratama, and Professor R. N. Roland Holst. De Bie Leuveling Tjeenk informed Van Doesburg:

The exhibition Commission and the Selection Committee have very seriously considered the question whether collective submissions will be admitted, but have decided that the artists will have to submit individually. According to the Terms of Participation, which have been established by the Heldring Commission in conjunction with the Exhibition Commission, the placement of all works of art will be by, and under the responsibility of, the Exhibition Commission. To your question whether your group can be granted a separate section and portion of the available monies, I must therefore give a negative answer.

It was naturally completely unacceptable to Van Doesburg to give these men the last say in the selection and placement of works by him and any others who would be willing to participate in a De Stijl section. In a surviving fragment of a letter, presumably written in reply to De

Bie Leuveling Tjeenk, he made it clear that he was willing to compromise only on the financial side by asking his co-workers to provide some of the necessary funds themselves. In his opinion it was necessary to provide a separate De Stijl section in order to demonstrate the complete cooperation of painter and architect. For this demonstration he requested 'at least 10,000 guilders (70,000 francs)' from the official funds. He continued that:

It would be very regrettable if the De Stijl group, which has already influenced the development of modern architecture here, had to abandon its substantial participation, the more so since the exhibition was established in order to demonstrate the spirit of renewal in architecture and the related arts, as written in art. 4 of the 'conditions générales d'admission' ('sont admises à l'exposition les oeuvres d'une *inspiration nouvelle* et d'une *originalité réelle*' etc.).[2]

The amount of money he requested makes it plain that Van Doesburg had great plans for the exhibition, very possibly the building of a small separate pavilion for the exhibition of much of the material shown in the Rosenberg gallery.

De Bie Leuveling Tjeenk's reply was polite but firm. He denied both that the commissioners were missing a great opportunity and that completely unrelated works would just be thrown together. Reflecting the same sort of loose collectivity demonstrated by *Architectura* and *Wendingen* at the close of the Hollandsche Werkbond debate, he remarked that 'collectivity, as we see it, is however a completely different one from yours'.[3]

Van Doesburg's hopes were dashed, but characteristically he did not let the matter rest there. In late 1923 he had received encouragement from the Dutch Ambassador in Paris and, after the refusal by the committees of his terms, he brought the affair to the notice of the public in *Het Bouwbedrijf* (II, no 4, April 1925) and of course in *De Stijl* (no 10/11, 1925). In his article 'The Preparation of the "Exposition des Arts Décoratifs", Paris 1925' in *Het Bouwbedrijf* (pp. 151–53) he again quoted article IV of the Regulations for Admission and asked 'What have the style-compotes . . . to do with "oeuvres d'une inspiration nouvelle"?' He reserved his praise for the Russians, Perret, and Mallet-Stevens, the last of whom had been criticised in *Architectura* for his submissions and subsequent critique of the Dutch section.[4] Van Doesburg was able to be much sharper in his remarks in *De Stijl*. There he interpreted the Dutch section as a direct counter-attack by the Wendingen group on De Stijl after its success in Paris at the Rosenberg gallery. He complained that 'France too has had a menu of Berlage-hash, Roland Holst-marmalade, with Konijnenburg-sauce set before her, but served as tastefully as possible'.[5] Van Doesburg had also circulated a petition of protest 'contre le *refus* de la participation du groupe "De Stijl"', and had received support from Perret, Loos, Tzara, Schwitters, Gropius, Marinetti, Wils, and Mallet-Stevens, amongst others. De Stijl had been taunted in the Dutch press because, while the group had not participated as such, Wils and Oud had participated individually. This, of course, led to yet another attack by Van Doesburg on Oud:

The Dutch artistic press . . . might also have referred to the fact that the architect Oud has in spirit and deed joined the Wendingen group, and thereby supported the principle of suppression and exclusion of the New. Further, the artists of De Stijl have not considered him to be amongst their colleagues for years.[6]

The statement is clearly unfair, since Oud had participated in the Rosenberg exhibition. Wils was left out of the attack since he at least had supported the petition. The Dutch journalist had called the signatories of the petition 'unprofessional outsiders' and here Nelly van Doesburg joined the fray with an open letter in *De Stijl* addressed to the journalist. She defended De Stijl and protested that Gropius, Mallet-Stevens *et al.* could hardly be called 'unprofessional outsiders'.[7]

At the time this argument was taking place, late 1924 and early 1925, Van Doesburg was in the first stages of producing a design for painting a small 'chambre à fleurs' for the Hyères villa designed by Rob Mallet-Stevens for the Vicomte de Noailles. Van Doesburg had come into contact with the Vicomte through their common interest in modern art (he lived only a few doors away from Rosenberg's gallery), and Van Doesburg was invited for discussions of the theory behind De Stijl. The Vicomte had been in contact with many artists and architects, including Le Corbusier, Mies van der Rohe, Lipchitz, and Giacometti, in connection with building and furnishing a new home for himself and his bride on a parcel of land given to them by his mother. The Vicomte's impressions of Van Doesburg were positive, but perhaps his enthusiasm for Van Doesburg's radical ideas was commensurate with the fact that the room placed at his disposal was tiny (1.20 m × 1.46 m) and very dark.

It may be precisely because the room was so small that the solution was indeed a radical departure even for Van Doesburg. There he concentrated all the results of his architectural work with Van Eesteren in combination with his recently-begun series of counter-compositions in painting. In a letter of 27 August 1925 he wrote to César Domela:

As always I am hard at work. On Belle-Ile I finished my piece on colour theory and am now beginning the second section on Plastic art. There is, however, still a lot of work to be done on it before I can offer it to my publisher. I am also, for want of architectural work, furiously working on my painting. A completely new, independent means of expression has developed out of the last stretch of work, which I completed with the large black and white counter-composition. These are primarily diagonal things in opposition to the 'construction terrestre' with dominant horizontals and verticals. Two of these are already coming into stride, and the other still in sketch form, but I'm going this very day to Paris, to order half a dozen canvases. After all my disappointments with architecture and her so terribly noble representatives, I'm really enjoying painting, which is for the moment the only art-form in which one can demonstrate the NEW independently and without compromise. I have had five chances to build something, but in the final analysis they have been cancelled as a result of the fact that I couldn't point to any 'architecture completely and independently carried out by me'. As if I hadn't inspired the fruition of the whole of the New architecture in Holland; nobody lets that bother them, and the architects (of such character) will certainly keep that to themselves with an easy conscience! Still, I was pleased to see an excellent house (in the photo) by

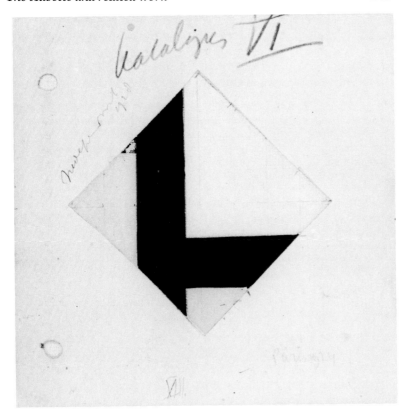

72 Theo van Doesburg,
Sketch of *Counter-Composition
VIII*, 1924 (pencil, ink and
gouache on graph paper,
5.5 cm × 5.5 cm measured
diagonally); Van Doesburg
Collection, R.B.K. (AB 4149 I)

Rietveld, whom I consider amongst the most honest and talented of architects along with Van Eesteren. The house is the application of our most recent principles.

There is still a possibility, however, that I shall soon build a model house with my own funds on the Côte de Phare, in St-Raphaël.

The letter is full of interesting points. First, Van Doesburg himself has answered Jaffé's question 'whether or not Van Doesburg may have started his series of diagonal counter-compositions with a work closely resembling and preceding Mondrian's lozenge compositions of 1925: the 1924 composition which is now in the Art Institute of Chicago'[8] (fig. 72). Because of the ambiguities in Van Doesburg's grammar the text can be interpreted as saying that 'These [counter-compositions, ending with the one in black and white, no VIII] are primarily diagonal things' (hung diagonally, or painted diagonally is really the question), but when he continues that 'two of these [diagonal works] are already coming into stride', it seems clear that *Counter-Composition VIII* was, as suggested to Jaffé by markings on the old canvas, conceived as a lozenge-shaped canvas with horizontal and vertical lines, and that the subsequent canvases were hung square and painted diagonally.[9]

Secondly, the letter emphasises Van Doesburg's dissatisfaction with the limitations imposed on him by practice. The flower-room was a nice little experiment, but it was not a room in which one could do much moving or living. He was frustrated by the limitations and compromises imposed on him in practice and wanted a full-scale architectural project where he would be given a completely free hand, and at the same time prove his ability to carry out architectural work on his own. As far as work for the Vicomte de Noailles is concerned, this patron did not even hang his own collection of paintings, including Picasso, Gris, Braque, and Léger, on the walls:

les toiles . . . ont fait retraite dans les armoires. Elles en sortent quand on veut les voir … Non qu'elles soient jugées trop anecdotiques: les noms de leur auteurs nous sont garants qu'elles ne pêchent pas par excès de réalisme mesquin. Mais des tableaux accrochés troublent les surfaces murales et retiennent la poussière. La disparition des toiles est sans doute la conséquence extrême du culte de l'hygiène, de l'ivresse de netteté qui règnent partout dans la villa d'Hyères. Les seules ornements qu'on tolère ici, ou plutôt qu'on aime, sont des fleurs. Une petite pièce spéciale a été aménagée par Van Doesburg pour couper les tiges et grouper les arums ou les roses dans les vases au cristal limpide.[10]

There was also, in fact, a mural on one of the outside walls on the terrace, but the Vicomte was not the man to give Van Doesburg free rein with his ideas.

The final point which Van Doesburg's letter to César Domela brings into question is the relationship of the design for the flower-room to the counter-compositional paintings and their relative dating. The painting of the flower-room was Van Doesburg's first use of painting on the diagonal in architecture.[11] It may well have been suggested by the use of the 45-degree angle in the axonometric drawings for the projects with Van Eesteren, but there the colour was to be applied orthogonally with the horizontal and vertical planes of the architecture. The use of diagonals in painting the wall surface was, however, consonant with his long-held theory that architectural form is closed and that painting should break that solidity and open the planes. This method of confirming the planar quality of the architecture and at the same time denying the natural structure was an important advance beyond the methods used at De Vonk or during 1923. It is difficult to conceive of this breakthrough taking place in architecture before painting, but the drawing for Hyères is signed and dated 1924–25, implying that it was produced during the winter, while the letter to Domela announcing the breakthrough in painting is dated 27 August 1925. As will be seen later in the discussion of the '*ville de circulation*', Van Doesburg sometimes gave outside dates to projects, the earlier date indicating when the ideas behind the project were first taking shape. In this case, he had come into contact with the Vicomte in 1924 when they discussed art together. When he wrote to Domela, the series ending with *Counter-Composition VIII* and including *Counter-Composition V* (fig. 73) had been completed (he dates them to 1924), and two diagonal compositions were then under way. This suggests that the breakthrough came possibly in June or July after which *Counter-Composition V* was literally 'turned' into an environmental painting.

When the large Van Doesburg exhibition of 1969 was being prepared Jean Leering discovered that the flower-room as carried out was quite

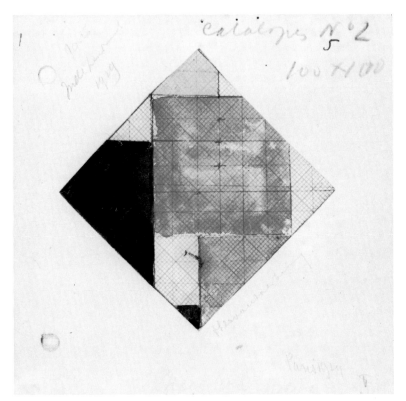

73 Theo van Doesburg, Sketch of *Counter-Composition V*, 1924 (pencil and gouache on graph paper, 6 cm × 6 cm measured diagonally); Van Doesburg Collection, R.B.K. (AB 4149 F)

different from Van Doesburg's design.[12] The artist had drawn a reflected ceiling plan with the related walls folded out and thus also reflected (fig. 74). This confused the painters who, in the absence of the artist, duly reflected the design for the ceiling so that the red triangle was correctly orientated in relation to the door and the window (or hatch since it is actually on an inside wall), but did not reflect the designs for the walls, thereby disturbing the relationships amongst the wall-planes (fig. 75). In producing such a drawing Van Doesburg again demonstrated his misunderstanding of the conventions of professional architectural practice.

The ideas Van Doesburg was developing in painting were, as before, the determining factors of his architectural work, but now more than ever before the converse was also true; architecture was a determining factor in his painting. The breakthrough in the two fields was virtually simultaneous. This is demonstrated in his article 'Painting: from Composition to Counter-Composition', dated Paris, 1926.[13] In the introduction to the article he confirmed that 'in 1924 I closed the period, which I now consider to be of classical-abstract composition, with the white-black-grey composition [no *VIII*]' (p. 17). He devoted the body of the article to the explanation of the theory and the meaning of his new counter-compositional method.

On the one hand the idea 'counter-composition' is opposed to the classical, albeit 'abstract' composition and plastic expression.

74 Theo van Doesburg,
*Croquis pour la petite chambre
de fleurs . . . construction de
couleurs . . . (1924–25)*
(pencil, ink and gouache on
tracing paper,
54 cm × 61 cm); in the
collection of the Stedelijk Van
Abbemuseum, Eindhoven

75 Theo van Doesburg,
Chambre de fleurs as executed,
Villa Noailles, Hyères

On the other hand it is opposed to the fundamental, all-embracingly dominating structural elements, both of nature and of architecture.

Naturally the last named were of importance for development ... but still after a long period man arrives at a recognition of his own nature and his own time. It is our own time which has produced the need for contrast. This contrast was not just realised in the external appearance of colour and the plastic formation of materials, but also and primarily in the tempo of life and in the technical aspect of the daily, mechanical function of living: in standing, moving, driving, lying down, and sitting up, that is in everything that is a determinant of architecture.

The vertical walls of our house, the horizontal planes of the ceiling and floor, and the horizontals and verticals of the intervening objects such as a table, a chair, a cupboard, a bed, etc., all provide satisfactory evidence of this. The movements I have named, insofar as they were related to industry, have all been taken over by machines.

In short, we carry out our physical movements in horizontal and vertical directions.

By the continuous repetition of these natural movements they have become more or less mechanical. Instinct has become mechanised. Our spirit takes no part in this process. Inasmuch as our spirit has not become petrified along with our physical existence, it resists this natural 'mechanisation' and assumes a totally different dimension. [pp. 18–23]

Van Doesburg considered this introduction of the diagonal to be a significant development in his visual philosophy. The classical balance of Neo-plasticism was consonant with the natural opposition of horizontal and vertical. The first introduction of contrast on what he saw as a spiritual level was in his use of colour dissonances and contrasting triads of colour. Natural form and movement in the physical world were becoming mechanised and standardised, and the classical Neo-plastic painting as *the reflection of the essential nature of the natural world* (which was previously the definition of the spiritual aspect of art) was no longer adequate as a reflection of the more highly evolved spirit which was in essence opposed to strictly mechanised material existence. The visual representation of this opposition was the diagonal. In the lozenge-shaped canvases of the earliest counter-compositions the edges of the canvas were the first literal diagonals (he had used implied diagonals in earlier architectural projects), tectonically opposed to the horizontal-vertical painting. The composition itself was still an analogy of nature, but when turned on its side became an analogy of spirit. The whole counter-compositional method was about architecture as a built analogy of the physical life. No matter how good the architecture, it was incomplete as an analogy of the complete life without the spiritual analogy provided by coloured counter-composition as a fully constituent part. The introduction of diagonal elements in architecture was not acceptable within the confines of his theory, 'since our physical and functional existence is carried out in H[orizontal] V[ertical], it follows that as long as this function has not yet been taken over by machines, the architecture which is the best is that which is wholly based on H.V.'[14] Functionally appropriate architecture may be the best, but Functionalist architecture was not appropriate for the whole man because it ignored his spiritual development and froze his life in the physical/mechanical realm. It seems that Van Doesburg was slipping back into a dualistic view of the world, but he protested that 'the spirit is the natural enemy of Nature (however paradoxical that sounds), without necessarily having to posit a dualism between the two' (p. 25).

The Elementarist counter-composition belonged in architecture, and elementary architecture was not complete without it. Rietveld's Schröder house of 1924 was the best example of a fully realised elementary project (see fig. 48). The elements of the architecture are kept visually separate by means of the application of colour and the control of structure. The structural composition coincides perfectly with the visual composition. The external walls have been treated as smooth, discrete planes with a hint of *trompe-l'oeil* treatment in the use of white or varying shades of grey. The window mullions become red or blue lines, and even the I-beam supporting the balcony and cantilevered eave, and the downpipe for rainwater have been fully integrated into the Neo-plastic composition. As evidenced by his letter to Domela, Van Doesburg admired this architecture enormously, but there were now further possibilities.

The new manner of painting can only have meaning as a procedure for the expression of the spiritual when it is placed in opposition to the organic/natural and the architectural structure instead of in agreement with it. This agreement was expressed by the totally H.V. determined painting in the H.V. determined construction of the architecture. The former reinforced the latter. The extension of the colour-plane and the line was in the same direction as the natural and closed architectural structure. (See fig. III and IV [fig. 76] in which the hatched bands represent the natural or architectural structure based on H.V., and the black lines represent the structure of the classic-abstract painting.) In the contrast painting (the counter-composition), this extension moves in opposition to the natural and architectural structure, that is to say it is in contrast to the latter.
Both these two radical possibilities offer a great number of additional potentialities. [pp. 26–27)

Van Doesburg had long used an implied diagonal in his painterly and architectural compositions, and in his designs for Van Eesteren's University Hall he had even placed the design for the ceiling and the floor diagonally in respect to each other. However, in the University Hall the compositions were always placed orthogonally in respect to the architectural axes and as the main hall was itself an octagon the compositions were prevented from forming a contrast with the architecture itself.

In 1926, the year he wrote 'Painting: from Composition to Counter-Composition', Van Doesburg received a unique opportunity to realise in practice the theories he had consolidated in the article:

En septembre 1926, j'entrai pour la première fois en rapports directs avec l'aubette, par l'entremise de M. Arp. Messieurs Horn me firent venir à Strasbourg, et ici je trouvai la faculté de réaliser sur une large échelle mes idées dans le domaine de la construction d'intérieurs, et de transformer les plus belles salles dans le sens moderne.[15]

The background of the Aubette is well known through Van Doesburg's articles in the Aubette Number of *De Stijl* (nos 87–89, Series XV (1928))

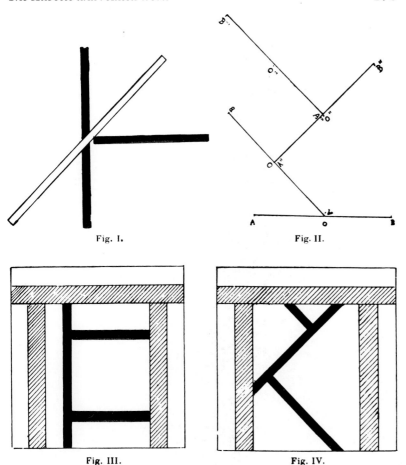

Fig. I.   Fig. II.

Fig. III.   Fig. IV.

76 Theo van Doesburg, Diagrammatic explanation of Neo-plastic and counter-compositional 'Monumental Painting' (from 'Schilderkunst: van kompositie tot contra-kompositie', *De Stijl*, VII, nos 73–74, Series XIII (1926), 17–28 (p. 28))

and in 'Architectural Renewal Abroad; the Reconstruction of the Aubette in Strasbourg' in *Bouwbedrijf* (VI, no 6 (15 March 1929)).These two articles provide the following important background information. The Aubette as it stood in 1926 had been changed very little, as far as the facade was concerned, since the time of Blondel who had designed and built the edifice between 1764 and 1767. He had designed the work as a military headquarters and the name originated from the fact that the soldiers were mustered there at dawn (*l'aube*) to receive their orders for the day. The Aubette was situated in a commanding position on the main square of Strasbourg and when it ceased to be used for military purposes it housed a café from 1845. In 1847 a concert-hall was added in the room which Van Doesburg later converted into the '*Ciné-Dancing*'. In 1869 the building came into the possession of the city and some of the rooms were made over into an art museum. One year later the museum was burnt by the Germans. In 1911 a competition was held to restore the building, but with little result. The modern history of the Aubette began in the early 1920s when the brothers Paul and André Horn and Ernest Heitz bought a ninety-year lease on the building. Paul

77 Documentary photograph
of the Aubette after the
alterations (note Van
Doesburg's neon signs); Van
Doesburg Archive, R.B.K.

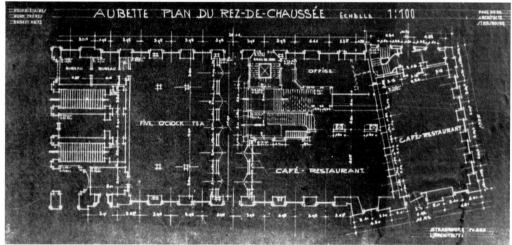

78 Paul Horn, Survey
drawing of the *Aubette Plan du
Rez-de-Chaussée*, 1926 (blueprint,
35.5 cm × 67.5 cm); Van
Doesburg Collection, R.B.K.
(AB 5138)

Horn was himself an architect and carried out the most necessary renovations, such as the consolidation of the foundations, but other than a few general changes he was unsure what ultimate form the complex should have. At that point, through Arp, he brought Van Doesburg to Strasbourg and responded very sympathetically to Van Doesburg's latest theories.

The city was not as sympathetic to Van Doesburg's ideas. They had declared the Aubette to be an historical monument and were very strict about the treatment of Blondel's facade (fig. 77):

Originally I wanted to dominate the whole of the facade with neon signs, but the municipal government refused permission. Even now [March 1929] they have taken the contractors ['for whom Paul Horn is the architect', the original drawing was signed by Horn but on the print in the Van Doesburg Archive the signature has been crossed out in pencil and signed *Théo van Doesburg 1927*] to court because the strict dominant line of the awning for the street café has not been kept in the style of the eighteenth century.[16]

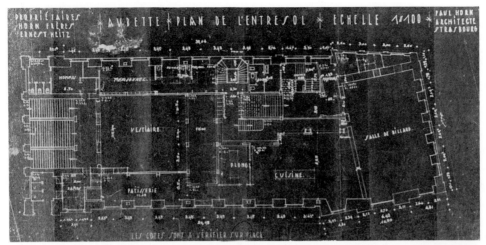

79 Paul Horn, Survey drawing of the *Aubette Plan de l'Entresol* (blueprint, 33 cm × 63 cm); Van Doesburg Collection, R.B.K. (AB 5140)

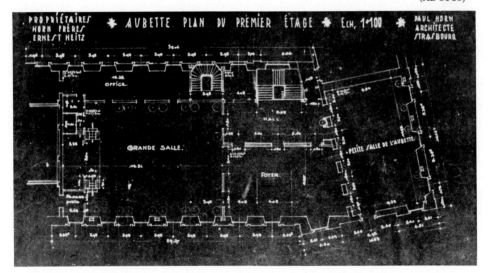

80 Paul Horn, Survey drawing of the *Aubette Plan du Premier Étage* (blueprint with red pencil, 34 cm × 60 cm); Van Doesburg Collection, R.B.K. (AB 5141)

The role of Paul Horn in the re-fitting of the Aubette is already becoming evident.

In the planning of the Aubette, Van Doesburg considered the building to be a '*bâtiment de passage*' and as such did not want to hinder the free circulation of visitors by making them choose only one or two of the function rooms for their visit. It has been claimed that he added a staircase 'which did not exist in the plans of Paul Horn' in order 'to permit the clientele to circulate freely within the entire establishment and thus avoid a rigid specialisation of different rooms and halls'.[17] The writer, Théo Wolters, also thought that the stair was between the ground floor and the first floor. A comparison of the plans by Horn of the Aubette as Van Doesburg found it (figs 78, 79 and 80) and the plans for the

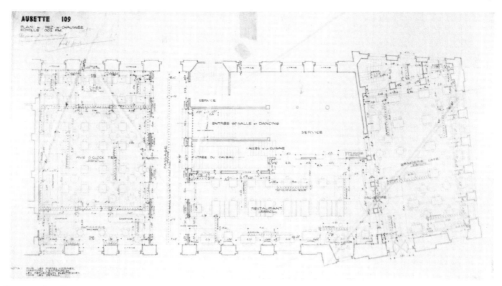

81 Theo van Doesburg,
*Aubette 109, Plan du Rez-de-
Chaussée*, 1927 (pencil, red
pencil and ink on tracing
paper, 55.5 cm × 100 cm);
Van Doesburg Collection,
R.B.K. (AB 5170)

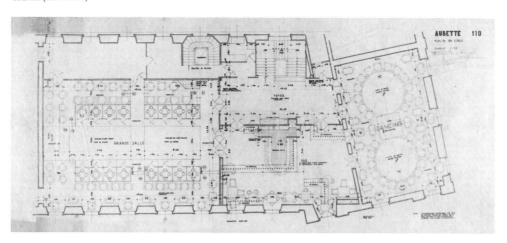

82 Theo van Doesburg,
*Aubette 110, Plan du Premier
Étage*, 1927 (pencil, red pencil
and ink on tracing paper,
52 cm × 109.5 cm unevenly
cut); Van Doesburg
Collection, R.B.K. (AB 5171)

latter's own designs (figs. 81 and 82) reveals that the staircase concerned
was there prior to Van Doesburg's involvement and that it connected
the *entresol*, the first floor, and the second floor. In fact Van Doesburg
carried out very few essential changes to the fabric of the building, con-
centrating on the distribution of activities amongst the existing rooms
and the organisation and detailing of the spaces themselves.

The staircase in question (fig. 83) was decorated by Hans Arp, but
the control exercised by Van Doesburg can be seen both in the stepped
balustrade reminiscent of the staircase at De Vonk, and in the use of
vertical bands rising as a complement to the visitor's movement between

83 Theo van Doesburg, architect, Hans Arp, colour-scheme, Staircase in the Aubette, 1926–27; contemporary photograph in the Van Doesburg Collection, R.B.K. (© ADAGP 1985)

the floors, and in Sophie Taeuber-Arp's simple rectilinear design for the stained-glass window (fig. 84). In spite of the fact that it was again a group effort, this time Van Doesburg was very much in control within certain agreed limitations. Concerning the co-operative work with Arp and Taeuber-Arp, Van Doesburg wrote in 'Notices sur l'Aubette à Strasbourg' in *De Stijl*:

Comme nous étions des hommes de direction différente à collaborer ici, nous pôsames pour principe que chacun était libre de travailler d'après ses idées. Ainsi p[ar] ex[emple] dans le caveau-dancing peint par Arp, on s'inspirait d'une imagination débridée; il en fut de même pour l'éclairage de la salle précédente (bar-américain), où la colonne ronde provenant d'une architecture antérieure, servait de leitmotiv. Les murs, et en particulier la longue paroi antérieure, furent également composés d'après une conception 'prémorphiste' [fig. 85].[18]

The rooms of which he spoke were separated sufficiently from the rest not to provide too much of a disturbance to the unity of the whole. Arp himself seems to have confirmed the fact that Van Doesburg had complete control over the project; when Karl Gerstner was writing his article on the Aubette for *Werk* he wrote to Nelly van Doesburg that 'Monsieur

84 Sophie Taeuber-Arp,
Stained-glass window for the
staircase in the Aubette,
1927; contemporary
photograph in the collection
of the Musée d'Art Moderne
de Strasbourg

85 Hans Arp, *Tableau mural
du Caveau-Dancing*, Aubette,
1927; contemporary
photograph reproduced in *De
Stijl*, VIII, nos 87–89, Series
XV (1928), p. 14 (© ADAGP
1985)

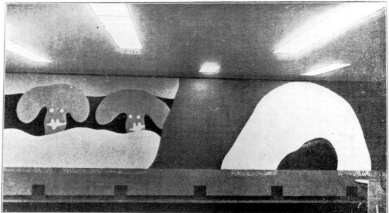

Arp m'a raconté que votre mari avait lui-même conçu tous les détails d'intérieur, depuis l'éclairage jusqu'aux cendriers'.[19] Van Doesburg did indeed pay infinite attention to the integration of detail in this project, in everything from the radiators to the fuse and switch boxes. To make orientation within the complex easier, he designed a special signboard in his 'Aubette script' (fig. 86) with the numbering of each room in a separate colour, and placed the sign at the main entrance. The names and coloured numbers were then repeated next to the entrance to the room concerned.

The progress of the work can to a great extent be seen in the list of drawings kept more or less progressively throughout the project.[20] Some confusion arises because entries were sometimes added in groups and appear in three different hands, beginning with that of Van Doesburg, the body of the entries were kept by an assistant (presumably Honneger or an assistant from Horn's office), and ended with additions by Taeuber-Arp. The list remains for the most part chronological. The first thirty-one

87 Theo van Doesburg,
Sketch design for the gallery
wall, *Ciné-Dancing*, first floor,
Aubette, 1926 (pencil and
gouache on tracing paper,
5.4 cm × 18.8 cm); this and
fig. 88 in the collection of the
Musée National d'Art
Moderne, Paris (cat. nos 10
and 9 respectively); clichés
Musée National d'Art
Moderne, Paris

88 Theo van Doesburg,
Sketch design for the gallery
wall, *Ciné-Dancing* (pencil,
charcoal and gouache on
tracing paper,
14.3 cm × 23.7 cm)

spaces have been left empty and most probably represent the survey
drawings, the working drawings for the services ('number 39' is the
last of this essential set and is described as 'Relevé pour la conduite d'eau
ch[aude] (caves)'), and Van Doesburg's first studies for the
colour-schemes.

Amongst these initial studies for the colour-schemes are two studies
for the wall with the gallery in the *Ciné-Dancing* (figs. 87 and 88). They
show a similar planar division of the wall with the stairs reversed. The
placing of the doorways in the room (for which see fig. 82) necessitated
the use of a staircase of the form shown in figure 88, and the definitive
design (fig. 89) of course shows such a stair, but with a mirror image
of essentially the same planar division as in the two studies. It was
between those two drawings,[21] then, during the initial stages of the
design of the Aubette between the end of September and about the middle
of November 1926, that Van Doesburg finally discovered the mistake
in his drawing technique which had such unfortunate consequences
the year before in the execution of the flower-room.

By the last week of November, less than three months after the beginning of Van Doesburg's involvement with the project, more than fifty
drawings had been completed, determining the servicing, fixing the
circulation patterns, and broadly determining the nature of the colour-
schemes for the most important rooms, the *Ciné-Dancing* and the *Petite
Salle de l'Aubette* on the first floor, and the *Café-Restaurant* and *Café-
Brasserie* on the ground floor. The latter two were adjoining rooms separated only by a few columns and steps, and were therefore treated as

86 Theo van Doesburg, *Table
d'indication* for the Aubette,
1927 (pencil, ink and
gouache on tracing paper,
92.2 cm × 27 cm); in the
collection of the Musée
National d'Art Moderne, Paris
(cat. no 29); cliché Musée
National d'Art Moderne, Paris

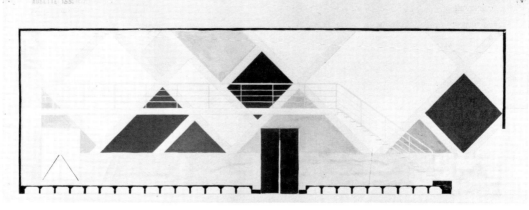

89 Theo van Doesburg,
Definitive design for the
gallery wall, *Ciné-Dancing:
'Aubette 160 Premier Étage
Grande Salle Face Côté Cour de
l'Aubette'* (photo-process print,
pencil, ink, gouache and silver
paint, 46 cm × 105 cm); Van
Doesburg Collection, R.B.K.
(AB 5209)

90 Theo van Doesburg,
Sketch design for the *Mur-
écran, Ciné-Dancing* (pencil,
charcoal and gouache on
tracing paper,
13.1 cm × 26.7 cm); this and
fig. 91 in the collection of the
Musée National d'Art
Moderne, Paris (cat. nos 12
and 11 respectively); clichés
Musée National d'Art
Moderne, Paris

91 Theo van Doesburg,
Sketch design for the *Mur Côté
Bar et Foyer, Ciné-Dancing*
(pencil and gouache on
tracing paper,
6.4 cm × 13.3 cm)

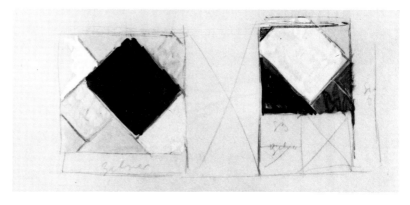

92 Documentary photograph of Van Doesburg's studio in Strasbourg; on the table is a 'maquette' of the *Ciné-Dancing*, 1927; Van Doesburg Archive, R.B.K.

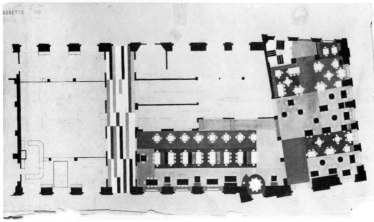

93 Theo van Doesburg, Definitive colour-scheme for the *Rez-de-Chaussée*, Aubette, 1927 (photo-process print, pencil, ink and gouache, 52.9 cm × 98.7 cm); this and fig. 94 in the collection of the Musée National d'Art Moderne, Paris (cat. nos 1 and 8 respectively); clichés Musée National d'Art Moderne, Paris

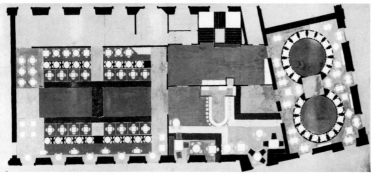

94 Theo van Doesburg, Definitive colour-scheme for the *Premier Étage*, Aubette, 1927 (photo-process print, pencil, ink and gouache, 49.4 cm × 94.2 cm)

a single unit. Through-circulation and waiter service were separated as much as possible, and the colour-scheme for the linoleum served to punctuate movement through the space and further to articulate the arrangement of the areas of seating (fig. 93). Different colour-schemes

were produced for the ceiling, the most important plane of this relatively low and long space. A comparison of two designs for the *Café-Brasserie* (figs. 95 and 96) demonstrates how Van Doesburg adjusted and controlled the character of the space by the size, distribution, and colour range of the constituent planes. The ventilators, represented by the black circles, have been carefully worked into the composition, as has the lighting which was suspended below the reflectors, indicated by the panels painted in silver in figure 97 (the *Café-Brasserie* is on the far right, labelled *Café-Restaurant*, but see also fig. 81). This constituted the design which was eventually executed, as can be seen in contemporary photographs. Since the ceiling was low in these rooms, the walls were given a very negative treatment: they were either given over to windows, doors, glass showcases, and other openings, or were painted in a neutral colour since they defined the horizontal band of what Van Doesburg designated 'the activity zone'.[22] The materials he used in these spaces, and throughout the Aubette, were chosen for their clean, smooth, or sparkling finish:

The chief materials in which the interiors have been carried out according to the demands of modern life are concrete, iron, mirror-glass, aluminium, nickel, hard rubber (here for the first time used by me for handrails and door-pushes), terrazzo tile, 'rabitz', linoleum, parquet, tiles, 'duralumin', 'lincrusta', 'rapolin', non-reflecting glass, rubber, leather, enamel, sheet silver, etc. As far as possible the use of wood has been avoided; the doors have all been made in metal and mirror-glass in full sheets, not broken down into panes. The doors and windows onto the passage have been carried right up to the ceiling, which gives a maximum of light, 'transparency', and visual connection between the spaces [*over-*

96 Theo van Doesburg,
Colour-scheme for the ceiling
of the *Café-Brasserie*, 1927
(pencil, ink and gouache,
23.8 cm × 37.6 cm); in the
collection of the Musée
National d'Art Moderne, Paris
(cat. no 6); cliché Musée
National d'Art Moderne, Paris

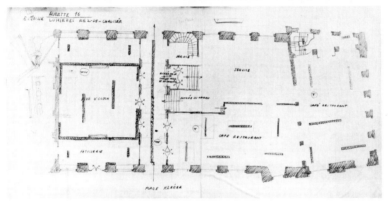

97 Theo van Doesburg,
*Aubette 96, Esquisse Lumières
Rez-de-Chaussée*, 1927 (pencil
and coloured pencil on
tracing paper,
55.5 cm × 109 cm unevenly
cut); Van Doesburg
Collection, R.B.K. (AB 5158)

zichtelijkheid]. It also removes the disturbing solid plane between the ceiling and window, or the ceiling and the door.[23]

Most of the intervening circulation spaces in the building, such as the passage by Taeuber-Arp, the monumental staircase by Arp, and the foyer-bar by Taeuber-Arp, were designed by Van Doesburg's associates in consultation with him,[24] while the subsidiary rooms such as the billiard-room (Arp), the tea-room (Taeuber-Arp), the *Bar-Américain* (Taeuber-Arp), and the cellar-bar (Arp) were left much more to their own discretion. Van Doesburg had reserved the centre-pieces, the *Petite Salle 'Dancing'* and the *Grande Salle 'Ciné-Dancing'*, for his own designs. The list of drawings in the Aubette note-book registers some collaboration, mostly in connection with the detailing of the lighting and such things as the gallery staircase in the *Ciné-Dancing*, but the colour-schemes bear the unmistakable hand of Van Doesburg.

To treat the lighting first, Van Doesburg's own description of his intentions and detailing is concise and complete:

L'éclairage a demandé une étude toute spéciale. Elle s'inspire de la destination spéciale de chaque salle. Je tâchai d'arriver à un éclairage régulier, plein, et

98 Documentary photograph
towards the windows on the
Place Kléber showing
reflections of the murals in the
mirrors above the radiators;
Van Doesburg Archive, R.B.K.

qui, néamoins, n'éblouisse pas les yeux et qui évite les ombres. L'éclairage centralisé a été écarté tout à fait. L'éclairage direct a été pratiqué dans la petite et dans la grande salle de fêtes [*Petite Salle 'Dancing'*], dans le salon de thé et dans le couloir, l'éclairage indirect dans le café-brasserie, dans le restaurant et dans le ciné-dancing. L'éclairage direct dans la grande salle de fêtes a été réalisé avec des plaques d'émail, dans lesquelles sont visées les ampoules. (sur 1.20, × 1.20, 16 ampoules). Les mesures de ces plaques d'émail, dans lesquelles sont vissées [l]es ampoules (surface/dimension la plus petite: 1.20 × 1.20). Il en est de même pour les ventilateurs. Dans le ciné-dancing, l'éclairage a été réalisé au moyen de réflecteurs fixés sur des tuyaux de nickel. Au début, je voulais éclairer les salles au moyen de la lumière-néon, mais je dus y renoncer, parce que, pour la lumière blanche, on n'a pas encore obtenu de bons résultats avec ce genre d'éclairage. Dans le café-restaurant et dans le brasserie, j'ai aussi employé l'éclairage sur plaques d'aluminium, laquelle, pratiquée sur les murs à côté des mirroirs, donne des effets très vifs.[25]

The intention was to dispel the gloom and romantic half-light usually found in night-clubs and to replace it with a new sparkling liveliness. He considered the romantic gloom to be a symptom of an outdated mentality. The bright, shadowless rooms with their Elementarist compositions were intended to give a new intellectual stimulation.

The rooms Van Doesburg designed were to provide an ambiance for a more conscious way of living. This is the reason that he reserved the rooms destined for the greatest amount of activity for himself. Movement was a controlling factor throughout the Aubette. It had determined the layout and the placement of the colour-planes in the *Café-Restaurant* and the *Café-Brasserie*, but nowhere was its influence stronger than in the vast *Ciné-Dancing* and in the *Petite Salle 'Dancing'* where there were to be people dancing to modern jazz in the rooms and even moving pictures on the wall. One very interesting aspect of his treatment of the *Ciné-Dancing* was his completely neutral treatment of the '*Face côté Place Kléber*' (the wall broken by all the existing windows). Rather than continuing the Elementarist compositions along this wall, he instead placed

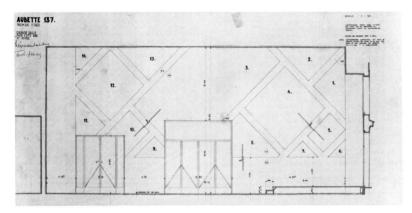

99 Theo van Doesburg, *Aubette 137, Premier Étage Grande Salle Face Côté Bar et Foyer*, 1927 (pencil, red chalk and ink on tracing paper, 44.5 cm × 86 cm); Van Doesburg Collection, R.B.K. (AB 5190)

large mirrors above the radiators to reflect the compositions on the other walls, in effect producing counter-compositions in literal movement relative to the visitor's own movement through the space (fig. 98).

Of the diagonal counter-compositions themselves in the *Ciné-Dancing* Van Doesburg wrote:

Animer cette salle par les couleurs était chose extrêmement difficile. Je n'avais à ma disposition aucune surface ininterrompue. Le mur de devant était interrompu par l'écran et par la porte de secours, le mur de derrière par la porte d'entrée, par la porte de la petite salle de fêtes et par les ouvertures de l'appareil cinématographique ainsi que par le réflecteur; à gauche la surface était coupée par les fenêtres montant presque jusqu'au plafond, et à droite par la porte des offices. Or, comme les éléments architectoniques se basaient sur des rapports orthogonaux, cette salle dut s'accommoder d'une répartition oblique des couleurs, d'une contre-composition, qui fût de nature à résister à toute la tension de l'architecture. Et ainsi la galerie qui traverse du côté droite obliquement la composition, fut plutôt un avantage qu'un désavantage pour l'ensemble. Elle accentue le rythme de la peinture.

Les surfaces sont relevées de 4 cm sur le plâtre et séparées l'une de l'autre par des bandes situées à une profondeur de 4 cm et large de 35 cm. Si on me demandait, ce que j'avais en vue lors de la construction de cette salle, je pourrais répondre: opposer à la salle matérielle à trois dimensions un espace oblique surmatériel et pictural.[26]

The general nature of the scheme for the *Ciné-Dancing* had been established during the first three months of Van Doesburg's work on the project, between September and November 1926. Two other drawings belonging to the same set as figure 87, the reflected sketch for the gallery wall, also show the *mur-écran* (fig. 90) and the entrance wall (fig. 91) reflected, as can be seen in the squares indicating the position of the doors. The catalogue of the exhibition 'Projets pour l'Aubette' (which contains those drawings presented to the French government from the estate of Nelly van Doesburg) lists figure 91 as a study for the wall containing the film screen. A close examination of the reflected countercompositions placed on either side of the vertical band (ostensibly showing the positing of the screen) indicates that it was in fact a study for the entrance wall (see also the '*maquette*' in figure 92). This means that Van Doesburg had originally intended that these opposing walls should

100 Theo van Doesburg, Colour-scheme, *Aubette 160, Premier Étage Grande Salle Face Côté Bar et Foyer*, 1927 (photo-process print, gouache, pencil, ink and silver paint, 44.5 cm × 89 cm) Van Doesburg Archive, R.B.K. (AB 5208)

101 Documentary photograph of the *Grande Salle Face Côté Bar et Foyer*; Van Doesburg Archive, R.B.K.

102 Theo van Doesburg, Colour-scheme, *Aubette 159, Premier Étage Petite Salle 'Dancing', Face Rue des Gdes Arcades* (photo-process print, red chalk, gouache, 39 cm × 106.5 cm); Van Doesburg Collection, R.B.K. (AB 5205)

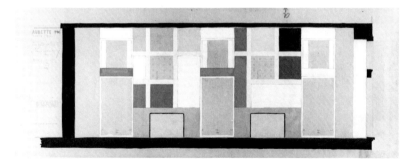

have a similar treatment with two independent counter-compositions on each. A similar idea was carried out in the *Petite Salle 'Dancing'* on the *Face rue des Grandes Arcades* (fig. 102) where the wall is broken by the tall windows. In the early sketches for the *Ciné-Dancing* the coloured planes are bounded by black lines but by the end of 1926 at least

103 Theo van Doesburg, Early colour-scheme for the *Petite Salle 'Dancing'*, Aubette, 1926 (pencil, gouache and collage, 52.6 cm × 31 cm); in the collection of the Musée National d'Art Moderne, Paris (cat. no 17); cliché Musée National d'Art Moderne, Paris

(fig. 103, dated 1926[27]) the decision had been made to separate them by broad neutral bands. In the final designs the bands are indicated as producing relief. Van Doesburg gave two reasons for this: 'en premier lieu, parce que j'atteignais ainsi une surface mieux définie et que le super-rayonnement des couleurs fut évité; en second lieu, parce que la fusion de deux couleurs était absolument impossible'.[28] His treatment of the relief in the two rooms was opposite: in the *Ciné-Dancing* the white bands were inset, leaving the colour-planes protruding and visually floating in space; while in the *Petite Salle 'Dancing'* the planes were recessed into the walls with the neutral bands providing a stronger visual structure in the space. The range of colours in the two rooms was the same, and the opposition was produced by the use of different hues of the same colour in neighbouring planes of a similar format. These pairs can be considered to be a familiar format if they have an implied extension beyond the bounds of the counter-composition into the neutral area, as in the blue-green and red-orange pairs on the gallery wall of the *Ciné-Dancing*. Van Doesburg had been experimenting with colour dissonances consistently throughout the De Stijl years, in his *Composition in Discords* of 1918, his 'musical' compositions in Drachten, and his *Counter-Composition XVI* of 1925. These polarities, of colour, in the treatment of relief, and most important in his counter-structural use of the diagonal in the *Ciné-Dancing*, were fundamental to the new Elementarist treatment of architecture. These two important rooms were monumental realisations of the opposing schemas presented and explained in his article 'Painting: from Composition to Counter-composition' (fig. 76). There he had stated that both methods opened up enormous possibilities and in these two rooms he exploited both to the full. He explained his constant use of contrast, which he used on ever-increasing scales in the Aubette, in 'Painting and Plastic Art: Concerning Counter-composition and Counter-form' (written in July 1926, about two months before beginning work on the Aubette): 'as opposed to all religious dogma, the Elementarist sees life as a *"transformation perpétuelle"*, and the creative subject as a contrasting phenomenon'. Later in the article he continued, saying that Elementarism

sets the negative colours, white, black, and grey, in contrast to the positive colours, and if these do not prove to be efficient, elementary *variants* of colour or line are added. . . . The very elementary earth-colours and ochres can also serve as 'variants'.

After this he moved on to a discussion of sculptural form, concluding that the Cubists

exaggerated natural gravity even more than their predecessors. In order to avoid this, a need for a new dynamic arose, whether provided for by moving figures, or by the use of elementary forms. It was namely a wish to create a contrast to the stiff axis of the static.

ELEMENTARISM is preparing the way for an elementary COUNTER-PLASTIC FORM and the initial work to be done is the destruction of this static axis resulting from the worship of the Euclidean idea of the world. . . .

There are already important examples to hand in figurative works (think of a few of the sculptures of Archipenko, such as *The Dance* [*Torso*] which was reproduced in *De Stijl* in its first year, and also his *Gondolier*, further there are many works by Boccioni, Brancusi, and Laurens). However, there are almost no elementary works which can serve as examples of counter-plastic form.[29]

In the *Ciné-Dancing* and the *Petite Salle 'Dancing'*, Van Doesburg aimed to produce a spatial work which fulfilled these ends. Visual movement had been introduced in a number of different ways, and the independence of the compositions and counter-compositions maintained

104 Documentary photograph of the *Petite Salle 'Dancing'*, Aubette, during building operations, 1927; Van Doesburg Archive, R.B.K.

a 'relativity' amongst his sections through 'universal space'.

Van Doesburg's basic considerations when approaching the architectural problem presented by the Aubette had been concerned with function. Circulation, seating arrangements, and the design of furnishings had been carried out in the simplest and most direct way possible. The chairs were of the bent-wood 'Thonet' type, because they were produced from a minimum of elements, or of simple chrome-steel types, because they were the epitome of the use of that principle, and in the most modern materials. He integrated his colour-schemes with the architectural solution by basing both on a grid of 1.20 m by 1.20 m (taken from the size of the radiators) and subjecting the ventilation, lighting, other fixtures, his grey 'neutral zone' and the colour-planes to the norm. As in his previous architectural projects, this method had a touch-stone

105 Documentary
photograph showing Hans
Arp, Sophie Taeuber-Arp and
the architect Honneger in the
studio on Place Kléber, 1927;
Van Doesburg Archive, R.B.K.

in a Rationalist and Constructive conception of architecture, but he had
moved far beyond the approaches themselves. In his series of articles
in *Bouwbedrijf* on 'Stained-Glass in the Old and the New Architecture',
in his series in *Binnenhuis* on 'The Creation of the Interior', and in his
article on 'Farben im Raum und Zeit', he repeated over and over that
perfection of function and of a constructive architecture might be sufficient for a purely material life, but that 'nothing is more useful and
there is nothing that we need more than precisely these "useless" works
of art because it is through these that man evolves'. In the Aubette,
his main concern was with nurturing the intellectual in man: 'the creative interior must be based on the play of contrasts. On the one hand
the interior, which responds fully to these demands, must set us at our
ease, and on the other hand it must stimulate us to spiritual
attentiveness.'[30]

As a result of his work on the Aubette, Van Doesburg was given two
more commissions in Strasbourg: in September and October 1927 he
redesigned André Horn's flat near the Aubette, and in the spring and
early summer of 1928 he designed the interior for a *'Magasin de
Linoleum'*[31] in the rue du Vieux-Marché-aux-Poissons for a Mr Meyer.
Van Doesburg had been away from Strasbourg several times during the
building of the Aubette and this had led to a number of minor problems.
In a letter of 16 March 1927 Arp wrote to Van Doesburg:

honneger und hor wollten einige würste [*sic*] in die originalpläne eintragen aber
kein plan wor zu finden. H[a]st du denn alle pläne mitgenommen. Heute kam
der gibsen und wollte neue abzüge von den wandplänen da seine verloren sind.[32]

It seems that Paul Horn was acting as site architect with the assistance
of Honneger (see fig. 105). In spite of Van Doesburg's absences and
Horn's participation, important decisions were left to Van Doesburg.
Honneger produced many of the drawings but was only employed on

106 Sophie Taeuber-Arp, Stained-glass window for the apartment of André Horn, Strasbourg, 1927; in the collection of the Musée d'Art Moderne, Strasbourg

a temporary basis. Some time in the spring of 1927 Honneger had left for Paris. On 11 July 1927 Horn wrote to Van Doesburg in Biarritz, where he was recovering from hay-fever, to request that Honneger be recalled from Paris to produce the rest of the necessary drawings. Further, Horn felt unable to make decisions which would affect aesthetic matters:

Ich bin seit 14 Tagen ohne Unterstützung von Seiten meiner Künstler, Schon öfters hätte ich Sie oder Herrn und Frau Arp befragen müssen. Es kann so nicht mehr weiter gehn. Deshalb bitte ich Sie, Ihre Reise nach Strasbourg am keinen Tag mehr zu verschieben.[33]

The problems which arose from Van Doesburg's absences seem not to have been serious enough to discourage Paul's brother André Horn from using Van Doesburg's services to refurbish his flat. The project was by no means as adventuresome as the Aubette, seemingly only using localised colour in the form of stained-glass windows by Van Doesburg and Sophie Taeuber-Arp (fig. 106).[34] Other than these individual colour compositions, Van Doesburg seems to have been restricted to the design of the lighting, the circular stair, fittings for the bar, and display cases for Horn's works of art. The drawings for this section of the work are dated between 24 September and 27 October 1927, but furniture designs for Horn are dated 1928.

Of the drawings for Magasin Meyer only one is dated, and that simply with '1928'. However, a letter from Van Doesburg to a furniture manufacturer in Strasbourg refers to the making of '*la caisse*' and is dated 23 June 1928.[35] The Aubette was opened in February so it is likely that the reference was to a design for Meyer and would therefore provide a more specific dating for the project. The designs themselves give no particular new insight into Van Doesburg's ideas, but they do serve to illustrate in a very compact way his use of colour and lighting to circulation and the use of space. The series of figures 107 to 110 shows even

107 Theo van Doesburg,
Plan for the *Transformation du
Magasin de Mr Meyer
Strasbourg*, 1928 (pencil and
coloured pencil on tracing
paper, 60 cm × 83 cm); Van
Doesburg Collection, R.B.K.
(AB 5275)

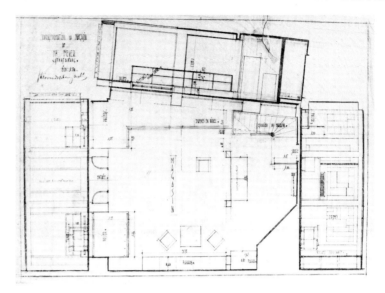

108 Theo van Doesburg,
Sketch design for the ceiling of
the Magasin Meyer indicating
the placement of non-
coloured planes and lighting,
1928 (pencil on tracing
paper, 49.5 cm × 53 cm); Van
Doesburg Collection, R.B.K.
(AB 5280)

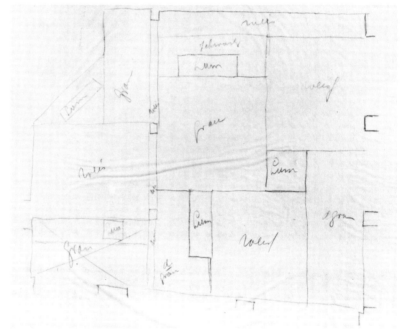

more clearly than the restaurants in the Aubette Van Doesburg's use
of the ground plan (fig. 107) and the resulting pattern of use dictated
by the plan as the controlling factor for the lighting (fig. 108), and in
the instance of the shop for Meyer, the distribution of non-colour-planes
in the circulation area and colour-planes on the display platform (figs.
109 and 110). The first and last of these also show the placement of
stained-glass windows to provide a focus for the scheme. The last drawing of the series includes one of Van Doesburg's tesseracts as an analysis
of the internal space resulting from these factors.

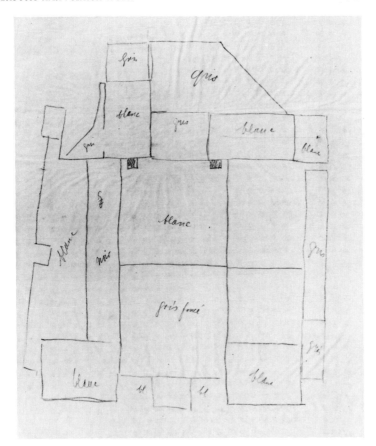

109 Theo van Doesburg,
Sketch design for the floor of
the Magasin Meyer indicating
the placement of non-colour
planes, 1928 (pencil on
tracing paper,
60 cm × 46 cm); Van
Doesburg Collection, R.B.K.
(AB 5277)

The Aubette had been the crowning achievement of Van Doesburg's
promotion of collaborative effort, but it also marked the end of such
work. *De Stijl* had become less and less the voice of even a loosely allied
group, with the result that the special issue on the Aubette was the last
produced by Van Doesburg. Van Eesteren had driven the point home
as early as the end of 1926 when in reply to Van Doesburg's complaint
that he had been collaborating in Oud's publication of *De 8 en Opbouw*,
Van Eesteren countered that it was not specifically meant as an attack
on *De Stijl*.

> When judging the magazine you mustn't forget that *De Stijl* has become an
> entirely personal expression of Van Doesburg, with all the related consequences.
> *De Stijl* has become a kind of private correspondence between you and the
> readers. As such it is important but along with that it has ceased to be the organ
> of the so-called De Stijl group.[36]

De Stijl was finished, but even if Van Doesburg had not succeeded in
welding together a unified group his efforts through *De Stijl* had been
successful in presenting a unified body of theory which had become a
common source of inspiration (ultimately both a positive and negative
inspiration) for a considerable group of artists.

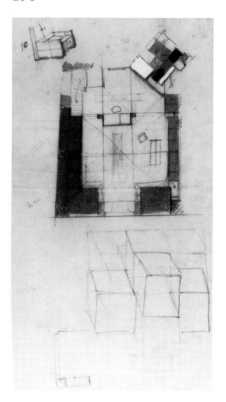

As the culmination of *De Stijl*, the Aubette was for the most part well received in the artistic press and, perhaps even more pleasing to Van Doesburg, it was accepted on his own terms. As one critic wrote in a local paper:

La nouvelle 'décoration', négligeant les apparences particulières dont le monde et l'esprit sont occupés ordinairement, plantes, bêtes, et gens, est, au milieu de ce monde, comme le témoignage d'un autre monde, ou bien un exemple d'une structure et d'une durée qui ne sont pas celles des êtres, mais celles des formes et des lois.[37]

Felix del Marle, artistic editor of *Vouloir*, was even more categorical in his praise. In a letter dated 19 December 1927, about two months before the official opening of the Aubette, he wrote to Van Doesburg:

J'ai vu vos très intéressants travaux en cours et j'ai longuement causé avec Monsieur Horn l'architecte qui m'a donné beaucoup de détails. Je suis certain que ce sera en effet une date dans l'histoire de l'art moderne mais nous aurons j'espère l'occasion d'en parler ensemble et sur place car aussitôt l'Aubette ouverte je dois aller pour faire un long article pour un journal de Paris dont je suis devenu correspondant.[38]

Van Doesburg was less than happy with the final result, partly because of the restrictions imposed by practice, and partly because of the public reaction to the interiors. The opening itself, on 16 February 1928, had been a great success, but the sense of occasion, the glittering newness, and the type of public had all been contributing factors. However, later in the year, on 7 November, he wrote to Adolf Behne:

die aubette in strasbourg hat mich gelehrt, dass die zeit für eine 'gesamtgestaltung' nicht reif ist. wenn die aubette fertig war, bevor die eröffnung, war es wirklich gut und bedeutend als erste realisierung unserer seit jahren gepflegten aufgabe: des gesambtkunstwerks. aber sofort, als die inhaber sich auf das urteil des publikums (das sie natürlich kalt und ungemütlich fand) verliessen, wurde alles hineingetragen, was nicht hinein gehört. das publikum kann seine 'braune' welt nicht verlassen und lehnt die neue 'weisse' welt hardnäckig ab. das publikum will in dreck leben und soll in dreck verrecken. mag der architekt für das publikum schaffen, der künstler schafft über das publikum hinaus und fordert neue verhältnisse, welche diametral den alten gewohnheiten gegenüberstehen, und deshalb enthält jedes kunstwerk eine zerstörende kraft, . . . die architektur ist ein irrweg, ebenso wie die angewandte kunst . . .[39]

When Van Doesburg complained publicly, he laid the blame for his disappointment squarely on the proprietors of the Aubette, claiming that they were speculators who did not make available the money given by the city for the works. Because of this he had had to cut necessary expenses. Through the use of 'ersatz' materials, economic constraints, and haste, a good deal of the unity of the work was lost. Further, inadequate upkeep and 'the rough manner in which the public of Strasbourg acted' took their toll on what Van Doesburg had managed to accomplish.[40]

Van Doesburg was so bitter about the economic constraints placed on him because in the end he was placed in serious financial difficulties as a result of his architectural work in Strasbourg. In August 1928 he was compelled to write to Moholy-Nagy to ask if Moholy would publish more of his works in the Bauhaus series: 'durch grosser geldknappheit bin ich dazu gezwangen, das, für jede auflage [of Van Doesburg's Bauhaus book 6], aus gemachte honorar zu beanspruchen. durch meine arbeit in strasbourg mit arp, habe ich etwa Fr. 20,000 frank verloren . . .' Besides inquiring about a second printing for his Bauhaus book 6, Van Doesburg offered a number of manuscripts for publication. He continued the letter with a full explanation of his situation and experiences, ending with a final plea:

durch ein aufenthalt von etwa 2 jahre in strasbourg, habe ich alle verbindungen einfach verloren und muss jetzt wieder ganz vom neuen anfangen. ich war ausserdem sehr überarbeitet und es fehlte mich an geld um, wie sonst, ans meer zu gehen. auch mit wohnung hätte ich schwierigkeiten, da ich mein schöne atelier in clamart verlor. ausser die aubette, hätte ich noch eine umbau und viele andere architektonische sachen in strasbourg zu erledigen. ich habe mich mit gewalt von strasbourg losreissen müssen. gerade war ich, mit viel mühe in Paris installiert, oder ich bekam den antrag zwecks einen grossen bausiedlung, nach strasbourg zurück zu keren. ich habe mich nicht enschliessen können, erstens weil der praxis mich einleuchtet gezeigt hat, dass auch die beste architektur die schöpferische intelligenz unbefriedigt lässt und zweitens weil eine gewissenhafte ausführung immer geld kostet. ich habe schon soviel an die aubette verloren, dass ein millionen projekt, wie sie jetzt vorliegt, mir vollständig ruinieren werde . . .

... bitte überlegen sie mit herr gropius, ob sie in die bauhaus bücherreihe nicht eine oder mehrer brochuren von mir bringen können. ... habe ich das richtig gehört, dass einen herr hannes meyer jetzt direktor des bauhauses ist ?[41]

Whether or not because his ideas were so antipathetic to those of Meyer, Van Doesburg's offer of manuscripts for publication was not taken up. Van Doesburg was clearly disillusioned once again with architecture and exhausted by the work in Strasbourg. He was still unable to come to terms with the compromises of architectural practice, but he had long wished to build his own house. For some time he had been discussing with Arp the possibility of joining together to build a double studio house. Having lost his studio in Clamart, he would make one more attempt to master architectural practice on his own terms.

7

◇◇◇

The full compass of architecture: from the private house to the new image of the city

The first mention of a wish to build a house for himself in France was in Van Doesburg's letter of 27 August 1925 to Domela about the development of the counter-compositional technique. About the same time Nelly van Doesburg had inherited a considerable amount of money, 'about fl. 16,000', and as Van Doesburg wrote to a Dutch friend: 'the best investment is naturally to build for oneself; that is a sure investment, especially in France'.[1] One of his motives was to produce a work of 'architecture completely and independently carried out by me'. The Aubette had provided him with much-needed professional architectural experience (not always to his liking), but in building his own house he would be free of the constraints imposed by other architects or their clients. The first step was to acquire a piece of ground, which he did in 1926,[2] in the name of his wife. In 1927 they and the Arps decided that they would build a double studio house on the plot in Clamart, bordering on Meudon near Paris. In April 1927 Van Doesburg produced the first designs for the house. The land was a long thin strip running back from the road, which presented terrible problems for the layout. The drawings, which are not in Van Doesburg's hand, show two side-by-side, linear-planned houses, each the width of one room plus hallway. Although the site was so restricted, the houses were large and quite commodious. The cross-section of the design gives an idea of the planning of the two virtually identical houses. On the ground floor at the front was the garage, followed by service rooms, a large covered patio, and finally the back garden. On the first floor was a sitting-room, the kitchen and pantry, a fairly anonymous room (probably meant as a music room for Nelly), and the studio. The second floor had a bedroom on a mezzanine above the studio, opening on the other side onto a large roof-terrace.

The second set of drawings for the same site was dated May 1927. In this set Van Doesburg experimented with different ways of treating the main entrances, placing both beside the party-wall, or one near the party-wall and one at the side (see fig. 111). He also attempted to demonstrate that, even within the strictures of planning for the site, the needs of both couples could be met. Arp seems to have been convinced, except about the finances. On 28 May 1927 he sent a postcard to Van Doesburg, who was again absent from the works in Strasbourg:

199

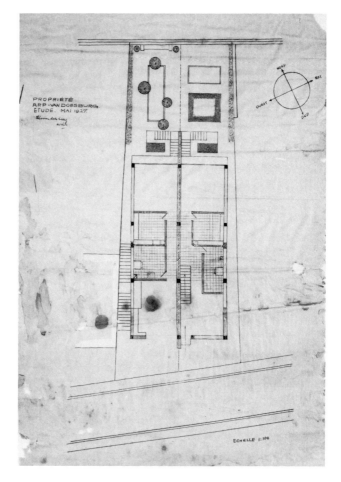

je te prie de m'envoyer au plus tôt l'adresse du notaire à Meudon, chez lequel je dois signer l'achat du terrain. J'aimerais encore une fois insister sur ce que la maison n'osera en aucun cas dépasser le prix de 60000 frs. C'est pourquoi je te prie avant de faire établir les Werkzeichnungen de me rassurer que la maison d'après ces plans ne reviendra pa [sic] plus cher.[3]

Van Doesburg was running into disappointments even in the building of his own house. Arp's next letter about a month later gives a very intimate glimpse of the nature of their relationship and Van Doesburg's motives:

nu. was ist los. zum teufel warum antwortest du nicht auf meinem brief. hat dir eine meerkuh deine contrequadrate abgebissen. begreifst du nicht dass für mich das haus nicht nur ein gegenstand theoretischer betrachtungen und übungen bleiben soll. willst du überhaupt bauen. ich kann dir nun mit wichtigen erfahrungen auf dem gebiete der arsch- ARSCH- arschitektur dienen.[4]

From the tone of the letter it would seem that Van Doesburg had in the intervening month already presented Arp with a design based on completely different principles and requiring another plot of land. This design used three interlocking cubes: one for the double dwelling, and

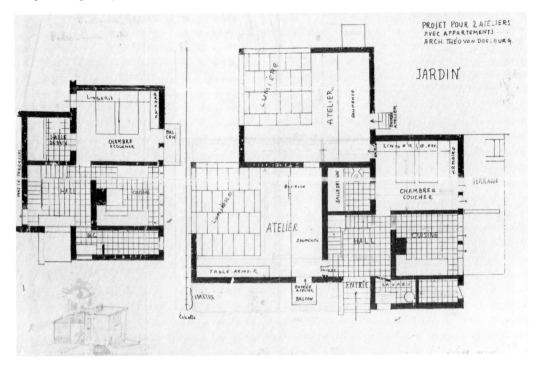

one each for the adjoining studios (fig. 112). The idea was to keep discrete geometrical forms for different functions, while the areas where the squares overlapped provided circulation routes which reintegrated the forms and the functions. The principle was quite neat, but in practice there was a problem of access to the back studio, which had to be approached either through the front studio or one of the bedrooms.

The project is important because here for the first time when working independently and in control *ab initio*, Van Doesburg can be seen to be extending the control of mathematics and geometry into the three-dimensionality of the layout. The spatial conception bears a strong resemblance to his 'tesseracts', and through them both to the Paris models and a study of the elementary means of architecture. A series of drawings for that last study shows the development from strongly shaded cubes of different dimensions placed in relationship to each other, with the addition in stages of secondary forms and architectural elements in response to specific function. (See figs. 113–115.)

Whatever the theoretical considerations, Arp did not want to build the house, so Van Doesburg converted the scheme into his '3rd design, Meudon' (written in another hand on sketch design AB 5343, Van Doesburg Collection, R.B.K.). This was a simplified version of the last scheme, based on two cubes (again one for the living area and one for the studio) with a connecting through-hallway.

The site in Meudon was too narrow to allow the use of interconnecting cubes on plan and, reconciling himself to the fact, Van Doesburg returned to a layout not unlike that of the first double house. This new

112 Theo van Doesburg, Two plans and a sketch axonometric for a *Projet pour 2 Ateliers avec Appartements*, June 1927 (pencil, blue pencil and ink on tracing paper, 32.5 cm × 50 cm); Van Doesburg Collection, R.B.K. (AB 5342)

113 Theo van Doesburg,
Composition with five cubes,
*Das elementare Ausdrucksmittel
der Plastik*, c. 1923 (pencil,
gouache, 20.6 cm × 9.7 cm);
Van Doesburg Collection,
R.B.K. (AB 5001)

114 Theo van Doesburg,
Elementary Means of
Architecture, c. 1923 (pencil
and ink, 25 cm × 19.5 cm
unevenly cut); Van Doesburg
Collection, R.B.K. (AB 5103)

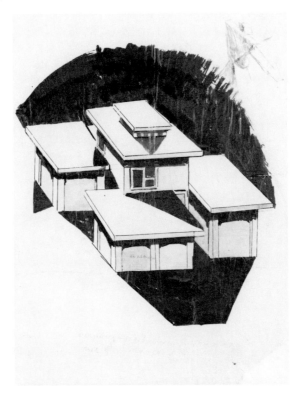

115 Theo van Doesburg, *Pavilion for relaxation and refreshment in the middle with 4 open verandas*, c. 1923 (pencil, ink and gouache on tracing paper, 31 cm × 23 cm unevenly cut); Van Doesburg Collection, R.B.K. (AB 5104)

plan probably dates from around the first week of November 1927. In the Aubette sketchbook (Van Doesburg Collection, R.B.K.), he kept accounts of his daily expenses, where, opposite the page for 3 to 7 November which included a meeting with Arp, there is a sketch of the Meudon house (MS p.7r). In cross-section he was still using separate cubes for separate functions. On plan these cubes are approximately 7.5 m by 5.5 m, essentially describing a golden section in the studio when the width of the entrance and internal staircase are subtracted. On plan the main entrance is shown at the side of the house, but in section the possibility of a front entrance is also indicated. The bedroom and the music room are situated next to the studio and separated only by a movable screen, or more likely a curtain. This was to develop into an important feature in the final scheme. In late 1927 Van Doesburg worked these ideas out in more accurate drawings (AB 5346 and AB 5348, now in the Van Doesburg Collection, R.B.K.). Here he experimented with the positioning of the house on the plot of land, tried different arrangements for the internal and external stairs, and returned to the use of a through-hallway in anticipation of the necessity of a front entrance.

The project then seems to have lain dormant until May 1929 when, with the assistance of a student, A. Elzas, Van Doesburg produced thorough and accurate plans, sections, and elevations (fig. 116). In the meantime the arrangement of the ground floor had been fixed, the end

116 Theo van Doesburg, *Plan d'ensemble Studio avec petit appartement en ciment-armée ou en brique*, May 1929 (pencil and coloured pencil on tracing paper, 65 cm × 82 cm); Van Doesburg Collection, R.B.K. (AB 5349)

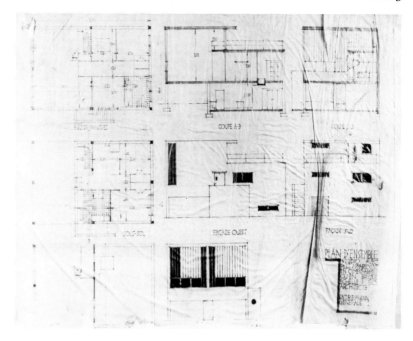

of the hall on the first floor had been blocked off to provide built-in closets, and a circular stair and gallery had been added in the studio to give access to a roof-terrace above the living block. The side elevation shows that he was still successful, if only to a restricted degree, in basing the architecture on interlocking cubes.

Elzas's arrival in 1929[5] brought a flurry of activity. In June 1929 the Meudon house took its final shape (fig. 117). The first change was the elimination of the side entrance. It might have just been possible to fit it onto the site, but then there would have been no access to the back garden except through the house, which was entirely unacceptable. The through-hallway appeared again on the first floor to accommodate the front entrance, and the garage was repositioned accordingly. The bedroom was removed to the front of the house above the garage, leaving the music room and library beside the studio. These two rooms were now separated by large swinging panels which could be positioned to seclude both of the rooms, leaving the hallway as a straight run to the front door, or both panels could be thrown across the hallway, creating one large room taking up the full width of the house (figs. 118 and 119). Van Doesburg had by very simple means created an adaptability of function and a changeability in spatial configuration.

The axonometrics in this series of drawings show a strong similarity to work by Le Corbusier, in particular his 'Maison Citrohan' (see fig. 120). Considering Van Doesburg's earlier quarrels with Le Corbusier over the use of primary and secondary elements in art, the differences in the basic assumptions behind Elementarist and Purist architecture, and finally Van Doesburg's statement that the aesthetic promoted by Le Corbusier was 'flat and without expression', Van Doesburg's return

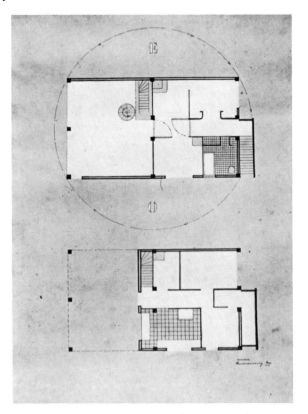

117 Theo van Doesburg, Plans for the ground floor and first floor for the Meudon house, June 1929 (ink and poster paint, 61.5 cm × 46 cm); Van Doesburg Collection, R.B.K. (AB 5361)

from an open and active form (represented by the Paris models) to a closed and passive form (as in Le Corbusier's *'prisme pur'*) seems almost inconceivable. However, as should be clear from the foregoing discussion, the development of the Meudon house was always in terms of a geometrical and functional separation/integration dichotomy, and the site had forced the application of this theory more and more into the internal arrangement, almost precluding any expected consequences in an external aesthetic.[6]

There is another slightly puzzling aspect of the aesthetic of the Meudon house. A good deal of the development of the design had taken place while the Aubette was being built, and the house had taken its final shape not much more than a year after the completion of the Aubette, so it might be expected that colour or even counter-compositions would play a larger role than the elementary use of colour-planes placed orthogonally in relation to the architecture. As in the Aubette, Van Doesburg used floor compositions in response to the fixed patterns of use established in specific areas, notably in the bathroom and kitchen. Flexibility of use or spatial configuration precluded such a treatment and, by the same token, the 'activity zone' in the Aubette had been given a neutral colour. In an article written for the special number of *De 8 en Opbouw* dedicated to Van Doesburg (no 17, 17 August 1935), Elzas noted that the walls were painted in varying tones of grey, giving an excellent ground

118 Documentary
photograph with a view from
the library into the music
room (arranged as a bedroom,
on the left) and the studio
(right); Van Doesburg
Archive, R.B.K.

119 The same view with the
panels swung across the
hallway to create one large
room; Van Doesburg Archive,
R.B.K.

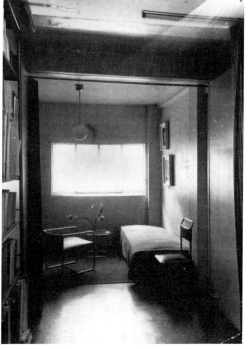

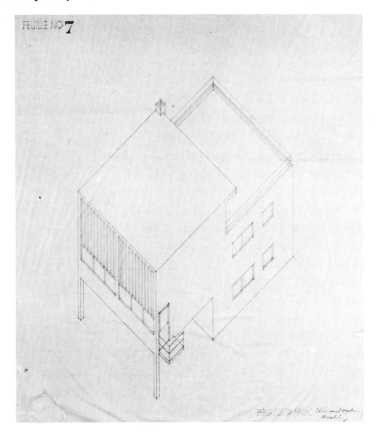

FEUILLE NO 7

120 Theo van Doesburg,
Axonometric of the Meudon
house, June 1929 (pencil on
tracing paper,
60 cm × 53 cm); Van
Doesburg Archive, R.B.K.
(AB 5357)

for exhibiting paintings.[7] That article was a re-worked version of one he had written for the *De Stijl* memorial number, where he had carefully explained:

In this house Van Doesburg realised a concept which he had often written about, namely to drop any notion of 'arranging the furniture' in a room, and thus came to an organic whole where 'house' and 'arrangement' are the same. He established the constantly repeated functions, such as cupboards and tables, by making them monolithic parts of the building. He attempted to give them 'independent energy' by painting them in different colours, so that all together they would produce a clear and pure impression, which he considered to be the mark of the 'creative interior'.[8]

Van Doesburg had seemingly returned to a constructive use of colour in architecture. As always before, the clue to new developments in his architectural ideas can be found amongst the recent developments in painting. In figure 121 a sketch for the dimensioning of the studio is seen beside a sketch for one of his '*formes universelles*'. It is somewhat difficult to see the specific relationship (that is whether the one was used in working out the other) but the general relationship is abundantly clear. They were both explorations of relationship created within interlocking square geometries. In 'Commentaires sur la base de la peinture concrète', published in his newly-founded periodical *Art concret*, Van

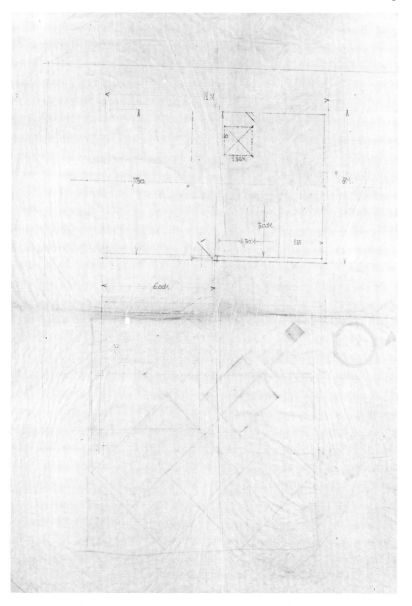

Doesburg announced, 'nous inaugurons la période de peinture pure, en construisant la *forme-esprit*' (p. 2). He described how this was to be accomplished: 'nous travaillons avec les données des mathématiques (euclidiennes ou non euclidiennes) et de la science, c'est-à-dire avec les moyens intellectuels' (p. 3). The final version of the *forme universelle* was used to illustrate 'Les Problèmes de l'art concret; art et mathématiques', Jean Hélion's contribution to *Art concret*. In that he outlined the principal aim of the group:

Pour que le tableau soit universel, il faut que les relations réciproques de ses éléments soient déterminées par des constructions géométriques exactes, c'est-à-dire qu'il existe entre les éléments des relations numériques déduites d'un module originel.

Ce qui est vrai pour la forme doit l'être (logiquement) pour la couleur. . . . Nul doute qu'il existe une géométrie de la couleur correspondant à la géométrie de ses dimensions; ce n'est que lorsqu'on aura déterminé toutes ses lois, qu'on pourra ordonner les couleurs aussi universellement que les formes et cesser de compter avec l'intuition et l'expérimentation.

Géométrie de la couleur, géométrie de la forme: il est nécessaire d'ouvrir une académie où l'on enseignera la technique de ces matériaux de la peinture, comme on enseigne partout la technique des matériaux de l'industrie. [p. 8]

Had he lived, Van Doesburg intended to use his house as just such a centre for his new group, *Art concret*, and also for students (partly as a source of much-needed income). He had outlined his plans for an academy, and also his new theory for painting and its relationship to architecture, in a letter of 3 January 1930 to Antony Kok:

What I am attempting to realise is a universal form, which corresponds absolutely to my spiritual conception. . . . This type of universal form is still under control since its structure is mathematical. I also wish to establish a similarly controlable structure for painting, for sculpture, and for architecture. My last canvas, on which I have already been working for a very long time, is in black, white, and grey. It has a controlled structure, an *established* surface without accidentals or individual caprice. Without fantasy? Yes. Without feeling? Yes. But not without spirit, and not without the universal . . .

I have made a sketch [possibly R.B.K.: AB 4932] for the next painting. I can make a *thousand paintings* on the basis of this temporal/spatial form since the 'universal' is inexhaustible! The new painting will have the following planar relationships: 8:16:32:56, and the colour must be in agreement with that. . . .

The house in Meudon is moving along quickly, but it is a great worry. The workers think we have money. One day they will find out just how much effort it takes for us to maintain our position. However, thanks to the house I hope to be able to undertake a lot of new things – a kind of Bauhaus or Academy for new art. [Van Straaten, p. 169]

The house itself represented a new theoretical departure as well as proof of professional competence as an architect. It was then just the beginning of his independent professional career, but it was also the end. He was exhausted by work on the Aubette, but had never slowed his pace. His asthma became worse, rest cures more frequent and he died on 7 March 1931, before the house was entirely finished.

Van Doesburg had finally come to terms with architectural practice. The practical experience he gained during his work on the Aubette, particularly in the use of concrete, was applied in his house in Meudon with confidence, and the detailing was of a high quality. Here again Van Doesburg employed an architectural assistant, but Elzas himself says that he was acting as 'Van Doesburg's pencil'.[9] In a draft copy of the specifications Van Doesburg described the method of construction:

Comme les plans indiquent, la construction sera élevé sur des piliers en ciment armé, de façon que ces piliers avec les poutres, solives (pour un plafond . . .) formera une espèce d'ossature qui garantie assez de résistance pour la charge du dallage des murs, des cloisons, et une étage éventuelle. (Voir fondation.)

Lorsque cette ossature est terminée elle forme une espèce de cage de béton

122 Documentary
photograph of the Studio
House in Meudon under
construction; Van Doesburg
Archive, R.B.K.

armé et il ne reste plus qu'à remplir les vides avec panneau de solomite (épaisseur
à discuter). Ces panneaux de solomite sont à l'extérieur couvert d'une couche
de ciment Portland (ciment *dur*) et à l'intérieur d'une couche de plâtre [see
fig. 122].[10]

The detailing of the house was carried out in November 1929 and building began in the same year.[11]

Van Doesburg's emphasis on the importance of the structure, and the
relationship of the form to the patterns of use in the different developmental stages of the Meudon house, were also the essential ideas behind
his plans for the '*ville de circulation*'. Since about 1923 he had become
progressively interested in city planning. According to his sixteen-point
architectural programme written in the winter of 1923/4 the same laws
held for urban design as for the 'prototype' houses he and Van Eesteren
had produced for Rosenberg. The use of elementary means in an aggre-
gation of multifarious structural, functional, and aesthetic elements
would create a unified plastic whole on an urban scale. His idea of the

prototype, however, was quite different from the standard type or unit which would simply be multiplied or stacked until the required number had been reached. In a special number of *Architecture vivante* (Spring, 1925), the Spangen designs were described as follows:

L'architecture extérieure est basée sur la répétition du même type d'habitation ainsi que sur une normalisation des accessoires comme portes, fenêtres, lucarnes, etc. Ceux-ci de couleurs très vives animent les surfaces architecturales. La plastique des façades est obtenue par l'avancement ou le recul des blocs de maisons. [p. 11]

Van Doesburg did not object to normalisation and standardisation *per se*. In 'The Renewal of Architecture Abroad' in *Het Bouwbedrijf* (IV, no 4 (February 1927), p. 90) he explained that '*Normalisation* was the first reform that led to simplification and uniformity. *Standardisation* as a consequence of the machine was the second phase, which can be seen in the way articles of use are made.' He went on to say that standardised proportions or modules would become a significant aid to design. The aim was 'uniformity in detail, variation in combination' (p. 91). In his review of the *Weissenhofsiedlung* in the same series of articles (*Het Bouwbedrijf*, IV, no 24 (25 November 1927), 556–59 (p. 558)) he wrote of Mies van der Rohe's work:

The Glass Hall in the *Gewerbehalle* is an expression of a deep-thinking and sensitive man. The same is true of his housing complex which made an instantaneous impression on me, when walking round the *Siedlung*, by the powerful way it is put together. The interiors were further proof of the impression. Although the flats are kept separate from each other, they still do not give the desolate impression of uniform cells placed next to each other. When will the risk be taken to gather together in a central building a great variety of housing types, and place under a single roof a number of functions (to a certain extent the way the skyscrapers in America have done)? Just as the tendency in mass housing will be towards a *unified dwelling*, standardised according to a unified measure (the module). At that point, the hopelessly tedious repetition of one and the same dwelling type will also die out.

He made essentially the same point earlier in the series of articles (*Het Bouwbedrijf*, III, no 5 (May 1926), p. 192) when he stated that a method of construction had to be developed which would allow for transformability of spatial configuration to overcome the transitory nature of the type and allow for a more 'elastic' city. Fixed planning according to a Taylor system, as espoused by the Functionalists, could only lead to a petrification of a way of life (p. 193). Van Doesburg's own answer to this problem lay in the use of structure in combination with montage, and transformable planning as demonstrated in the Meudon house.

In 'Art and Architectural Renewal in Italy' (*Het Bouwbedrijf*, VI, no 17 (16 August 1929), 341–44), Van Doesburg gave a more complete explanation of his own alternative structural system and its development. He described the evolution of the structure through four stages: the first was the traditional load-bearing wall (fig. 123a); the second was a concrete post and beam construction with light infill (fig. 123b); the third was a type of 'domino frame' with supports placed at the corners

123 Theo van Doesburg, Series of drawings showing the 'Historical development of structure', 1929; Van Doesburg Collection, R.B.K. (AB 5391–5) (a) Traditional load-bearing wall (pencil and ink on tracing paper, 18.5 cm × 13.5 cm) (b) Concrete post and beam structure with light infill (pencil and ink on tracing paper, 17 cm × 12 cm) (c) Type of 'domino frame' with supports at the corners (pencil and ink on tracing paper, 20 cm × 14 cm) (d) Pillars recessed from the facade to separate the functions of support and enclosure – 'domino frame' (pencil and ink, 19.5 cm × 13 cm) (e) Van Doesburg's new structural system (pencil and ink on tracing paper, 20 cm × 15 cm)

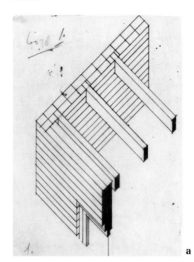

a

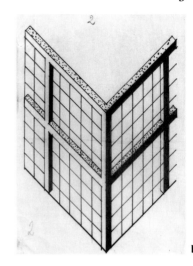

b

c

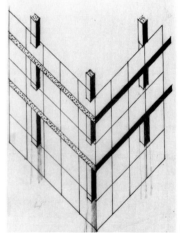

d

e

(fig. 123c); and the fourth was a variation of the third, but with the pillars recessed from the facade of light curtain walling in order to separate further the functions of support and enclosure (fig. 123d). This last development was basically Le Corbusier's 'domino frame' which he had applied so successfully in his Villa Savoie.

The connection with Le Corbusier is of great importance. In Van Doesburg's estimation, the aesthetic promoted by Le Corbusier was 'flat and without expression', but his skilful use of space within the open plan was worthy of further consideration.[12] To Van Doesburg, the real importance of Le Corbusier's work was not his experiments with the private dwelling alone, certainly not his aesthetic, nor just the constructive system he was applying with such success. Van Doesburg summed up Le Corbusier's importance with the statement:

Without a doubt the ambitious plans which represent a radical renewal of architecture in France, even though they are not the invention of the French spirit, will achieve an excellent result on a French basis under French auspices. These plans are not limited to the building of a few free-standing villas, such as those by Mallet-Stevens and Le Corbusier-Saugnier ... These can only be seen as studies for the solutions of the problems of building which have occupied modern architecture and which are developing from the private house, to the '*immeuble*' and beyond to the complex and to the new image of the city.[13]

Le Corbusier's great importance in Van Doesburg's eyes lay in his consistent development of prototypes for multiple housing, his continual thinking ahead 'from the private dwelling to the new image of the city'.

It is significant that Van Doesburg dated his own plans '1924–1929'. He intended to suggest that he first started developing the ideas which lay behind his designs in 1924, while the designs themselves were produced in the five years that followed. Le Corbusier's book *Urbanisme* was published early in 1924, and in the January 1925 number of *Het Bouwbedrijf* Van Doesburg published an article which in effect was a review of the book. Not satisfied with designing housing complexes which could be tacked onto the outskirts of existing cities, Le Corbusier diagnosed the causes of the problems of urbanisation, then tailored a whole new urban system to take into account the changing nature of the city. As Van Doesburg said:

The architect who is most deserving of consideration when it comes to theoretical work concerning city planning is the Swiss Le Corbusier-Saugnier. It is obvious that with the destruction during the war on the one hand, and technical and hygienic improvements on the other, the problem of city planning demands our attention more than ever. What I include under the heading 'city planning' is quite different from the addition of houses or even housing complexes onto the edges of cities. That is only architectural 'knitting' which has little do do with an *organic, geometrical traffic system.*

For Le Corbusier, the city-planning problem is a scientific question which rests on the painstaking study of circulation, hygiene, ethics, relaxation, etc., which have been changed by the discoveries of the last few years. Le Corbusier has applied himself like a physician or surgeon. He endeavours to heal the sickness of the metropolis, giving a diagnosis and operating as though on a sick body. [p. 32]

In this article, Van Doesburg's central criticism of the 'City of Tomorrow' was that it had not been decentralised. At heart it remained a 'plan for urban transformation and growth rather than a principle for a modern urbanism', as Van Doesburg would have it (p. 34). From the dating of the project for the '*ville de circulation*', Van Doesburg's own design can be seen as an attempt to make good the shortcomings of the 'City of Tomorrow'.

The European city could not function properly as the hub of modern society because its own centre was inherited from the Middle Ages, and as such was the result of the traffic system prevailing at that time. Its centre was the church and the market-place which concentrated the spiritual and economic life in one area with narrow streets radiating outwards. Haussmann's boulevards had been an important step because they indicated that a simple street layout with a number of different centres would facilitate the movement of increased traffic. Van Doesburg felt that Le Corbusier had dealt inadequately with the closed-facade architecture of the street, which was the result of this two-dimensional arterial circulation system inherited from mediaeval and classical cities.

An essential change (as many cities in America already show) can only occur when, as a consequence of local and through traffic, a totally *new building method* is used. In the first place the *street* must disappear, because it is precisely these tubes formed by the classical street facades which are the cause of the increasing traffic congestion. Le Corbusier has also realised this mistake and has tried to do away with the street by a system of parks between the enclosed buildings. The question is, however, if this can be carried into practice. Within this systematic division of planted and built-up area, an enormous amount of ground area is lost, which in turn causes an extraordinarily high cost for building.[14]

Van Doesburg had analysed the chief functions of the city to be production, distribution, and consumption. As a consequence he demanded that agriculture be integrated into the fabric of the city. Disappointingly the article did not elaborate on his alternative, but presumably he intended to use the green spaces between the decentralised urban areas for this purpose.

The articles Van Doesburg contributed to *Het Bouwbedrijf* gave only a very sketchy impression of his own alternative proposals for city planning, but his discussion of the evolution of structure in the 16 August 1929 issue did fill in some of the gaps. The fifth and final stage of this evolution was put forward as the 'totally new building method' promised earlier (fig. 123e). Here all supporting elements have been placed at the corners of the building to free internal areas for unrestricted planning, and ground-level areas for the unrestricted movement of traffic.

Precisely what is interesting about a method of construction with freely-placed concrete columns is that it distributes the load evenly over the whole surface and it uses concrete floors, so that the plans for the upper storeys can be completely different from the lower part of the building. Because of this there is a greater *constructive and also aesthetic freedom* available to the architect in the design of his project. This independence from bearing walls did not just revitalise the concept of the storey, but also the concept 'facade'. The latter is now counted simply as the skin which has been stretched over a skeleton of concrete or iron.[15]

He was demanding nothing less than the complete independence of 'structure' and the function of 'enclosure' from one another. Non-load-bearing walls could be placed at will within the structural cage to 'elasticise' the living spaces, the facade could be broken wherever necessary for windows and doors, or left out entirely for terraces or at ground level for the penetration of traffic. This structural system was in a very real sense the meeting point for his solutions to the two fundamental problems of the modern city – collective housing and collective circulation. A further possibility stressed by Van Doesburg was that different floors could be given completely different layouts. The advantage of this is, of course, that different functions within the urban system could be layered vertically. Years earlier he had praised the architect Ludwig Hilberseimer for at least taking a small step in that direction when he designed a complex in which trains were underground, commerce and vehicular traffic were at ground level, and housing and pedestrian traffic were elevated.[16] But Hilberseimer's solution was still inadequate. Like other modern architects, he had not gone far enough.

Schon um 1914 hat der futuristische Architekt Sant'Elia eine Zukunftsstadt entworfen: La Città-Futurista, und schon heute sieht dieses Projekt weniger utopisch aus wie damals. Nach ihm haben in allen Ländern die jungen Architekten sich auf das Problem des Städtebaus gestürzt: In Deutschland Mies van der Rohe, Hilberseimer, die Brüder Rasch, Rading u.a. In Frankreich erst viel später Pierre Jeanneret und Corbusier, in Holland Oud, Eesteren und Stam. Trotz allen diesen und noch vielen hier nicht erwähnten Versuchen blieb di Frage, welche Voraussetzungen für eine engültige Erneuerung der Stadt in Betracht gezogen werden müssen, unbeantwortet.[17]

Van Doesburg's answer was that instead of depending on a classical conception of the city, based on Roman prototypes as was the case for Le Corbusier, the tube-like 'corridor street' should be replaced by the vertical street and streets in the air to create a viaduct city where traffic could move in three dimensions.

The American skyscraper, as an architectural solution which maximised land use, was a great influence on European architecture at the time. But rather than solve traffic problems, the skyscraper aggravated them. Van Doesburg still considered tall buildings to be necessary and his reason for this is revealing: 'Vor allem wollen wir frische Luft. Die neue Stadt soll auch unseren Lungen etwas bringen.'[18] 'Air and light' was more than a catch-phrase for Van Doesburg with his worsening asthma.

Skyscrapers as such, or 'Americanisation' as he put it, were not the answer – again the emphasis is on decentralisation:

Wenn wir die verschiedenen und vielversprechenden Projekte, die in den letzten 10 Jahren entstanden sind, etwas näher betrachten, so sehen wir, dass es sich meistens um die Transformation oder Amerikanisierung der Herz- und Adernstadt handelt. Vornehmlich trifft dies für das Stadtprojekt von Jeanneret [and Corbusier's design for Paris of 1925] zu, wobei es sich nur um eine amerikanisierte klassische Stadt handelt, die fest in der Erde verankert ist, wie Herkulanum oder Pompeji.[19]

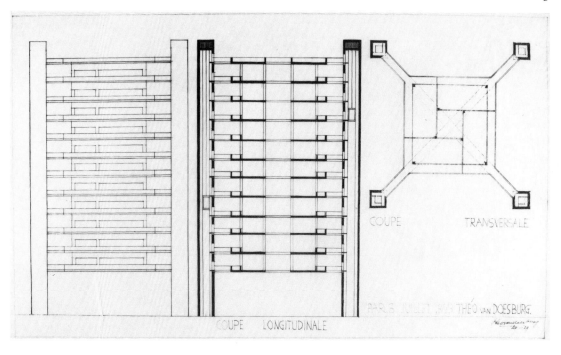

COUPE   TRANSVERSALE

PARIS JUILLET 1929 THÉO van DOESBURG

COUPE   LONGITUDINALE

124 Theo van Doesburg,
Plan, section and elevation of
a tower-block for the *ville de
circulation*, July 1929 (pencil
and ink on tracing paper,
39.5 cm × 66.5 cm); Van
Doesburg Collection, R.B.K.
(AB 5399)

The growth of traffic, coupled with the advances in technology, pointed in another direction. Reinforced concrete did away with the limitations of stacking bricks and opened up the possibility of adopting a montage system. In his article 'Die Verkehrsstadt' of 1929, Van Doesburg again emphasised the importance of separating structure and the function of enclosure. His proposal was to remove all structure to the corners of the building in the form of piers with a hollow cross-section of plus or minus four metres (fig. 124). Practically speaking, the cost of a structure with such a clear span would be prohibitive, but this extreme example did provide a diagrammatic representation of the possibilities afforded by the application of the principles involved.

The hollow piers were to be integrated as a vertical component in the traffic system and act secondarily as ducts for services. Van Doesburg had two main reasons for developing this structural system: first, the newly created 'sites' on the floors hung between the piers were uninterrupted by structure, allowing complete flexibility in use; secondly, in place of the 'corridor street', in his opinion unsuccessfully dealt with by Le Corbusier, the city was to be opened up for 'free' traffic in three dimensions. The most complete account of Van Doesburg's ideas concerning urban planning is contained in section III ('L'Urbanisme et la cité de demain') of a lecture he delivered at the '*Conference 88, Madrid-Barcelona 1930*', 'L'Esprit fondamental de l'architecture contemporaine' (dated Paris, April 1930). There he outlined the problems presented by the *ville frontale* and went on to describe his solution in terms of a three-dimensional traffic system:

125 Theo van Doesburg, Diagrammatic comparison between the *ville frontale* and the *ville de circulation* (pencil and ink on tracing paper, 46 cm × 40.5 cm); Van Doesburg Collection, R.B.K. (AB 5404)

L'automobile a discipliné la circulation et a dressé les rues par la ligne droite. L'aéroplane nous a montré la ville en projection et nous avons pu constater que les rues ne sont que des tuyaux étroits, ou la circulation automatique ne pouvait se développer que linéaire, donc en deux dimensions. A présent la circulation horizontale est à son plus haut dégré et on peut constater que la surface terrestre est utilisée jusqu'au bout. La circulation sous-terrain nous a aidé sans doute à différer la catastrophe de la circulation, mais ce n'était qu'un délai – le problème de l'Urbanisme reste sans solution définitive. Nul doute que la nécessité, toujours à la base de chaque invention – (rappelons le 'Schwebebahn' à Elberfeld, le Ponte Vecchio à Florence, etc) – nous donnera la solution qu'il nous faut. Ce que nous avons appris parmi de nombreuses expériences c'est que:

1. L'ancienne forme de la ville, gréco-romaine ou gothique est en contradiction avec le fonctionnement de la vie moderne et n'a aucun rapport avec notre intelligence et avec notre physique;
2. La ville frontale empêche une circulation libre. Se développant en façade, la circulation restait limité au *horizontalisme* en 2 dimensions;
3. Pour éviter la catastrophe de la ville moderne, c.à.d. la *stagnation totale* de la circulation, nous serons forcés de percer les façades de rues, pour donner libre accès aux véhicules automatiques en créant une ville de circulation.[20]

A drawing in the Van Doesburg Collection (R.B.K., fig. 125) indicates the difference between the traffic systems of the modern *ville frontale* and the *ville de circulation*. The former, shown above on the drawing, indicates an increasing density of activity towards the centre of the city by an increase in the size of the skyscrapers. Traffic is forced through the dark canyons between the buildings, or into subways. The *ville de circulation*, shown above in the drawing, remains open at ground level to allow the movement of vehicular traffic around and under the buildings, as can just be made out by the building third from the right. On the same building, a lift has been indicated, and a cable-car or *Schwebebahn* connects the whole of the complex. The intention was to separate private and short-distance traffic from commercial and long-distance traffic.

All the technical means for the structural and traffic systems were already available, if terribly expensive, but even the most detailed of the drawings (fig. 124) gave very little specific information as to how the systems were to be integrated. For instance, how was the ground-level traffic to be regulated if not in a linear way similar to the system in the *ville frontale*, and could a cable-car service between buildings laid out on a grid be operated in such a way that it would be time-effective, let alone cost-effective? Van Doesburg had illustrated a radical abstract principle for urban planning, but he had neither applied that principle to an existing urban fabric to demonstrate its real advantages, nor had he started afresh and designed a whole new city from first principles to represent the ideal application. In the concluding paragraph of 'L'Urbanisme et la cité de demain' he tried to answer the latter criticism:

Il était à mon avis une erreur de vouloir renouveler des cités entières, comme la projeté. Le Corbusier par exemple, parce que nous ne savons pas vers quelle direction la vie se développera. Il s'agit plutôt de trouver une méthode qui mettra en vigueur cet esprit fondamental de notre architecture moderne: de convaincre l'inertie de la matière.[21]

From April 1930, when this was written, Van Doesburg was hindered from taking his ideas concerning urban planning into any greater detail by the demands on his time in building the Studio House and by the increased attacks of asthma. He had, however, pursued his ideas concerning circulation, structure, function, and adaptability consistently from the private Studio House to the *ville de circulation* and a new image of an 'elastic' city. Van Doesburg finally accepted the compromises of professional practice when confronted by the practical necessities involved in building the Studio House. He had become an architect of high quality as well as a theoretician of great influence. His city planning remained on a theoretical level in a very early developmental stage, and he was not to be given time to carry it into practice.

Letter of 7 February 1929 from Van Doesburg to the pacifist Bart de Ligt and his wife

Dear friends,

. . . I must work like a madman just to stay alive, and can hardly stop to catch my breath. Besides the large number of articles for architectural journals and all sorts of other papers, I must also spend time writing books. When I returned from Strasbourg, financially as good as ruined, my morale stunned by all the beer and Alsace sauerkraut, beggarly and intellectually plundered, I was as good as finished and therefore had to start all over again from square one, just as in 1923. *De Stijl* was not going badly, but still the last issues, the 'Jubilee issue' and 'Aubette issue' had absorbed so much money that the funds were exhausted. Any money that I received unfortunately had to be used for other things and I could not go on with the situation as it was. Otherwise things had been successful enough – special publications on the work of De Stijl are scheduled to appear in Japan and in Germany. The interest in Tokyo, Japan is especially great and subscriptions are arriving by the bundle. I am now negotiating with a large publisher in Germany to try to publish *De Stijl* through him on an increased scale and in different languages. If that doesn't work then I'll have to wait until there is enough money again so that I can clear up my debt to the funds. Naturally I will not give up, and in the meanwhile, until the new series is definite I am going to publish a pamphlet with Arp, Del Marle, and others, which will take up a position against the domination of the snobbishness here. In Paris everything is simply a passing fashion. The snobs have the upper hand and all the '*artistes*' are upstarts who earn masses of money with rubbish. Still, relatively speaking, I can't complain about my exhibitions. I am singled out for discussion even though the remarks are anything but intelligent. Every day I am more taken aback by how silly and conservative they are here. They are superficial and a-cultural, exactly the opposite of the Germans . . .

Naturally we have read your book *Contre la guerre nouvelle* with great interest. I've actually read it twice. . . . I agree with you on most points, and believe in the Principle. Still, for all that I wonder why it is that intellectual activity was actually increased through and after the war? . . . Was Marinetti really correct when he said that war is the only means for purifying Mankind? . . . I know for a fact that anti-militarism is an ideal, and thus a fiction, and just like an '*Art Pur*' cannot be carried

219

through as a rule or way of life. It remains, thus, a deed that can never be regarded highly enough when one throws one's whole being behind an idea and cultivates noble ambitions. . . .

As you undoubtedly know, Arp is also here in Paris and things are going quite well with him. With us, however, it is worse than miserable. Everything is going against us. Since the Aubette there has not been a single architectural commission, and because of the terrible decline in painting, for which the art dealers are primarily to blame, there is not the remotest possibility of sales for Mondrian and me. What little money we have left will consequently soon be finished, and then what? Financially it would have been better if the Aubette had not been wedged in, and I had thought that I would get more commissions as a result of that gigantic work. And yet there was nothing – nothing. To return to Holland is also impossible. It is impossible to survive the life there under the domination of a stupid, presumptuous, plebeian mentality – a terribly annoying fanaticism with half-festering left-overs of religion. Anything that still has a bit of good blood and spirit has been able to save itself from that nest of stupid minor prophets by leaving for Paris. Just about everyone of any worth is here. . . .

Van 't Hoff should be back in Holland occupied with humanism, the moral life, and practical communism, or some such anglicised Tolstoi-ism, 'without buttons on his coat' (preferably homespun) since buttons are made from bone, and bones come from an animal, and animals from God, etc. . . . [Ellipses in original.] It's too bad, he could have been a good meat-eating architect.

I never eat meat, because I . . . just don't have the money. Through this letter you now have an idea what is going on here. . . .

Yours,
Does/Nel

[Letter in the Van Doesburg Archive, R.B.K.]

Conclusion

Van Doesburg's letter of 7 February 1929 to Bart de Ligt and his wife contains many intimate reflections touching on the artist's life and work. For instance, his oblique praise of De Ligt's high principles was also a *cri de coeur*. Van Doesburg felt that he himself had also thrown his whole being behind an idea, cultivated noble ambitions, and that as a result he was financially ruined, criticised, and deserted, while charlatans who stole his ideas were highly praised and successful. His idea was that at the base of each of the arts was a tectonic, elementary, mathematical structure; his was a 'universal stylistic idea'. He did not posit the primacy of theory or practice in the development of the style, they were necessary concomitants. Art was not an end, and there was no end to art. Painting, architecture and the other arts for Van Doesburg were continually in development, in 'becoming', because the life which they reflect, embody, and envelop are in constant movement. The universals of art, like the universals of nature, can be synthesised in an infinite number of ways and still retain their universal expression.

Van Doesburg had pursued his idea relentlessly and vigorously in the pages of *De Stijl*, *Mécano*, *Art concret* and in a wide spectrum of magazines and books to reach an audience as widely dispersed as the Netherlands and Japan. He had first developed and tested theory in practice with Oud and Wils when, as a correlative to the architectonic nature of painting, the painterly conception of architecture emerged. Work with De Boer provided Van Doesburg with the opportunity of exploring a musical, or harmonic mathematics of form and colour, in order to articulate more fully 'the process of separation [into constituent elements] and reconstruction, which our architecture needs', as Oud defined 'Cubism' in architecture. This analytical process was completed in Van Doesburg's work with Van Eesteren on the models for the 1923 exhibition at Rosenberg's Galleries in Paris. The full integration of aesthetic and functional elements within painterly tectonics was synthesised in the Maison d'Artiste, or third model, and found its ultimate realisation in Rietveld's Schröder–Schräder house in Utrecht in the following year.

Never satisfied, never stagnant, and always questioning the role and nature of art, Van Doesburg moved beyond painterly tectonic composition, on canvas and in architecture, and proposed the dialectics of counter-composition. In the Aubette Arp's 'prae-morphist' painting con-

221

trasted with the architectonics of Van Doesburg's work. Van Doesburg
in his turn used colour both to reinforce the architectural structure, as
in the *Petite Salle 'Dancing'*, and to form a highly active contrast to the
architecture as in the *Ciné-Dancing*. This contrast was to emphasise the
intellectual and spiritual function of art, as opposed to the natural and
material forces resolved in the literal architectural structure.

Work on the Aubette had been a costly venture for Van Doesburg,
in terms of his health as well as financially. Fortunately, in less than
a year his financial position was easing slightly and he was able to write
more hopefully to Kok on 23 January 1930 that 'undoubtedly there
is more sympathy for my work since the collectors and connoisseurs
began to take an interest. I think that it is the result of the continued
success of so-called abstraction' (Van Doesburg Archive, R.B.K.). Despite
the less stringent circumstances it was still a rather precarious existence,
and the burden of building a house for himself and for Nelly was a strain.
Even so, he continued to experiment with the mathematical basis of
painting and architecture, creating in the process his first work of 'architecture completely and independently carried out' (letter to Domela, 27
August 1925, Van Doesburg Archive, R.B.K.). As he wrote in a typescript dated Paris 1930 and headed 'De l'intuition à la certitude': 'La
mathématique n'était pas seulement la base de toutes les sciences, mais
aussi le fondement des arts des grandes époques.'

Van Doesburg had consistently pursued this idea from his first incur-
sions into the practice of architecture. Within a year of writing 'De l'intuition à la certitude' on 7 March 1930 Van Doesburg died, and death
robbed him of the recognition for which he had longed. The former
leader of De Stijl had become a very disillusioned man before his death:
for all his successes, for all his efforts in Strasbourg, and notwithstanding
the influence of his theoretical work, he was not recognised as an architect. He barely managed to earn a living as a painter.

Despite Van Doesburg's achievements his career was also dogged by
failure, much of it the result of his often abrasive temperament. He had
always aimed at a collaborative effort, but De Stijl was never a very
closely knit group. Even their early correspondence, dating from 1918,
is for a large part concerned with the discussion of deviations of members
such as Hoste, Van der Leck, Van 't Hoff, Vantongerloo, Huszar, and
Wils from the party line. Hoste had praised the work of an 'enemy of
De Stijl'; Van der Leck had disagreed with Van Doesburg about the inclusion of architects in the group and thus had a different idea about the
basic aim of De Stijl; Van 't Hoff, who had given considerable financial
support to the magazine, disagreed on social and religious questions;
Vantongerloo had different ideas concerning colour and form; and
Huszar and Wils had collaborated with the 'enemies of De Stijl' in *Architectura* and *Wendingen*. Disintegration had begun even before the work
on De Vonk was finished. In a postcard dated 21 May 1918 (Van
Doesburg Archive, R.B.K.), Van Doesburg wrote to Oud:

Saturday night I was at Huszar's, as you know. Even before the fight began
(and why fight?), Huszar declared that the causes were the result of the Van

der Leck incident . . . The Unity of De Stijl had been fundamentally *broken*, broken for good. A lot has happened and it is difficult to describe it all. I'll tell you *all* about it in person. I am terribly down.

Van Doesburg felt all of these rifts very deeply and saw the conflicts as attacks on himself, which many probably were. He was a very difficult man whose criticism of other artists was often reduced to a very personal level. Over the years these conflicts contributed to the development of a certain degree of paranoia in Van Doesburg; he had the idea that the 'enemies of De Stijl' were constantly plotting against him and the logical development towards the style of the future. Later he thought that even the friends of De Stijl were intellectual parasites on him for their own, often financial, ends. On 11 November 1924, he wrote again to Oud:

> For many 'to belong to De Stijl' simply means good credit. Van Eesteren, whose career I launched having first brought him up (breast-fed him, you might say!), became a well-known architect in one jump, and can now work wherever he likes.
> The De Stijl group is most certainly both Mondrian and Van Doesburg, but it is more Van Doesburg than Mondrian because the latter has been left intellectually 'in the red' through the restrictions of Theosophy.
> Naturally (hand on my heart) I regret that I lost you. How splendid our beginning together was in little Leiden am Rhein. (*'Ein Rheinischen Mädchen und Rheinische Wein – dass muss ja ein Himmel auf Erde sein.' Bis. Aber es ist nicht wahr!*) Because our contrasting temperaments were complementary, there were endless possibilities. But even when I was in Weimar I felt that something was coming between us, that something must occasion a definitive conflict. And the conflict occurred. In spite of the fact that you claimed that you wanted to keep colour out of architecture (which I can understand, if not accept), you now paint all your doors blue, window-frames yellow, etc. . . . Is that consistent? Is that a colour solution for architecture? What possibilities did I have within the enormous restrictions, then, in Spangen? No other than that which I had consistently developed. *Aber, merde* – that is all in the past. As long as I don't have real possibilities I will experiment on paper or in the form of models. The results will in any case be put into practice – by others.
> [Letter in the Van Doesburg Archive, R.B.K.]

Van Doesburg's break with Oud and Van Eesteren, and the break with Mondrian which at that time was already brewing, would leave Van Doesburg alone in his struggle towards the new style. The group effort was finished, but the De Stijl group was not. Notwithstanding the personal invective and the continuing arguments about the finer points of theory, the counter-compositions by Van Doesburg, the compositions painted in the late 1920s by Mondrian, and the Café 'De Unie' in Rotterdam by Oud all belong to the De Stijl group *oeuvre*. In his letter of 11 November 1924 to Oud, Van Doesburg took a much stronger position: 'What is the De Stijl group? It is the whole of creative Europe and soon the whole of America! Everyone, without exception, has experienced not only the influence of the De Stijl idea, but also the De Stijl idea as a living source of energy.' Van Doesburg's remark was justified to the extent that *De Stijl* was followed with interest, and often with dedication, in the main artistic centres of Europe, and remained a force to be reckoned with because of its following of young artists.

Van Doesburg's letter to De Ligt re-emphasises the third major point made in his letter of 11 November 1924 to Oud when he placed such personal emphasis on his theoretical work, saying that 'the results will in any case be put into practice – by others'. In the end, ideas, not specific buildings, constituted Van Doesburg's great contribution to architecture. These ideas were concerned with colour and the elements of form under the control of mathematics. He attacked the problem in its purest and freest form in painting. There he could be entirely consistent and uncompromising, but gradually he came to realise that his '"*Art Pur*" cannot be carried through as a rule or way of life', and he finally came to grips with the realities and compromises of architectural practice. Theory, painting, and architecture went hand in hand in his work, and an understanding of the philosophical and theoretical background is essential for a complete assessment of his experiments in, and eventual practice of, architecture.

Philosophy, theory, painting, and the practice of architecture all developed in parallel in Van Doesburg's work. His radical theoretical position, culled from his formal experiments in painting, could not be ignored by anyone but a convinced historicist architect. He questioned all the basic assumptions of architectural practice and, like the Dadaists, tried to purge contemporary culture of its artistic, social, and architectural 'holy cows'. In his role as an experimentalist, practitioner, propagandist, and general dealer in ideas, he contributed significantly to the complete reassessment of the fundamental principles of architecture which was taking place during the 'heroic years' of the Modern Movement.

Notes

Introduction

1 'Der Kampf um den neuen Stil', *Neue Schweizer Rundschau*, 1929, translated in Cees Boekraad *et al.*, *Het nieuwe bouwen: de Nieuwe Beelding in de architectuur – De Stijl* (Delft, 1983), 17–37 (pp. 18–19 and 26).

2 Many of the most important documents from the Van Doesburg Archive (Schenking Van Moorsel) have been reprinted in Evert van Straaten, *Theo van Doesburg, 1883–1931: een documentaire op basis van materiaal uit de Schenking Van Moorsel* (The Hague, 1983). Unless otherwise noted all translations from the Dutch are my own.

3 'Schilderkunst: van kompositie tot contra-kompositie', *De Stijl*, VII, nos 73–74, Series XIII (1926), 17–28 (p. 17).

4 'Van "natuur" tot "kompositie"', *De Hollandsche Revue*, XXIV, no 8 (25 August 1919), 470–76 (p. 470).

5 Just Havelaar, *De symboliek der kunst* (Haarlem, 1918), p. 1.

6 G. W. F. Hegel, *The Philosophy of Fine Art*, translated by F. P. B. Osmaston, 4 vols (London, 1916), I, pp. 9 and 139.

7 Arthur Schopenhauer, 'The Metaphysics of Fine Art', in *The Essential Schopenhauer* (London, 1962), p. 29. The importance of Schopenhauer's conception of the contemplation of art by a pure, will-less subject of knowledge, for Mondrian's artistic theory, is amply illustrated by Mondrian's own direct references. See 'De nieuwe beelding in de schilderkunst', *De Stijl*, I, no 5 (March 1918), p. 52; 'Het bepaalde en het onbepaalde', *De Stijl*, II, no 2 (December 1918), p. 18, n. 3; and 'Natuurlijke- en abstracte realiteit', *De Stijl*, II, no 10 (August 1919), p. 110.

8 Hans Hess, *Pictures as Arguments* (London, 1975), p. 133.

9 Translated in H. L. C. Jaffé, *De Stijl* (London, 1970), p. 149.

10 Arthur Schopenhauer, *The World as Will and Representation*, translated by E. F. J. Payne, 2 vols (New York, 1969), II, see pp. 444–45.

11 A. Pit, *Het logische in de ontwikkeling der beeldende kunsten*, Utrechtsche bijdragen voor letterkunde en geschiedenis, volume VI (Utrecht, 1912), p. 8.

12 J. J. P. Oud, 'Over cubisme, futurisme, moderne bouwkunst, enz.', *Bouwkundig Weekblad*, XXXVII, no 20 (16 September 1916), pp. 156–57.

13 Theo van Doesburg, *Principles of Neo-plastic Art*, translated by Janet Seligman (London, 1968), pp. 16–17.

14 Theo van Doesburg, 'Open brief aan Bernard Canter', *Holland Express*, X, no 37 (12 September 1917), p. 441. Canter's obituary for Thijs Maris appeared in *Holland Express*, X, no 35 (29 August 1917), p. 411. Canter's editorial reply to Van Doesburg was in the 12 September issue, pp. 441–43; the quotation is from p. 442.

15 Van Doesburg's defence took the form of a letter to the editor entitled 'Repliek aan den heer H. C. Verkruysen en zijns gelijken', in *Architectura*, XXV, no 5

(3 February 1917), pp. 32–33. The quotations from Worringer are to be found in the 1948 German edition on pp. 56 and 42–43 respectively, and in Michael Bullock's translation (London, 1953) on pp. 44 and 31 respectively.

16 Georg Simmel, 'Die Ruine', *Philosophische Kultur*, second edition (Leipzig, 1919), 125–33, translated in *Georg Simmel, 1858–1918*, edited by Kurt H. Wolff (Columbus, Ohio, 1959), 259–66 (p. 259).

17 Simmel, 'Der Henkel', *Philosophische Kultur*, 116–24, translated in Wolff, 267–75 (pp. 272–73).

18 Heinrich Wölfflin, *Principles of Art History: the Problem of the Development of Style in Later Art*, translated by M. D. Hottinger (New York, 1950), p. 27.

19 H. L. C. Jaffé, *De Stijl 1917–1931: the Dutch Contribution to Modern Art* (London, 1956), p. 148.

20 *Drie voordrachten over de nieuwe beeldende kunst* (Amsterdam, 1919), p. 5.

21 Theo van Doesburg, *De nieuwe beweging in de schilderkunst* (Delft, 1917), p. 25.

22 Piet Mondrian, 'De l'art abstrait', 1931, quoted in Charles Biederman, *Art as the Evolution of Visual Knowledge* (Minnesota, 1948), p. 368.

23 Theo van Doesburg, *Klassiek – barok – modern* (Antwerp and Amsterdam, 1920), p. 12.

24 Wassily Kandinsky, *Concerning the Spiritual in Art*, translated by Francis Golffing, Michael Harrison, and Ferdinand Ostertag (New York, 1947), p. 28.

25 H. L. C. Jaffé, *Piet Mondrian* (London, 1970), p. 9; Herbert Read, *The Philosophy of Modern Art* (Greenwich, Connecticut, 1952), p. 142.

26 Wilhelm Worringer, *Abstraction and Empathy*, translated by Michael Bullock (London, 1953), pp. xiv–xv.

27 Karston Harries, *The Meaning of Modern Art: a Philosophical Interpretation* (Evanston, 1968), p. 106.

28 *Concerning the Spiritual in Art*, pp. 52 and 53 respectively. His emphasis.

1. The early years of *De Stijl*; national and international contexts

1 Alex Booleman, in the review article '*De Stijl*', *De Wiekslag*, I, no 8 (December 1917), 86–88 (p. 86).

2 'Ter inleiding', *De Stijl*, I, no 1 (October 1917), 1–2; his emphasis.

3 J. P. Mieras, '*De Stijl*', *Bouwkundig Weekblad*, XXXVIII, no 47 (24 November 1917), 273.

4 See in particular Van Doesburg's review of their exhibition, in *Holland Express*, X, no 14 (4 April 1917), 167. Note also that his criticism of their work is based primarily on his idea that perspective painting is incompatible with the modern conception of architecture.

5 Alex Booleman, in the review article '*De Stijl*', art. cit.

6 H. Th. Wijdeveld, 'Jaarverslag van de redactie', *Architectura*, XXV, no 50 (15 December 1917), 387.

7 H. Th. Wijdeveld, '*Wendingen*', *Wendingen*, I, no 1 (January 1918), 1–2 (p. 1).

8 *De Stijl*, IV, no 6 (June 1921), 87–88.

9 'Leden van het Genootschap "Architectura et Amicitia" op 1 januari 1918', *Architectura*, XXV, no 51 (22 December 1917), 391–94.

10 'Schilderkunst, naar aanleiding der eerste tentoonstelling van de Leidsche kunstclub "De Sphinx" te Leiden', *Eenheid*, no 348 (3 February 1917), 2–3; his emphasis; the article is dated 'Leiden, 22 January 1917'. Note however, his comments on the architectural submissions of Oud and Wils. Van Doesburg sees a possibility of the development of a 'pure religious architecture' from the work of Oud especially, and this was to form the foundation of their subsequent collective efforts in De Stijl, as will become clear in the discussion of the holiday house 'De Vonk' in Noordwijkerhout.

11 Pp. 148–56 (pp. 149–50); his emphasis; see also *De nieuwe beweging in de schilderkunst* (Delft, 1917), p. 29.

12 'Schilderkunst: vereeniging "De Sphinx", 1ste tentoonstelling, Leiden', *Holland Express*, X, no 5 (31 January 1917), 58–59 (p. 58).

13 Van Doesburg. 'Ter inleiding', *De Stijl*, I, no 1 (October 1917), 1.

14 In a letter to the editor, *Holland Express*, X, no 38 (19 September 1917), 455; the letter is dated 'Leiden, 16 September 1217 [*sic*]'.

15 In a letter to the editor, *Holland Express*, X, no 40 (3 October 1917), 479; his emphasis; the letter is dated 'Leiden, 29 September 1917'.

16 A. Elzas, 'Theo van Doesburg', *De 8 en Opbouw*, no 17 (17 August 1935), 173–82 (p. 179); Elzas's quotation seems to have a number of sources: the sentences preceding those quoted here are a paraphrase of Van Doesburg's editorial 'Overzichtelijke beschouwing bij de intrede van den derden jaargang', *De Stijl*, III, no 1 (November 1919), 1–5 (pp. 1–2); and Elzas's later comments are related to the editorial 'Data en feiten (betreffende de invloedsontwikkeling van *De Stijl* in 't buitenland) die voor zich spreken', *De Stijl*, VII, nos 79–84, Jubilee Series XIV (1927), 53–71. The comment comparing the roles of Severini and Apollinaire is prefigured in Van Doesburg's 'Revue der avant-garde', *Het Getij*, VI, no 1 (1921), 109–12 (p. 109).

17 *De Stijl*, I, no 8 (June 1918), 94–95 (p. 95); his emphasis.

18 *De Stijl*, I, no 10 (August 1918), 118–21 (p. 121).

19 *Bouwkundig Weekblad*, XXXVII, no 20 (16 September 1916), 156–57 (p. 156).

20 *Het schoone en de kunst* (Amsterdam, 1906), p. 50.

21 W. T. Stace, *The Philosophy of Hegel* (New York, 1955), p. 453; see also Hegel, *Aesthetics: Lectures on Fine Art*, translated by T. M. Knox, I (Oxford, 1975), pp. 303, 372, and 438: 'Therefore, the representations of symbolic art which were intended to be expositions of the content remain themselves only enigmas and problems, and they testify only to a wrestling for clarity and to the struggle of the spirit which continually invents without finding repose and peace.' Hegel discusses Symbolic art in connection with Classical art as necessarily a representative, naturalistic art. Van Doesburg's and Oud's use of the term 'symbolic' refers to the use of abstract means as being fully adequate to the expression of abstract content. The appeal to Bolland and implicitly to Hegel is completely inappropriate as support for their argument.

22 *Zuivere rede en hare werkelijkheid*, third edition (Leiden, 1912), §50, p. 579.

23 Ibid., p. 1047.

24 'Moderne wendingen in het kunstonderwijs', *De Stijl*, II, no 11 (September 1919), 127–32 (p. 131).

25 Bolland, *Zuivere rede*, pp. 577–78.

26 Antonio Sant'Elia, in the Futurist manifesto of architecture, as quoted by Robert van 't Hoff in 'Aanteekeningen bij bijlage XX', *De Stijl*, II, no 10 (August 1919), 114–16 (p. 115).

27 'Moderne wendingen in het kunstonderwijs', *De Stijl*, II, no 11 (September 1919), 127–32 (p. 131).

28 'Architectonische beschouwingen bij bijlage III', *De Stijl*, II, no 11 (September 1919), 127–32 (p. 131).

29 *Drie voordrachten over de nieuwe beeldende kunst* (Amsterdam, 1919), pp. 22 and 23.

30 'Architectonische beschouwingen bij bijlage III', *De Stijl*, III, no 3 (January 1920), 25–27 (pp. 25–26).

31 *Amerikaansche reisherinneringen* (Rotterdam, 1913), p. 42.

32 Ibid., pp. 40–41.

33 Ibid., p. 44; his discussion of the 'plastic effect' is to be found on p. 45; full

acceptance of the machine, on p. 42; and the restraints set by economy, on p. 43.

34 Frank Lloyd Wright, as quoted by Robert van 't Hoff, in 'Architectuur en haar ontwikkeling', *De Stijl*, II, no 4 (February 1919), 40–42 (p. 40).

35 'Architectonische beschouwing bij bijlage VIII', *De Stijl*, I, no 4 (February 1918), 39–41 (p. 41).

36 Some of the more important comparisons occur in: H. L. C. Jaffé, *De Stijl 1917–1931* (London, 1956), pp. 51–53, and *De Stijl* (London, 1970), pp. 28 and 29; Bruno Zevi, *Poetica dell'architettura neoplastica* (Milan, 1953), p. 68 following; Giovanni Fanelli, *Moderne architectuur in Nederland* (The Hague, 1978), pp. 135 and 140; Gunther Stam, *The Architecture of J. J. P. Oud, 1906–1963*, exhibition catalogue (Tallahassee, Florida, 1978), p. 25; Joost Baljeu, *Theo van Doesburg* (London, 1974), pp. 29–31, 46, and 52–53; Daniele Baroni, *Gerrit Thomas Rietveld: Furniture* (London, 1977), pp. 21 and 41 following; etc.

37 'Aanteekeningen bij de bijlagen VI en VII', *De Stijl*, III, no 5 (March 1920), 44–46 (p. 45).

38 J. J. P. Oud, 'Architectonische beschouwing bij bijlage VIII', *De Stijl*, I, no 4 (February 1918), 39–41 (p. 39); Berlage's comments were in *Amerikaansche reisherinneringen*, pp. 46–47; Van Doesburg notes a similar lack of tradition in the two countries, in 'Vernieuwingspogingen der Oostenrijksche en Duitsche architectuur', *Het Bouwbedrijf*, II, no 6 (June 1925), 225–27 (p. 225).

39 *Kultuur en kunst* (Amsterdam, 1911), pp. 36–37; the 'cultural aristocracy' is referred to on p. 37.

40 See Theo van Doesburg, 'Tien jaren stijl: algemeene inleiding', *De Stijl*, nos 79–84 (1927), 2–9 (p. 7); and Sergio Polano, 'Notes on Oud: Re-reading the Documents', *Lotus International*, no 16 (September 1977), 42–54 (p. 49), quoting from J. J. P. Oud, *Mein Weg in De Stijl* (The Hague, 1960), pp. 12–27.

41 'Architectonische beschouwing: A. massabouw en straatarchitectuur', *De Stijl*, II, no 7 (May 1919), 79–82 (p. 80, n. 1).

42 Editorial, 'Prof. Behrens over moderne Nederlandsche bouwkunst', *Bouwkundig Weekblad*, XLIII, no 44 (4 November 1922), 426; continued from the previous issue, p. 424.

43 Editorial, 'De "Deutsche Werkbund" tentoonstelling', *Architectura*, XXII, no 41 (10 October 1914), 298; the Muthesius exhibition was announced in *Architectura*, XXII, no 16 (18 April 1914), 127–28.

44 'Kroniek LIX: de Duitsche Werkbund en zijn beteekenis voor Nederland', *Bouwkundig Weekblad*, XXXIV, no 26 (27 June 1914), 311–15 (p. 315).

45 'De Duitsche Werkbund en een Hollandsche Driebond: Duitsche Werkbund', *Bouwkundig Weekblad*, XXXIV, no 28 (11 July 1914), 339–41 (p. 340); taken from *Het Orgaan van de Ned. Vereeniging voor Ambachts- en Nijverheidskunst*.

46 Editorial, 'Berichten', *Bouwkundig Weekblad*, XXIV, no 27 (4 July 1914), 334; see also 'Een Hollandsche Werkbond', *Architectura*, XXII, no 27 (4 July 1914), 221. Penaat and a *Hollandsche Werkbond* are also discussed in Frans van Burkom, 'Kunstvormgeving in Nederland', in *De Amsterdamse School, 1910–1930*, in the series 'Monografieën van de Stichting Architectuur Museum' (Amsterdam, 1979), pp. 71–108 (p. 71).

47 See C. Smit, *Nederland in de eerste wereldoorlog (1899–1919)*, 3 vols, vol. III, 1917–1919 (Groningen, 1973), p. 49.

48 See the replies to the questionnaires in *Architectura*, 18 August, 25 August, 1 September, and the discussions in the *Driebond* issue of *Architectura*, 6 October 1917.

49 'Een verbond tusschen industrie, handel en kunst', *Architectura*, XXV, nos 39–40 (6 October 1917), 279.

50 Recorded by J. F. Staal in the 'Verslag van de 1398ste ledenvergadering van het Genootschap "Architectura et Amicitia", gehouden op Woensdag 24 October 1917', *Architectura*, XXV, no 44 (3 November 1917), 339–43 (p. 342); the debate over the *Driebond* issue is reported by J. F. Staal in the 'Verslag van de 1397ste ledenvergadering van het Genootschap "Architectura et Amicitia" gehouden op Woensdag 10 October 1917', in *Architectura*, XXV, no 42 (20 October 1917), 331.

51 *De Stijl*, II, no 10 (August 1919), 113–14 (p. 113).

52 In this connection see also Jan Wils, 'Beeldhouwkunst', *Wendingen*, I, no 6 (30 June 1918), 12–15.

53 'Moderne wendingen in het kunstonderwijs', *De Stijl*, II, no 6 (April 1919), 66–68 (p. 66).

54 J. G. Wattjes, *De verhouding van de bouwkunst tot wetenschap, techniek en kunst: rede uitgesproken bij de aanvaarding van het hoogleraarsambt in de architectuur aan de Technische Hoogeschool te Delft, op 27 September 1918* (Delft, 1918), pp. 12–13.

55 Ibid., pp. 20–21.

56 'Slotbemerkingen', *De Stijl*, II, no 10 (August 1919), 118–20 (p. 119).

57 R. N. Roland Holst, *Over kunst en kunstenaars* (Amsterdam, 1923), pp. 168–69; the lecture is dated '14 October 1918'. Note the reference to icons; this may have been an oblique reference to Van Doesburg's quarrel with Hoste (see Chapter 2, passim).

58 Ibid., p. 171.

59 'Moderne wendingen in het kunstonderwijs', *De Stijl*, II, no 11 (September 1919), 127–32 (p. 128).

60 Reported by Wijdeveld in the 'Verslag van de 1385ste ledenvergadering van het Genootschap "Architectura et Amicitia" gehouden op Woensdag 20 December 1916', *Architectura*, XXV, no 2 (13 January 1917), 8–10 (p. 9).

61 'Ingezonden', *Architectura*, XXV, no 3 (20 January 1917), 17–18 (p. 17); see also *Drie voordrachten*, especially pp. 8, 18, 25, and 31. Van Doesburg gave direct reply to Verkruysen in 'Ingezonden', *Architectura*, XXV, no 5 (3 February 1917), 32–33, where the argument was based on Worringer's *Abstraction and Empathy*. Verkruysen simmered for a year, then, taking Van Doesburg's advice to look into Worringer, he replied in 'De nieuwe schilderkunst', *Wendingen*, I, no 2 (20 February 1918), 8–11. Worringer was also quoted here, but the argument was founded more on Bolland (see *Zuivere rede*, p. 256 following). After another year had passed, Van Doesburg published the sections of 'Moderne wendingen in het kunstonderwijs' which contained the attack on Verkruysen (*De Stijl*, II, no 4 (February 1919). 44–48; and in no 5 (March 1919), 57–58).

2. Elementary means and the painterly conception of architecture

1 See Theo van Doesburg, 'Open brief aan Bernard Canter', *Holland Express*, X, no 37 (12 September 1917), 441; 'Antwoord aan mejuffrouw Edith Pijpers en allen, die haar standpunt innemen', *De Stijl*, I, no 6 (April 1918), 65–71; 'Moderne wendingen in het kunstonderwijs', *De Stijl*, II, no 4 (February 1919), 44–48.

2 *De Stijl*, I, no 11 (September 1918), 136. The correspondence also includes: Van Doesburg, 'Open brief aan den architect Huib Hoste', *De Nieuwe Amsterdammer* (6 July 1918), published in an altered form in *De Stijl*, I, no 9 (July 1918), 111–12; Hoste, 'Antwoord op een open brief', *De Stijl*, I, no 11 (September 1918), 135–36; Hoste, 'Het vacantiehuis te Noordwijkerhout', *De Telegraaf* (1 March 1919), evening edition; for the personal correspondence see Marcel Smets, *Huib Hoste, voorvechter van een vernieuwde architectuur* (Brussels, 1972), pp. 145–46.

3 'Antwoord op een open brief', p. 136.

4 Van Doesburg to Hoste, letter dated '20 July 1918' (see Smets as cited above in note 2); quoted by Hoste in 'Het vacantiehuis te Noordwijkerhout'.

5 See Jan Gratama, 'Vacantiehuis te Noordwijkerhout', *Klei*, XII, no 2 (15 January 1920), 13–19 (p. 14), where he quotes Oud's explanation of the layout.

6 'Aanteekeningen over monumentale kunst: naar aanleiding van twee bouwfragmenten (hall in vacantiehuis te Noordwijkerhout, bijlage I)', *De Stijl*, II, no 1 (November 1918), 10–12 (p. 12). I agree with Van Doesburg's judgement of the windows, but admit Beckett's contention that his criticism 'may reflect his disappointment at not receiving a commission for the windows' (see Jane Beckett, '"De Vonk", Noordwijk: an Example of Early De Stijl Cooperation', *Art History*, III, no 2 (June 1980), 202–17 (p. 216)).

7 Van Doesburg's claim is in *De Stijl*, (November 1918), p. 12, quoted and disputed by Hoste in *De Telegraaf* (1 March 1919).

8 'Orientatie', *De Stijl*, III, no 2 (December 1919), 13–15 (p. 15); quoted by Gratama in *Klei* (15 January 1920), p. 18. The influence of Van Doesburg is evidenced by Oud's article 'Over cubisme, futurisme, moderne bouwkunst, enz.', *Bouwkundig Weekblad*, XXXVII, no 20 (16 September 1916), 156–57.

9 Gratama, *art. cit.*, p. 18.

10 '"De Vonk", Noordwijk', pp. 214–15.

11 Quoted by Jean Leering in 'De architectuur en Van Doesburg', in the Stedelijk Van Abbemuseum catalogue *Theo van Doesburg 1883–1931* (1968), 19–25 (p. 20).

12 For comments on Van Doesburg's idea of positive/negative contrasts in paintings of the period see Robert P. Welsh, 'Theo van Doesburg and Geometric Abstraction', in *Nijhoff, Van Ostaijen, 'De Stijl': Modernism in the Netherlands in the First Quarter of the 20th Century*, edited by Francis Bulhof (The Hague, 1976), 76–94 (p. 86).

13 'Glas-in-lood van Theo van Doesburg', *Bouwkundig Weekblad*, XXXIX, no 35 (31 August 1918), 199–202 (p. 202). It is interesting to note that since this book was completed it has been suggested that the paired themes of *Composition II* are an abstraction from a nude study. See Carel Blotkamp, 'Theo van Doesburg', in Carel Blotkamp *et. al.*, *De beginjaren van De Stijl* (Utrecht, 1982), 14–46 (p. 26). It has also been suggested that the themes are taken from drawings of *A Girl in the Harbour* (see E. van Straaten, *Theo van Doesburg, 1883–1931: een documentaire op basis van materiaal uit de Schenking Van Moorsel* (The Hague, 1983), p. 67).

14 'Glas-in-lood van Theo van Doesburg', p. 201.

15 'Over cubisme, futurisme, moderne bouwkunst, enz.', p. 157. De Vonk represents the zenith of De Stijl's co-operative effort during this early period. At this time Oud still believed in Van Doesburg's 'painterly conception of architecture', as evidenced by his review of Otto Grautoff's book *Formzertrümmerung und Formaufbau in der bildenden Kunst* (*De Stijl*, II, no 10 (August 1919), 113–14) (see above p. 53). Sergio Polano's 're-reading of the documents' in his 'Notes on Oud' (*Lotus International*, no 16 (September 1977), 42–54) was incomplete and biased by the utter acceptance of Oud's short 1960 memoir of the period. They did achieve a significant degree of co-operation in this project; there was mutual support on theoretical issues but naturally with some deviations between some of the individual members; and there was a considerable amount of common ground in their theories and goals over the years between 1916 and 1919. Although articles in *De Stijl* committed them to a profound co-operative effort which they did not achieve for any sustained period of time, it is unreasonable to deny them the term movement or to place it between inverted commas (ibid., pp. 42 and 49, note 1), demanding a degree of 'homogeneity and compactness'

unheard of in other much more loosely allied groups such as the Expressionists who are quite sensibly recognised as a movement. All the article succeeds
in establishing is that theoretical differences arose at this time from practice
and occasioned irreparable rifts in the group. The fact that the group then
lost its cohesion is by no means a new discovery. Polano is correct, however,
in saying that De Stijl, if viewed over the full time-scale of 1917-31, must
be seen as an extension of Van Doesburg, 'who was the centre of that movement and the only element of effective internal continuity' (p. 47).

16 'De beteekenis van het glas-in-lood in de nieuwe bouwkunst', in *Glas-in-lood*,
   edited by W. F. Gouwe, in the series De toegepaste kunsten in Nederland,
   vol. 25 (Rotterdam, 1932), 37–38 (p. 37); the remarks are dated 'Paris, Villa
   Corot, 1930'.
17 'Antwoord op een open brief', p. 136.
18 'Aanteekeningen over monumentale kunst', p. 12.
19 On space see *Zuivere rede*, third edition (Leiden, 1912), p. 270; on Nature
   and God, p. 1131, no 234; on light, p. 1134, no 270; and on colour, p. 1134,
   no 272.

3. Work with De Boer: colour, mathematics, and music

1 'Een belangrijk kunsttijdschrift', *Het Getij* (June 1919), 164–65 (p. 165).
2 Both quotations are taken from *Principles of Neo-plastic Art*, translated by
   Janet Seligman (London, 1968), the first from pp. 29–30, the second from
   pp. 32–33. In 'Grondbegrippen der nieuwe beeldende kunst', *Tijdschrift voor
   Wijsbegeerte*, XIII, nos 1 & 2 (1919), the passages are to be found in no 2,
   pp. 176–77 and 179–80.
3 Theo van Doesburg, *Principles*, p. 33; and 'Grondbegrippen', p. 180.
4 Vilmos Huszar, 'Over de moderne toegepaste kunsten', *Bouwkundig Weekblad*,
   XLIII, no 7 (18 February 1922), 59–69 (p. 65).
5 Wilhelm Ostwald, quoted from Faber Birren, *The Color Primer* (New York,
   1969), pp. 65–66.
6 Theo van Doesburg, 'Over het zien van nieuwe schilderkunst', *De Stijl*, II,
   no 4 (February 1919), 42–44 (p. 43).
7 Vilmos Huszar, 'Iets over *Die Farbenfibel* van Ostwald', *De Stijl*, I, no 10
   (August 1918), 113–18 (p. 115).
8 Ibid., pp. 115–16.
9 See Piet Mondrian, 'De nieuwe beelding in de schilderkunst', *De Stijl*, I, no
   3 (January 1918), 29–31 (p. 31, note 1), and Van Doesburg's copy of *Die
   Farbenlehre* (Leipzig, 1919), p. 95, Van Doesburg Archive, R.B.K.
10 'Het glas-in-lood in de oude en nieuwe architectuur', *Het Bouwbedrijf*, VII,
   no 10 (9 May 1930), 202–5 (pp. 202–3).
11 Undated letter, return address Leiden (in the collection of Thom Mercuur,
   Franeker, Friesland, hereafter cited as coll. Mercuur).
12 These short phrases are all taken from the same undated letter.
13 Willem Brouwer to J. J. P. Oud in a letter dated 15 January 1920, Oud
   Archive, Nederlands Documentatiecentrum voor de Bouwkunst,
   Amsterdam.
14 For a more detailed discussion of Van Doesburg's colour-schemes for Spangen
   see Nancy Troy, *The De Stijl Environment* (Cambridge, Mass., and London,
   1983), pp. 82–91.
15 In a letter dated 1 September 1921, reproduced in K. Schippers, *Holland Dada*
   (Amsterdam, 1974), p. 176.
16 Drawing in the collection of Dirk Rinsema, Meppel, the Netherlands; since
   this book was written the drawing has changed hands.
17 See above, note 3.

18 Drawing in the collection of It Bleekerhûs Museum, Drachten, dwg no 572.

19 Sketchbook 2, *Holland en Duitschland en Belle-Ile 1925 en Caprie*, MS p.10r (acquisition number AB 4150 N), Van Doesburg Collection, R.B.K.

20 *De Stijl*, IV, no 3 (March 1921), p. 47.

21 *L'Esprit nouveau*, no 5, not paginated, but the quotation is taken from the penultimate paragraph.

22 Quoted above, note 6. Other drawings which make specific reference to the proportions 3.5.8 are 1973.345.g, 1973.345.h, and 583 in the collection of It Bleekerhûs Museum, Drachten.

23 Drawing in the collection of It Bleekerhûs Museum, Drachten, dwg no 1973.345.h.

24 See above, Chapter 2, p. 76.

25 Letter dated 8 January 1921 (in fact 1922) (coll. Mercuur).

26 For details see Troy, pp. 82–83.

27 In a letter dated 17 February 1922, N. Ober Weimar, MS p.1r and v (coll. Mercuur).

28 Letters reproduced in Schippers, *Holland Dada*, pp. 175 and 176 respectively.

29 See ibid., p. 177.

30 Quoted in H. R. Heite, 'Dada in Drachten', *Trotwaer*, special no 9/10 (November 1971), not paginated, but the quotation is to be found on the first page of the text.

31 See Schippers, *Holland Dada*, p. 186.

32 Support was mentioned in the letter of 8 January 1921 (in fact 1922), MS p.1r; opposition is discussed in a letter of 17 February 1922, MS p.1v (both in coll. Mercuur).

33 Schippers, *Holland Dada*, p. 106.

34 Coll. Mercuur.

35 Letter of 18 June 1922, reproduced in Schippers, *Holland Dada*, p. 178.

36 In a letter of 4 September 1922 (coll. Mercuur).

37 Compare the compositions in fig. 47 with the windows for the school in the catalogue *Mondrian und De Stijl*, Galerie Gmurzynska (Cologne, 1979), pp. 114–17.

38 In a letter of 24 April 1922, p. 5 (coll. Mercuur).

39 'Een oordeel over de hedendaagsche bouwkunst in Nederland', *De Bouwwereld*, XXI, no 28 (12 July 1922), 217–19 (p. 219).

40 The former quotation is from J. J. P. Oud, 'Bouwkunst en kubisme', *De Bouwwereld*, XXI, no 32 (9 August 1922), p. 245; the latter from Theo van Doesburg, 'Het kubisme voor het laatst', *De Bouwwereld*, XXI, no 35 (30 August 1922), p. 270.

41 'Van de esthetiek naar het materiaal', *Bouwkundig Weekblad*, XLIII, no 38 (23 September 1922), 372–75 (p. 373).

42 'Uitweiding bij eenige afbeeldingen', *Bouwkundig Weekblad*, XLIII, no 43 (28 October 1922), 418–24 (p. 420).

43 Letter dated 18 January 1920, Oud Archive, Nederlands Documentatie-centrum voor de Bouwkunst, Amsterdam.

4. Berlage and the new humanism

1 Theo van Doesburg, *Klassiek – barok – modern* (Antwerp, 1920), pp. 11 and 29. His emphasis.

2 H. P. Berlage, *Schoonheid in samenleving*, first edition (Rotterdam, 1919), p. 9.

3 Van Doesburg, *Drie voordrachten*, pp. 58 and 101.

4 H. P. Berlage, *Over de waarschijnlijke ontwikkeling der architectuur* (Delft, 1905), p. 33.

5 H. P. Berlage, 'Slotvoordracht en samenvatting', in *Zeven voordrachten over bouwkunst gehouden vanwege 't Genootschap Architectura et Amicitia*

(Amsterdam, 1908), 341–94 (p. 366). The lecture became the last chapter, 'Opmerkingen over bouwkunst', of Berlage's *Studies over bouwkunst, stijl, en samenleving* (Rotterdam, 1910). Here there are slight changes and the reference to Van der Pek becomes more oblique (see p. 115).

6 Van Doesburg, *Klassiek – barok – modern*, p. 28.

7 I. K. Bonset (pseudonym of Van Doesburg), 'Het andere gezicht', *De Stijl*, III, no 10 (August 1920), p. 85.

8 Theo van Doesburg, 'De taak der nieuwe architectur', first instalment, *Bouwkundig Weekblad*, XLI, no 50 (11 December 1920), 278–80 (p. 279).

9 H. P. Berlage, *Schoonheid in samenleving*, p. 12, quoting Hegel in 'Über Kunst und Kunstschönheit'; and pp. 24–25.

10 Theo van Doesburg, 'De taak der nieuwe architectuur', second instalment, *Bouwkundig Weekblad*, XLI, no 51 (18 December 1920), 281–85 (p. 283); both Berlage quotations are from p. 282; the second is verbatim from *Schoonheid in samenleving*, p. 140.

11 Theo van Doesburg, 'De taak der nieuwe architectuur', second instalment, p. 281.

12 I. K. Bonset, 'Het andere gezicht', p. 91; for Van Doesburg's (self-)contradictory statement see 'De taak der nieuwe architectuur', first instalment, p. 279.

13 Theo van Doesburg, 'De beteekenis der mechanische esthetiek voor de architectuur en de andere vakken', *Bouwkundig Weekblad* (in three instalments), XLII, nos 25, 28 and 33 (18 June, 9 July, 13 August 1921), pp. 164–66, 179–83, 219–21 in the respective issues; quoted from the first instalment, p. 166.

14 Editorial, 'Aanteekeningen bij bijlage IX', in *De Stijl*, III, no 7 (May 1920), p. 64. Compare Van Doesburg's remark in 'De beteekenis der mechanische esthetiek', third instalment, p. 220: 'not only the aesthetic, but the moral influence of the new work of art has increased greatly. Clarity and light, closed spaces accentuated by deep and pure colour, have a moral effect on the inhabitants, where the surroundings dominate all their business and thoughts.'

15 See for instance *Aratra Pentelici* (London, 1890), p. 15, §11: 'These abstract relations and inherent pleasantnesses, whether in space, number, or time, and whether of colours or sounds, form what we may properly term the musical or harmonic element in every art; and the study of them is an entirely separate science. It is the branch of art-philosophy to which the word "aesthetics" should be strictly limited . . .'

16 Attributed by Van Doesburg to Lenin, in *The Red Young Land*, I; used as an epigraph for the second instalment of 'De beteekenis der mechanische esthetiek'; the criticism of Ruskin and Morris follows in the text of the article, p. 179.

17 Le Corbusier, 'Trois rappels à Messieurs les architectes', *L'Esprit nouveau*, I (n.d.), p. 95; the emphasis used here is as it appears in *Vers une architecture* (Paris, 1923), p. 20.

18 Theo van Doesburg, 'De taak der nieuwe architectuur', second instalment, p. 281.

19 Theo van Doesburg, 'Der Wille zum Stil: Neugestaltung von Leben, Kunst und Technik', *De Stijl*, V, nos 2 and 3 (February and March 1922), pp. 23–32 and 33–41 respectively (see p. 37); and 'The New Architecture and its Consequences', manuscript unpublished in Van Doesburg's lifetime, but published in translation in Joost Baljeu, *Theo van Doesburg* (London, 1974), pp. 189–98, where it is dated 1930. The short quotation is from Theo van Doesburg, 'De taak der nieuwe architectuur', third instalment, *Bouwkundig Weekblad*, XLII, no 2 (8 January 1921), 8–10 (p. 9).

Letter to De Boer

1 The articles to which Van Doesburg is referring are both by Boeken: 'Huize Sevensteyn in Park Zorgvliet te 's-Gravenhage', *Bouwkundig Weekblad*, XLIII, nos 51–52 (December 1922), 496–504; and 'Aanteekeningen bij het beeld-houwwerk van Csaky', *Bouwkundig Weekblad*, XLIII, nos 51–52 (December 1922), 507–11.

2 The 'corner building' refers to the houses on the corner of the Oldenbarneveldlaan and Doornstraat around the corner from the Frankenslag (for which see the special issue of *Forum* on Duiker and Bijvoet by Jelles and Alberts, *Forum*, XXII, no 5 (1972), pp. 10–13). The concrete housing is by Pauw and Hardeveld, for which see 'Aanteekeningen bij de Rotterdamsche betonwoningen, architecten Pauw en Hardevelt', *De Stijl*, V, no 1 (January 1922), 11–12.

3 Illustrated in *De Stijl*, V, no 12 (December 1922), 215–16. Van Doesburg was at that time living at Klimopstraat 18 on the Daal en Berg estate (see Schippers, *Holland Dada*, p. 48).

4 The interiors were probably those for Dr Den Hartog in Maarsen, illustrated in *De Stijl*, VI, nos 3–4 (May–June 1923). The exhibitions under discussion resulted in Van Doesburg's 'Development Exhibition' at the Landesmuseum in Weimar, illustrated in *De Stijl*, VI, nos 6–7, Series XII (1924).

5 See the special Lissitzky issue of *De Stijl* (V, nos 10–11 (1922)).

6 Van Doesburg was in close contact with Evert Rinsema, keeping him up to date with progress in his own work, that of De Stijl, and the international art world in general.

7 These windows are now in private collections, but much documentary material, primarily in the form of photographs, is in the Van Doesburg Archive, R.B.K. Drawings for the windows include AB 5074 A and B, AB 5073, AB 5075, AB 5076, and most likely AB 5077 in the Van Doesburg Collection, R.B.K.

8 A group of artists in Groningen.

9 A club for artists in The Hague.

10 Thijs Rinsema, Evert's brother.

11 See Schippers, *Holland Dada*, p. 178.

Introduction to Part II

1 See above, pp. 82–83.

2 For the dating of the commission see below, pp. 153–54; this quotation is from a letter reproduced in Schippers, *Holland Dada*, p. 175.

3 Interview with Van Eesteren, 26 May 1979.

4 Letters between the two in the Van Doesburg Archive, R.B.K., are dated as early as 22 January 1918.

5 For a record of Van Doesburg's interest in Russia see for example *De Stijl*, II, no 6 (April 1919), p. 68; III, no 9 (July 1920), pp. 79–80; and III, no 11 (September 1920), p. 96. He discussed plans for a trip to Russia in a letter dated 24 April 1922 (coll. Mercuur), and the 1925 trip is mentioned in a letter from Schwitters reproduced in *Holland Dada*, p. 149.

6 *Mécano*, no 3, red issue (1922).

7 'The Literature of the Advance Guard in Holland', *The Little Review*, XI, no 1 (Spring 1925), 56–59 (p. 56).

8 'Caminoscopie, Boek III', *De Stijl*, VI, nos 3–4 (May–June 1923), 33–37 (p. 35).

9 'Dada complet', *Merz*, no 1 (January 1923), 4–22 (p. 5).

10 For which see Schippers, *Holland Dada*, pp. 82–84.

11 *Merz*, no 1 (January 1923), 4–11 (p. 6).

12 See Schippers, *Holland Dada*, p. 83.

13 For instance, as reproduced in ibid., p. 189.

14 The former quotation is from 'Caminoscopie; 'n antiphylosofische levensbeschouwing zonder draad of systeem', *De Stijl*, IV, no 5 (June 1921), 65–71 (p. 68); the latter is *art. cit.*, p. 69.

15 'Het andere gezicht', *De Stijl*, IV, no 4 (April 1921), 49–51 (p. 49).

16 Kurt Schwitters, 'Dadaismus in Holland: Dada complet', *Merz*, no 1 (January 1923), 3–11 (p. 9).

5. Towards an elementary architecture

1 'De beteekenis der mechanische esthetiek voor de architectuur en de andere vakken', *Bouwkundig Weekblad*, XLII, no 25 (18 June 1921), 164–66; no 28 (9 July 1921), 179–83; and no 33 (13 August 1921), 219–21.

2 See Baljeu, *Theo van Doesburg*, p. 62.

3 The three foregoing short quotations are from 'De beteekenis der mechanische esthetiek', p. 166.

4 'Over het wezen van het werktuig', *Nederlandsche ambachts- en nijverheidskunst jaarboek* (Rotterdam, 1922), 10–18 (pp. 11–12).

5 'Het andere gezicht', *De Stijl*, IV, no 4 (April 1921), 49–51 (p. 49).

6 'Over het wezen van het werktuig', p. 13.

7 A copy of De Groot's *Vormcompositie en centralisatie* (Amsterdam, 1922) is amongst Van Doesburg's books in the Archive, R.B.K.

8 I. K. Bonset, 'Balans van het nieuw', *De Stijl*, IV, no 12 (December 1921), 176–77 (p. 176).

9 'Van de esthetiek naar het materiaal', *Bouwkundig Weekblad*, XLIII, no 38 (23 September 1922), 372–75 (p. 373).

10 See *art. cit.*, p. 373, and also Theo van Doesburg, 'Von der neuen Ästhetik zur materiellen Verwirklichung', *De Stijl*, VI, no 1 (March 1923), 10–14 (p. 11).

11 Coll. Mercuur; Van Doesburg spoke again of the trip in a letter of 4 May 1922, in the same collection.

12 El Lissitzky, 'Proun', *De Stijl*, V, no 6 (June 1922), 81–85 (p. 82).

13 See El Lissitzky, *Russia: an Architecture for World Revolution*, translated by Eric Dluhosch (London, 1970), pp. 239–40.

14 See 'Zur elementaren Gestaltung', *G*, no 1 (July 1923), 1–2; and also 'Voorwaarden tot een nieuwe architectuur', *Architectura*, XXVII, no 27 (11 August 1923), 163–65 (p. 163, note 1).

15 'Balans van het nieuwe', *De Stijl*, V, no 9 (September 1922), 129–35 (p. 134).

16 *El Lissitzky*, exhibition catalogue of the Galerie Gmurzynska, Cologne (Cologne, 1976), p. 73. For the public criticism see for instance Van Doesburg's remarks in *De Stijl*, VII, nos 75–76, Series XIII (1926), p. 58, and 'Architectuurvernieuwingen in het buitenland', *Het Bouwbedrijf*, III, no 13 (29 October 1926), 424–27 (p. 426).

17 *De Stijl*, V, no 4 (April 1922), 61–64.

18 Jane Beckett, 'Dada, Van Doesburg and *De Stijl*', *Journal of European Studies*, IX (1979), 1–25 (p. 17).

19 Herta Wescher, 'Entretien avec Nelly van Doesburg', *Cimaise*, XVII, no 99 (November–December 1970), 35–41 (p. 36).

20 Catalogue of the Exhibition 'De Stijl' at the Stedelijk Museum, Amsterdam (6 July–25 September 1951), p. 44.

21 The former article is in *Het Getij*, VI, no 3 (September 1921), p. 51; the latter is 'De invloed van de Stijlbeweging in Duitschland', *Bouwkundig Weekblad*, XLIV, no 7 (17 February 1923), 80–84 (p. 83).

22 The sarcastic article is signed 'G.W.' and is entitled 'De Stijl-beweging in Duitschland', *Bouwkundig Weekblad*, XLIV, no 9 (3 March 1923), 103; the more soberly critical is A. Boeken, 'Staatliches Bauhaus in Weimar 1919–1923', *Bouwkundig Weekblad*, XLIV, no 52 (29 December 1923), 541–43. Behne's article formed part of the editorial 'De "Bauhaus" tentoonstelling te Weimar', *Klei*, XV, no 21 (1 November 1923), 245–54. The quotation is to be found on p. 246.

23 *Het Bouwbedrijf*, II, nos 5, 6, 7, and 10 (May, June, July, and October respectively, 1925), 197–200, 225–27, 262–65, and 363–66 respectively.

24 Ibid. (May issue), p. 199.

25 Ibid. (October issue), p. 364 for the former quotation; p. 366 for the latter.

26 Letter in the Oud Archive, Nederlands Documentatiecentrum voor de Bouwkunst, Amsterdam.

27 Letter from Moholy-Nagy to Oud, dated 17–20 August 1922, in the Oud Archive, Nederlands Documentatiecentrum voor de Bouwkunst, Amsterdam.

28 Coll. Mercuur. For a description of the Prix de Rome competition and Van Eesteren's very impressive entry see J. P. Mieras, 'Prijskamp in de schoone bouwkunst', *Bouwkundig Weekblad*, XLIII, no 1 (7 January 1922), pp. 2–8.

29 See R. Blijstra, *C. van Eesteren*, in the series Beeldende kunst en bouwkunst in Nederland (Amsterdam, 1968), pp. 8–9 and 9–10.

30 Mieras, 'Prijskamp', pp. 6–8, for basic information concerning the University Hall.

31 For Van Eesteren's reaction to the refusal of the Committee to grant the money for the second year of his travel see C. van Eesteren, 'Tentoonstelling Prix de Rome bouwkunst', *Bouwkundig Weekblad*, XLIV, no 13 (31 March 1923), pp. 144–47; for the short quotation see p. 145; for the long quotation, pp. 145–46. The article was in answer to J. P. Mieras, 'Tentoonstelling Prix de Rome bouwkunst', *Bouwkundig Weekblad*, XLIV, no 12 (24 March 1923).

32 For reproductions see Mieras, 'Prijskamp', pp. 2–8; the groundplan appears on p. 6; also *L'Architecture vivante* (Winter 1923), plates 44–47.

33 See also the version in *De Stijl*, VI, no 9, Series XII (1924–5), p. 121, and the coloured versions AB 5106 and AB 5108 in the Van Doesburg Collection, R.B.K.

34 'Voorwaarden tot een nieuwe architectuur', p. 164.

35 'Über das Verhältnis von malerischer und architektonischer Gestaltung', *Der Cicerone*, XIX, no 18 (1927), 564–70 (pp. 569–70); also paraphrased in 'Farben im Raum und Zeit', *De Stijl*, nos 87–89, Series XV (1928), 26–36 (pp. 33–36).

36 Quoted in the catalogue of the exhibition 'De Stijl' at the Stedelijk Museum, Amsterdam (6 July–25 September 1951), p. 72.

37 The former quotation is translated in R. Blijstra, *C. van Eesteren*, English version (Amsterdam, 1971), p. 8; this was confirmed in a personal interview on 26 May 1979; the letter of 15 August 1924 is in the Van Doesburg Archive, R.B.K., and is quoted in Jean Leering, 'De architectuur en Van Doesburg', in the catalogue of the exhibition 'Theo van Doesburg, 1883–1931', Stedelijk Van Abbemuseum, Eindhoven (13 December 1968 – 26 January 1969), 19–25 (p. 21).

38 *Art. cit.*, p. 20.

39 *Art. cit.*, p. 22.

40 Bajeu, *Theo van Doesburg*, p. 60.

41 Troy, *The De Stijl Environment*, pp. 106–8; quoted from Theodore M. Brown, *The Work of G. Rietveld, Architect* (Utrecht, 1958), p. 31.

42 Jaffé, *De Stijl*, 1956 edition, p. 166.

43 'Tentoonstelling Prix de Rome bouwkunst', p. 146.
44 Jaffé, *Theo van Doesburg*, p. 91.
45 Ibid, p. 95.
46 'De beteekenis der mechanische esthetiek voor de architectuur en de andere vakken', p. 165.
47 Letter in the Van Doesburg Archive, R.B.K.
48 See *Bulletin de l'effort moderne*, no 9 (November 1924), pp. 15–16; *Pásmo*, no 2 (1924); 'Ke Kollektivni Konstrukci', *Stavba*, III, no 2 (July 1924), pp. 29–31; and *Vouloir*, no 25 (1927), not paginated.
49 Letter in the Van Doesburg Archive, R.B.K.
50 From a Dutch transcription in the Van Doesburg Archive, R.B.K.
51 Theo van Doesburg, 'L'Evolution de l'architecture moderne en Hollande', *L'Architecture vivante*, III, no 9 (Autumn and Winter 1925), 14–20 (p. 16).
52 *Vouloir*, no 25 (1927), not paginated.
53 Letter in the Van Doesburg Archive, R.B.K.
54 Letter in the Van Doesburg Archive, R.B.K.
55 'Jury rapport: prijsvraag winkel-galerij met café-restaurant aan de Laan van Meerdervoort te 's-Gravenhage', *Het Bouwbedrijf*, I, no 4 (October 1924), pp. 165–69.
56 Letter in the Van Doesburg Archive, R.B.K.
57 Letter dated 26 December 1926, in the Van Doesburg Archive, R.B.K.
58 Letter dated 10 December 1924, in the Van Doesburg Archive, R.B.K.
59 *De Stijl*, VI, nos 10–11, Series XII (1924–5), p. 148, and ibid., no 12, p. 139.

6. The Aubette and related work

1 Letter of 4 September 1924, Van Doesburg Archive, R.B.K. Van Doesburg's letter of 18 October 1923 to Kok outlines his financial position after sharing the expenses of the exhibition at the Rosenberg Gallery with Van Eesteren.
2 Letter fragment undated, Van Doesburg Archive, R.B.K.
3 Letter of 7 October 1924, Van Doesburg Archive, R.B.K.
4 See Max Speyer, 'Indrukken van de Parijsche tentoonstelling', *Architectura*, XXIX, no 44 (31 October 1925), 386–88 (pp. 387–88).
5 'Het fiasco van Holland op de expositie in Parijs in 1925', *De Stijl*, VI, nos 10–11, Series XII (1925), 156–59 (p. 157). Van Doesburg was not just displaying a paranoid reaction in his interpretation of the situation. Yve-Alain Bois has traced the rancorous series of events leading to Van Doesburg's exclusion from the exhibition. See 'De Stijl in Paris', *Het nieuwe bouwen*, 101–27 (pp. 110–11). There he concludes that 'When one imagines everything Van Doesburg might have got up to, it is easy to see why it only took one quick step to setting the seal on the unanimous opposition of the concerted Dutch architects to any participation of De Stijl.'
6 *Art. cit.*, p. 158. The petition of protest is in the same issue of *De Stijl*, pp. 149–50.
7 'Open brief aan den heer Jhr. W. F. A. Roëll, correspondent van *Het Vaderland*', in the same issue of *De Stijl*, 151–52 (p. 151), where she also quotes Roëll's taunt.
8 H. L. C. Jaffé, 'The Diagonal Principle in the Works of Van Doesburg and Mondrian', *The Structurist*, no 9 (1969), 14–21 (p. 21).
9 This is also confirmed by the sketch in the Van Doesburg Collection, R.B.K. (AB 4149 I, fig. 73).
10 Léon Deshairs, 'Une villa moderne à Hyères', *Art et décoration*, no 54 (1928), p. 8; quoted in Troy, *The De Stijl Environment*, p. 208, note 14.
11 See below, p. 174.
12 Jean Leering, 'De architectuur en Van Doesburg', in the catalogue of the

exhibition 'Theo van Doesburg, 1883–1931', Stedelijk Van Abbemuseum, Eindhoven (13 December 1968–26 January 1969), 19–25 (p. 24).

13 *De Stijl*, VIII, nos 73–74, Series XIII (1926), pp. 17–28.

14 *Art. cit.*, p. 23.

15 Theo van Doesburg, 'Notices sur l'Aubette à Strasbourg', *De Stijl*, VIII, nos 87–89, Series XV (1928), 2–13 (p. 4).

16 'Architectuurvernieuwing in het buitenland; de ombeelding van de Aubette in Straatsburg', *Het bouwbedrijf*, VI, no 6 (15 March 1929), 116–22 (p. 116). The drawing concerned is AB 5147, Van Doesburg Collection, R.B.K.

17 Théo Wolters, 'The Aubette, a Monumental Expression of De Stijl', *Cimaise*, XVII, no 99 (November–December 1970), 49–56 (p. 55).

18 Van Doesburg, *Notices*, p. 13.

19 Letter dated 7 July 1960 in the Van Doesburg Archive, R.B.K. Karl Gerstner's article is 'Die Aubette als Beispiel integrierter Kunst', *Werk*, XLVII, no 10 (October 1960), 375–80; a design for the ashtrays is preserved in the Musée National d'Art Moderne, Paris (cat. no 30).

20 Van Doesburg Archive, R.B.K.

21 Or, to be more precise, within this set of drawings, since figures 88, 90, 91, and a ceiling plan were worked up and made into a 'maquette', as seen on the table in Van Doesburg's atelier in the Aubette in fig. 92 (Van Doesburg Archive, R.B.K.).

22 See 'Architectuurvernieuwing in het buitenland', p. 121.

23 *Art. cit.*, p. 120.

24 See also Edmée de Lillers, 'L'Aubette salle par salle', in the catalogue of the exhibition *Theo van Doesburg: Projets pour l'Aubette*, Centre National d'Art et de Culture Georges Pompidou, Musée National d'Art Moderne (12 October–12 December 1977), 10–19 (p. 14).

25 'Notices sur l'Aubette à Strasbourg', Aubette issue of *De Stijl*, p. 6; see fig. 97 for the general distribution of the lighting.

26 *Art. cit.*, pp. 7–8. See also fig. 99 for his handling of the relief.

27 See *Projets pour l'Aubette*, p. 39.

28 'Notices sur l'Aubette à Strasbourg', p. 6.

29 'Schilderkunst en plastiek; over contra-compositie en contra-plastiek – Elementarisme', *De Stijl*, VII, nos 75–76, Series XIII (1926), 35–43 (pp. 41–43); the earlier quotations are to be found on pp. 40–41.

30 For the first quotation see 'Het glas-in-lood in de oude en nieuwe architectuur', *Het Bouwbedrijf*, VII, no 6 (14 March 1930), 122–26 (pp. 125–26); for the second quotation see 'De beelding van het interieur', *Het Binnenhuis*, XII, no 16 (31 July 1930), 181–84 (p. 184). Further see 'De beelding van het interieur', *Het Binnenhuis*, XI, no 18 (29 August 1929), 205–8 (p. 207); ibid., XI, no 21 (10 October 1929), 241–43 (p. 241); ibid., XII, no 14 (3 July 1930), 157–61 (p. 157); 'Farben im Raum und Zeit', *De Stijl*, VIII, nos 87–89, Series XV (1928), 26–36 (p. 32), reprinted as 'Farben im Raum', *Die Form*, IV, no 2 (1929), 34–36.

31 Title of drawing AB 5298 in the Van Doesburg Collection, R.B.K.

32 Letter in the Van Doesburg Archive, R.B.K. Original orthography and grammar have been retained here and in the following letters. Their combination of Dada and an incomplete command of other languages would escalate correction into complete reinterpretation in many instances.

33 Letter dated 11 July 1927 in the Van Doesburg Archive, R.B.K.

34 See also Theo van Doesburg, 'Het glas-in-lood in de oude en nieuwe architectuur', *Het Bouwbedrijf*, VII, no 10 (9 May 1930), 202–5 (p. 205), fig. 6; and the catalogue *Les Vitraux des musées de Strasbourg* (Strasbourg, 1965), entry nos 158–60.

35 Van Doesburg Archive, R.B.K.

36 Letter from Van Eesteren to Van Doesburg dated 26 December 1926 in the Van Doesburg Archive, R.B.K.

37 Signed only H.A.C., 'Quelques considérations trés actuelles sur le cachet artistique de l'Aubette', *Les Dernières Nouvelles de Strasbourg*, LI, no 54 (23 February 1928), p. 4.

38 Van Doesburg Archive, R.B.K.

39 In V. Conrads and H. G. Sperlich, *Phantastische Architektur* (Stuttgart, 1960), p. 149; quoted from Clara Weyergraf, *Piet Mondrian und Theo van Doesburg* (Munich, 1979), pp. 95–96.

40 See Theo van Doesburg, 'Architectuurvernieuwing in het buitenland: de ombeelding van de Aubette in Straatsburg', *Het Bouwbedrijf*, VI, no 6 (15 March 1929), 116–22 (p. 122).

41 Letter dated Paris, 16 August 1928, Van Doesburg Archive, R.B.K.

7. The full compass of architecture

1 In a letter dated Clamart, 18 September 1925, to 'Liefste Mammie' (probably Helena Milius, his previous wife), Van Doesburg Archive, R.B.K.

2 See Baljeu, *Theo van Doesburg*, p. 88.

3 Letter in the Van Doesburg Archive, R.B.K.

4 Letter dated 22 June 1927, Van Doesburg Archive, R.B.K.

5 A letter of reference written by Van Doesburg for Elzas states that 'je peux déclarer que Mr A. E[lzas] qui a travaillé chez moi dans l'année 1929 . . .', Workbook 22, MS p. 21v.

6 For a more complete discussion of the relationship between Le Corbusier and Van Doesburg, see Allan Doig, 'Theo van Doesburg en Le Corbusier: rivaliteit, uitwisseling en ontwikkeling', *Wonen TABK*, 15/16 (August 1982), 28–36.

7 'Een atelier met woning te Meudon-Val-Fleury', *De 8 en Opbouw*, no 17 (17 August 1935), 183–84 (p. 184).

8 *De Stijl*, Van Doesburg memorial issue (January 1932), pp. 36–37; see also Van Doesburg's 'De beelding van het interieur', in *Binnenhuis*, particularly the instalment in the 14 February 1929 issue (p. 39).

9 Elzas's remark is quoted in Jean Leering's article 'De architectuur en Van Doesburg' in the catalogue of the exhibition 'Theo van Doesburg, 1883–1931', Stedelijk Van Abbemuseum, Eindhoven, 13 December 1968 – 26 January 1969, 19–25 (p. 24).

10 Notebook 18, MS p.2r, Van Doesburg Archive, R.B.K.

11 See A. Elzas, 'Atelier met woning te Meudon-Val-Fleury', *De Stijl*, last number (January 1932), 36–37 (p. 37).

12 'Vernieuwingspogingen in de Fransche architectuur', *Het Bouwbedrijf*, I, no 4 (October 1924), 173–77 (p. 175).

13 Ibid., no 6 (December 1924), 260–66 (p. 261).

14 'Vernieuwingspogingen in de Fransche architectuur', *Het Bouwbedrijf*, II, no 1 (January 1925), 32–38 (pp. 32–34).

15 *Art. cit.*, p. 34.

16 'Architectuurvernieuwing in het buitenland; Frankrijk, Duitschland, Oostenrijk, Tjecho-Slovakije', *Het Bouwbedrijf*, III, no 2 (February 1926), 74–78 (p. 78).

17 'Die Verkehrsstadt', *Architektur der Gegenwart*, no 3 (1929), 4–10 (p. 6).

18 *Art. cit.*, p. 7.

19 *Art. cit.*, pp. 7–8.

20 From a typescript in the Van Doesburg Archive, R.B.K., pp. 15–16.

21 Ibid., p. 19.

Select bibliography

Collections consulted

Archive Le Corbusier, Fondation Le Corbusier, Paris
It Bleekerhûs Museum, Drachten, Friesland, the Netherlands
City Archives, Drachten, Friesland, the Netherlands
Fondation Custodia, Institut Néerlandais, Paris
Musée d'Art Moderne, Strasbourg
Musée National d'Art Moderne, Paris
Oud Archive, Nederlands Documentatiecentrum voor de Bouwkunst, Amsterdam (N.D.B.)
Rijksbureau voor Kunsthistorische Documentatie, The Hague
Dirk Rinsema, Meppel, the Netherlands
Stedelijk Museum, Amsterdam
Stedelijk Van Abbemuseum, Eindhoven
Thom Mercuur, Franeker, Friesland, the Netherlands
Van Doesburg Archive and Collection (Schenking Van Moorsel), Rijksdienst Beeldende Kunst, The Hague (R.B.K.)

Books by Theo van Doesburg

Editor, *Art concret* (Paris, 1930)
Classique – baroque – moderne (Paris, 1920)
Drie voordrachten over de nieuwe beeldende kunst (Amsterdam, 1919)
Grundbegriffe der neuen gestaltenden Kunst, Bauhausbücher 6 (Munich, 1925)
Klassiek – barok – modern (Antwerp and Amsterdam, 1920)
De maskers af (Amsterdam, [1916])
De nieuwe beweging in de schilderkunst (Delft, 1917)
I. K. Bonset, *Nieuwe woordbeeldingen: de gedichten van Theo van Doesburg* (Amsterdam, 1975)
Principles of Neo-plastic Art, translated by Janet Seligman (London, 1968)
De schilder De Winter en zijn werk (Haarlem, 1916)
Editor, *De Stijl*, complete reprint (Amsterdam, 1968)

Articles by Theo van Doesburg

'Aanteekening bij bijlage IV', *De Stijl*, III, no 3 (January 1920), 32
'Aanteekeningen bij de bijlagen VI en VII', *De Stijl*, III, no 5 (March 1920), 44–46
'Aanteekening bij bijlage IX', *De Stijl*, III, no 7 (May 1920), 64
'Aanteekeningen bij de Rotterdamsche betonwoningen, architecten Pauw en Hardeveld', *De Stijl*, V, no 1 (January 1922), 11–12

'Aanteekeningen over monumentale kunst: naar aanleiding van twee bouwfragmenten (hall in vacantiehuis te Noordwijkerhout, bijlage I)', *De Stijl*,
II, no1 (November 1918), 10–12

(I. K. Bonset, *pseud.*) 'Het andere gezicht', *De Stijl*, III, no 10 (August 1920),
84–86; no 11 (September 1920), 90–92; IV, no 4 (April 1921), 49–51;
'Abstracte, sur-humanistische roman', *De Stijl*, VII, no 77, Series XIII
(1926), 66–70; VII, no 78, Series XIII (1926–7), 89–92; nos 79–84,
Jubilee Series XIV (1927), 13–18; VIII, nos 85–86, Series XV (1928),
107–15

(I. K. Bonset, *pseud.*) 'Antikunstenzuivereredemanifest', *Mécano*, yellow issue
(1922)

'Antwoord aan mejuffrouw Edith Pijpers en allen, die haar standpunt innemen',
De Stijl, I, no 6 (April 1918), 65–71

'De architect André Lurçat', *Het Bouwbedrijf*, III, no 4 (1926), 152–55

'De architect J. J. P. Oud "voorganger" der "Cubisten" in de bouwkunst?', *De
Bouwwereld*, XXI, no 30 (26 July 1922), 229

'Architectuur-diagnose: naar aanleiding der architectuur-tentoonstelling van
de "Stijl-groep" in de Galerie Rosenberg te Parijs', *Architectura*, XXVIII,
no 15 (17 May 1924), 61–63

'Architectuurvernieuwingen in het buitenland': 'Frankrijk, Duitschland,
Oostenrijk, Tjecho-slovakije', *Het Bouwbedrijf*, III, no 2 (February 1926),
74–78; no 5 (May 1926), 191–94; no 6 (June 1926), 228–31; no 7 (July
1926), 266–68; no 8 (August 1926), 296–98; no 10 (17 September
1926), 346–49; no 11 (1 October 1926), 371–72; no. 13 (29 October
1926), 424–27; no 15 (26 November 1926), 477–79; IV, no 2 (21 January 1927), 40–44; no 4 (18 February 1927), 88–91; no 9 (29 April 1927),
217–20;

'Italië', *Het Bouwbedrijf*, IV, no 15 (22 July 1927), 352–55; [the architecture
of Mallet-Stevens] *Het Bouwbedrijf*, IV, no 20 (30 September 1927),
468–72;

'De architectuurtentoonstelling "Die Wohnung" te Stuttgart', *Het Bouwbedrijf*, IV, no 24 (25 November 1927), 556–59;

'Kunst en architectuurvernieuwing in Sovjet-Rusland', *Het Bouwbedrijf*, V,
no 20 (September 1928), 395–400; no 22 (October 1928), 436–41; VI,
no 3 (1 February 1929), 49–53;

'Eenige nieuwe architectuurdemonstraties in Tjechoslovakije', *Het Bouwbedrijf*, V, no 26 (December 1928);

'De ombeelding van de Aubette in Straatsburg', *Het Bouwbedrijf*, VI, no 6 (15
March 1929), 116–22;

'Kunst en architectuurvernieuwing in Italië' etc., *Het Bouwbedrijf*, VI, no 9 (26
April 1929), 179–81; no 10 (10 May 1929), 201–03; no 13 (21 June
1929), 263–66; no 15 (19 July 1929), 305–08; no 17 (16 August 1929),
341–44; no 20 (27 September 1929), 401–04; no 24 (22 November
1929), 472–74; VII, no 3 (31 January 1930), 60–62; no 7 (28 March
1930), 145–49; no 11 (23 May 1930), 219–22;

'Kunst en architectuurvernieuwing in Polen', *Het Bouwbedrijf*, VII, no 18 (29
August 1930), 358–61; VIII, no 5 (27 February 1931), 87–90

(I. K. Bonset, *pseud.*) 'Archachitektonica: inscriptie voor het museum van Dr
Berlage te 's-Gravenhage', *Mécano*, blue issue (1922)

'L'Art collectif et son importance sociale', *Vouloir*, no 25 (1927)

(I. K. Bonset, *pseud.*) 'Balans van het nieuwe', *De Stijl*, IV, no 12 (December
1921), 176–77; V, no 7 (July 1922), 106–9; V, no 9 (September 1922),
130–35

'Base de la peinture concrète' (with Carlsund, Hélion, Tatundjian, and Wantz),
Art concret, I, no 1 (April 1930), 1

'Beeldende kunst: "grosze Berliner Kunstausstellung", Glasspalast, Berlin, Mei-September 1921', *Het Getij*, VI, no 3 (September 1921), 50–57; no 4 (October 1921), 73–76

'Beeldende kunst: tweede tentoonstelling van "Het Signal", "Binnenhuis", Raadhuisstraat, Amsterdam', *Holland Express*, X, no 14 (4 April 1917), 167

'De Beelding van het interieur', *Het Binnenhuis*, X, no 21 (October 1928), 279–83; no 26 (December 1928), 345–51; XI, no 3 (31 January 1929), 29–31; no 4 (14 February 1929), 39–42; no 5 (28 February 1929), 54–56; no. 6 (14 March 1929), 67–70; no 10 (9 May 1929), 111–14; no. 13 (20 June 1929), 145–48; no 16 (1 August 1929), 181–84; no 18 (29 August 1929), 205–8; no 21 (10 October 1929), 241–43; XII, no 9 (24 April 1930), 97–101; no 14 (3 July 1930), 157–61; no 16 (31 July 1930), 181–84

'Een belangrijk kunsttijdschrift', *Het Getij* (June 1919), 164–65

'Belangrijke nieuwe uitgaven over nieuwe architectuur', *Het Bouwbedrijf*, VII, no 20 (26 September 1930), 401–03

'De beteekenis der mechanische esthetiek voor de architectuur en de andere vakken', *Bouwkundig Weekblad*, XLII, no 25 (18 June 1921), 164–6; no 28 (9 July 1921), 179–83; no 33 (13 August 1921), 219–21

'De beteekenis van de kleur in binnen- en buitenarchitectuur', *Bouwkundig Weekblad*, XLIV, no 21 (26 May 1923), 323–34

'De beteekenis van het glas-in-lood in de nieuwe bouwkunst', in *Glas-in-lood*, edited by W. F. Gouwe, in the series De toegepaste kunsten in Nederland, vol. 25 (Rotterdam, 1932), 37–38

'Das Buch und seine Gestaltung', *Die Form*, IV, no 21 (1929), 566–71

(Aldo Camini, *pseud.*) 'Caminoscopie: 'n antiphylosophische levensbeschouwing zonder draad of systeem', *De Stijl*, IV, no 5 (June [actually May] 1921), 65–71; no 6 (June 1921), 82–87; no 7 (July 1921), 97–99; no 8 (August 1921), 118–22; no 12 (December 1921), 180–82; V, no 6 (June 1922), 86–88; VI, no 3/4 (May–June 1923), 33–37; IV, nos 6–7, Series XII (1924), 74–78

'Chroniek – Mécano: International Congres van Konstruktivisten en Dada 1922 in Weimar', *Mécano*, no 3, red issue (1922)

(I. K. Bonset, *pseud.*) 'Chronique scandaleuse des Pays-Plats', *Mécano*, no 3, red issue (1922)

'Classique – baroque – moderne', *L'Effort moderne*, no 21 (January 1926), 1–3; no 22 (February 1926), 1–3; no 23 (March 1926), 1–2

'Commentaires sur la base de la peinture concrète', *Art concret*, I, no 1 (April 1930), 2–4

Conference 88, Madrid–Barcelona 1930, unpublished MS in the Van Doesburg Archive, Schenking Van Moorsel, R.B.K., The Hague.

(I. K. Bonset, *pseud.*) 'Tot een constructieve dichtkunst', *Mécano*, nos 4–5, white issue (1923), n.p.

(I. K. Bonset, *pseudo.*) 'Dada Hollande I.K.B: manifest 0,96013', *Mécano*, blue issue (1922)

'Dadaïsme', *Merz*, no 2 (April 1923), 28–32

'Dadaïsme: I. Dada vormt zich', *Merz*, no 1 (January 1923), 16

'Dadaistische-vreemdelingenverkeer in Holland', *Merz*, no 2 (April 1923), 27–28

'Data en feiten (betreffende de invloedsontwikkeling van *De Stijl* in 't buitenland) die voor zich spreken', *De Stijl*, VII, nos 79–84, Jubilee Series XIV (1927), 53–71

'Denken – aanschouwen – beelden', *De Stijl*, II, no 2 (December 1918), 23–24

Editorial comment on an open letter from Huib Hoste, *De Stijl*, I, no 11 (September 1918), 136

'Eenige punten ter verklaring der moderne schilderkunst', lecture given 13 October 1929 in the Stedelijk Museum, Amsterdam, at the opening of the exhibition of Parisian art (*Esac*)

'C'est le spirituel . . .', *G*, no 3 (June 1924), 38

'Zur elementaren Gestaltung', *G*, no 1 (July 1923), 1–2

'Elémentarisme', *Abstraction – creation – art non-figuratif*, no 1 (1932), 39

'Das Ende der Kunst', *Pásmo*, nos 13–14 (1925), 8

'Van de esthetiek naar het materiaal', *Bouwkundig Weekblad*, XLIII, no 38 (23 September 1922), 372–75

'L'Evolution de l'architecture moderne en Hollande', *L'Architecture vivante*, III, no 9 (Autumn and Winter 1925), 14–20

'Evolution of Modern Architecture in Holland', *The Little Review*, XI, no 1 (Spring 1925), 47–51

'Expressionistisch-literaire komposities', *Het Getij* (February 1919), 37–39

'Farben im Raum', *Die Form*, IV, no 2 (1929), 34–36

'Het fiasco van Holland op de expositie in Parijs in 1925', *De Stijl*, VI, nos 10–11, Series XII (1925), 156–59

'Film als reine Gestaltung', *Die Form*, IV, no 10 (1929), 241–48

'Futurisme', *Eenheid*, no 127 (9 November 1912)

'Het glas-in-lood in de oude en nieuwe architectuur', *Het Binnenhuis*, XI, no 24 (21 November 1929), 279–81; no 26 (19 December 1929), 301–04; XII, no 3 (30 January 1930), 26–29; no 5 (27 February 1930), 49–52;
  also published in *Het Bouwbedrijf*, VI, no 26 (20 December 1929), 520–22; VII, no 2 (17 January 1930), 40–42; no 6 (14 March 1930), 122–26; no 10 (9 May 1930), 202–5

'Godenkultuur', *Het Getij* (April 1919), 93–94

'Grondbegrippen der nieuwe beeldende kunst', *Tijdschrift voor Wijsbegeerte*, XIII, no 1 (1919), 30–49; no 2 (1919), 169–88

'Grootmeesters der beeldende kunst', *Eenheid*, no 357 (7 April 1917); no 361 (5 May 1917); no 368 (23 June 1917); no 376 (18 August 1917); no 385 (20 October 1917); no 392 (8 December 1917)

'Grootmeesters der beeldende kunst: Michel Agnolo', *Eenheid*, no 469 (29 May 1919), 1384–85

'Het Hollandsche paviljoen op de Exposition des Arts Décoratifs te Parijs', *Het Bouwbedrijf*, II, no 6 (June 1925), 221

'Huszar's beeldend toneel', *Het Vaderland*, avondblad (23 February 1923)

'Ingezonden', *De Wiekslag*, I, no 10 (March 1918), 112

'Ter inleiding', *De Stijl*, I, no 1 (October 1917), 1–2

'De invloed van de Stijlbeweging in Duitschland', *Bouwkundig Weekblad*, XLIV, no 7 (17 February 1923), 80–84

'Karakteristiek van het Dadaïsme', *Mécano*, nos 4–5, white issue (1923), n.p.

'Ke Kollektivní Konstrukci' (with C. van Eesteren), *Stavba*, III, no 2 (July 1924), 29–32

'K Elementární Tvorbě', *Stavba*, III, no 2 (July 1924), 27–29

'Kort overzicht der handelingen van het Internationale Kunstenaarscongres te Düsseldorf (29–31 Mai 1922)', *De Stijl*, V, no 4 (April 1922), 49–64

'Het kubisme voor het laatst', *De Bouwwereld*, XXI, no 35 (30 August 1922), 270

'Kunst-kritiek: moderne kunst: Stedelijk Museum, Amsterdam, Expositie Mondriaan, Leo Gestel, Sluiters, Schelfhout, Le Fauconnier', *Eenheid*, no 283 (6 November 1915)

'The Literature of the Advance Guard in Holland', *The Little Review*, XI, no 1 (Spring 1925), 56–59

(I. K. Bonset, *pseud.*) 'Madapolan', *Mécano*, no 3, red issue (1922)

'Manifeste 2 de "De Stijl", 1920: la littérature', *L'Esprit nouveau*, no 2 (n.d.), 82–83

'Manifest Proletkunst' (with Kurt Schwitters, Hans Arp, Tristan Tzara, Chr. Spengemann), *Merz*, no 2 (April 1923), 24–25

'Moderne tuinplastiek (bloemenvaas)', *Bouwkundig Weekblad*, XL, no 51 (20 December 1919), 313

'Moderne wendingen in het kunstonderwijs', *De Stijl*, II, no 3 (January 1919), 34–35; no 4 (February 1919), 44–48; no 5 (March 1919), 57–58; no 6 (April 1919), 66–68; no 8 (June 1919), 91–94; no 9 (July 1919), 102–4; no 11 (September 1919), 127–32; no 12 (October 1919), 137–39

'The New Architecture and its Consequences', manuscript dated 1930, unpublished in Van Doesburg's lifetime, but published in translation in Joost Baljeu, *Theo van Doesburg* (London, 1974), 189–98

'De nieuwe architectuur', *Bouwkundig Weekblad*, XLV, no 20 (17 May 1924), 200–4

'De nieuwe beweging in de schilderkunst', *De Beweging*, XII, no 5 (May 1916), 124–31; no 6 (June 1916), 219–26; no 7 (July 1916), 57–66; no 8 (August 1916), 148–56; no 9 (September 1916), 226–35

'De nieuwe woordbeelding', *Het Getij*, VI (1921), 83–89; 120–28

'Notices sur l'Aubette à Strasbourg', *De Stijl*, VIII, nos 87–89, Series XV (1928), 2–13

'Nová Architektura Holandská', *Stavba*, III, no 5 (November 1924), 90–94

'Obnova Architektury', *Stavba*, III, no 2 (July 1924), 23–26

'Odnowienie Architektury', *Block*, no 5 (1924), 12–13

'Open brief aan Bernard Canter', *Holland Express*, X, no 37 (12 September 1917), 441

'Open brief aan den architect Huib Hoste', *De Nieuwe Amsterdammer* (6 July 1918)

'Open brief aan den architect Huib Hoste', *De Stijl*, I, no 9 (July 1918), 111–12

'Over het zien van nieuwe schilderkunst', *De Stijl*, II, no 4 (February 1919), 42–44

'Overzichtelijke beschouwing bij de intrede van den derden jaargang', *De Stijl*, III, no 1 (November 1919), 1–5

'Repliek aan den heer H. C. Verkruysen en zijns gelijken', *Architectura*, XXV, no 5 (3 February 1917), 32–33

'Réponse à notre enquête: "Ou va la peinture moderne?"', *L'Effort moderne*, no 3 (March 1924), 7–8

'Revue der avant-garde', *Het Getij*, VI, no 1 (1921), 109–12; no 2 (August 1921), 25–29; no 6 (December 1921), 138–41; un-numbered issue (1921), 193–200; VII, no 1 (January 1922), 13–15

'Rondblik', *De Stijl*, II, no 6 (April 1919), 68–70

'Rondblik', *De Stijl*, III, no 9 (July 1920), 78–80

'Rondblik', *De Stijl*, III, no 11 (September 1920), 95–96

'Rondblik: Holland – een wendingsche wending aanstaande', *De Stijl*, IV, no 6 (June 1921), 87–88

'Schilderkunst, naar aanleiding der eerste tentoonstelling van de Leidsche kunstclub "De Sphinx" te Leiden, 18–31 januari 1917', *Eenheid*, no 348 (3 February 1917), 2–3

'Schilderkunst: notities over Impressionisme, naar aanleiding van teekeningen, studies en etsen van Kees van Urk, te Leiden', *Eenheid*, no 362 (12 May 1917)

'Schilderkunst: van kompositie tot contra-kompositie', *De Stijl*, VII, nos 73–74, Series XIII (1926), 17–28

'Schilderkunst en plastiek: over contra-kompositie en contra-plastiek – Elementarisme', *De Stijl*, VII, nos 75–76, Series XIII (1926), 35–43

'La Signification de la couleur en architecture', *La Cité*, IV, no 10 (May 1924), 181–87

'Slotbemerkingen', *De Stijl*, II, no 10 (August 1919), 118–20

'Surrealistische letterkunde in Frankrijk (recherche Surréaliste)', *Groot Nederland*, XXIX, no 2 (February 1931), 201–11; no 3 (March 1931), 290–307

'De taak der nieuwe architectuur: naar aanleiding van *Schoonheid in samenleving* door H. P. Berlage', *Bouwkundig Weekblad*, XLI, no 50 (11 December 1920), 278–80; no 51 (18 December 1920), 281–85; XLII, no 2 (8 January 1921), 8–10

'Terrassenarchitectuur', *Het Bouwbedrijf*, II, no 1 (3 January 1930), 18–20

'Thijs Maris', *Eenheid*, no 380 (15 September 1917)

'Tien jaren stijl: algemeene inleiding', *De Stijl*, nos 79–84, Jubilee Series XIV (1927), 2–9

'Über das Verhältnis von malerischer und architektonischer Gestaltung', *Der Cicerone*, XIX, no 18 (1927), 564–70

'Is een universeel beeldingsbegrip thans mogelijk', *Bouwkundig Weekblad*, XLI, no 39 (25 September 1920), 230–31

'Van "natuur" tot "kompositie": aanteekeningen bij de ontwikkeling van een abstracte schilderij', *De Hollandsche revue*, XXIV, no 8 (25 August 1919), 470–76

'Die Verkehrsstadt', *Architektur der Gegenwart*, no 3 (1929), 4–10

'Vernieuwingspogingen der architectuur in Duitschland en Oostenrijk', *Het Bouwbedrijf*, II, no 5 (May 1925), 197–200; no 6 (June 1925), 225–27; no 7 (July 1925), 262–65; no 10 (October 1925), 363–66

'Vernieuwingspogingen in de Fransche architectuur', *Het Bouwbedrijf*, I, no 4 (October 1924), 173–77; no 6 (December 1924), 260–66; II, no 1 (January 1925), 32–38; no 3 (March 1925), 108–12

'Vers la peinture blanche', *Art concret*, I, no 1 (April 1930), 11–12

'Vers un style collectif', *L'Effort moderne*, no 4 (April 1924), 14–16

'Vers une construction collective', *L'Effort moderne*, no 9 (November 1924), 15–16

'Von der neuen Ästhetik zur materiellen Verwirklichung', *De Stijl*, VI, no 1 (March 1923), 10–14

'De voorbereidingen der "Exposition des Arts Décoratifs", Parijs 1925', *Het Bouwbedrijf*, II, no 4 (April 1925), 151–53

'Voorwaarden tot een nieuwe architectuur', *Architectura*, XXVII, no 27 (11 August 1923), 163–65

'De vrijwilliger', *Het Getij* (August 1919), 201–5

'Výzva!/Aufruf!', *Pásmo*, nos 7–8 (November 1924), 1

'Der Wille zum Stil: Neugestaltung von Leben, Kunst und Technik', *De Stijl*, V, no 2 (February 1922), 23–32; V, no 3 (March 1922), 33–41

Books by other authors

Apollinaire, Guillaume, *The Cubist Painters: Aesthetic Meditations* [1913], edited by Robert Motherwell, translated by Lionel Abel (New York, 1949)

Appollonio, Umbro, *Futurist Manifestos*, translated by Robert Brain and others (London, 1973)

Baljeu, Joost, *Theo van Doesburg* (London, 1974)

Baroni, Daniele, *Gerrit Thomas Rietveld: Furniture* (London, 1977)

Berlage, H. P., *Amerikaansche reisherinneringen* (Rotterdam, 1913)

Berlage, H. P., *Beschouwingen over bouwkunst en hare ontwikkeling* (Rotterdam, 1911)

Berlage, H. P., *Een drietal lezingen in America gehouden* (Rotterdam, 1912)

Berlage, H. P., *Over de waarschijnlijke ontwikkeling der architectuur* (Delft, 1905)

Berlage, H. P., *Over stijl in bouw- en meubelkunst*, second edition (Rotterdam, 1908)

Berlage, H. P., *Schoonheid in samenleving*, first edition (Rotterdam, 1919); second edition (Rotterdam, 1924)

Berlage, H. P., *Studies over bouwkunst, stijl, en samenleving* (Rotterdam, 1910)

Biederman, Charles, *Art as the Evolution of Visual Knowledge* (Red Wing, Minnesota, 1948)

Birren, Faber, *The Color Primer: a Basic Treatise on the Color System of Wilhelm Ostwald* (New York, 1969)

Blijstra, R., *C. van Eesteren*, in the series Beeldende kunst en bouwkunst in Nederland (Amsterdam, 1968)

Blijstra, R., *C. van Eesteren*, English version, in the series Art and Architecture in the Netherlands (Amsterdam, 1971)

Blotkamp, Carol, *et al.*, *De beginjaren van De Stijl* (Utrecht, 1982)

Boekraad, Cees, *et al.*, *Het nieuwe bouwen: de Nieuwe Beelding in de architectuur – De Stijl* (Delft, 1983)

Bolland, G. J. P. J., *Schelling, Hegel, Fechner en de nieuwere theosophie* (Leiden, 1910)

Bolland, G. J. P. J., *Het schoone en de kunst* (Amsterdam, 1906)

Bolland, G. J. P. J., *Zuivere rede en hare werkelijkheid*, third edition (Leiden, 1912)

Brown, Theodore M., *The Work of G. Rietveld, Architect* (Utrecht, 1958)

Campbell, Joan, *The German Werkbund: the Politics of Reform in the Applied Arts* (Princeton, 1978)

Christie, Manson and Woods Ltd, *Paintings from the Collection of Mr and Mrs Armand P. Bartos*, sold at Christie's, 27 June 1983

Conrads, V., and H. G. Sperlich, *Phantastische Architektur* (Stuttgart, 1960)

Theo van Doesburg, 1883–1931, catalogue of the exhibition in the Stedelijk Van Abbemuseum, Eindhoven (13 December 1968–26 January 1969)

Theo van Doesburg: Projets pour l'Aubette, catalogue of the exhibition in the Centre National d'Art et de Culture Georges Pompidou, Musée National d'Art Moderne, Paris (12 October–12 November 1977)

Fanelli, Giovanni, *Moderne architectuur in Nederland* (The Hague, 1978)

von Goethe, J. W., *The Theory of Colours*, translated by C. L. Eastlake (London, 1840)

Gouwe, W. F., *Glas in lood*, in the series De toegepaste kunsten in Nederland (Rotterdam, 1932)

Grautoff, Otto, *Formzertrümmerung und Formaufbau in der bildenden Kunst* (Berlin, 1919)

Harries, Karston, *The Meaning of Modern Art: a Philosophical Interpretation* (Evanston, Illinois, 1968)

Havelaar, Just, *De symboliek der kunst* (Haarlem, 1918)

Hedrick, Hannah L., *Theo van Doesburg: Propagandist and Practitioner of the Avant-Garde, 1909–1923* (Ann Arbor, 1973)

Hegel, G. W. F., *Aesthetics: Lectures on Fine Art*, translated by T. M. Knox, 2 vols (Oxford, 1975)

Hegel, G. W. F., *The Philosophy of Fine Art*, translated by F. P. B. Osmaston, 4 vols (London, 1916)

Henderson, Linda Dalrymple, *The Fourth Dimension and Non-Euclidean Geometry in Modern Art* (Princeton, 1983)

Hess, Hans, *Pictures as Arguments* (London, 1975)

Hitchcock, Henry-Russell, and Philip Johnson, *The International Style* (New York, 1966)

Hitchcock, H. R., *Painting toward Architecture* (New York, 1948)

Jaffé, H. L. C., *Theo van Doesburg* (Amsterdam, 1983)

Jaffé, H. L. C., *Piet Mondrian* (London, 1970)

Jaffé, H. L. C., *De Stijl* (London, 1970)

Jaffé, H. L. C., *De Stijl, 1917–1931: the Dutch Contribution to Modern Art* (London, 1956)

Kandinsky, Wassily, *Concerning the Spiritual in Art*, translated by Francis Golffing, Michael Harrison, and Ferdinand Ostertag (New York, 1947)

Knox, Israel, *The Aesthetic Theories of Kant, Hegel, and Schopenhauer* (New York, 1936)

Le Corbusier (C. E. Jeanneret), *Vers une architecture* (Paris, 1923)

Leliman, J. H. W., *Het stadswoonhuis in Nederland gedurende de laatste 25 jaren* (The Hague, 1920)

El Lissitzky, catalogue of the exhibition at the Galerie Gmurzynska, Cologne (9 April–30 June 1976)

Lissitzky, El, *Russia: an Architecture for World Revolution*, translated by Eric Dluhosch (London, 1970)

Mansbach, Steven, *Visions of Totality: Laszlo Moholy-Nagy, Theo van Doesburg, and El Lissitzky* (Ann Arbor, 1980)

De meesterwerken van J. en W. Maris, in the series Nederlandsche meesters, no 4 (The Hague, n.d.)

Mondrian und De Stijl, catalogue of the exhibition at the Galerie Gmurzynska, Cologne (May–August 1979)

Muthesius, Hermann, *Kultuur en kunst* (Amsterdam, 1911)

Ostwald, Wilhelm, *Einführung in die Farbenlehre* (Leipzig, 1919)

Ostwald, Wilhelm, *Der Farbenatlas* (Leipzig, 1918)

Ostwald, Wilhelm, *Die Farbenfibel* (Leipzig, 1917)

Ostwald, Wilhelm, *Die Farbenlehre*, 2 vols (Leipzig, 1918)

Ostwald, Wilhelm, *Farbkunde* (Leipzig, 1923)

Ostwald, Wilhelm, *Die Farbschule* (Leipzig, 1919)

Ostwald, Wilhelm, *Goethe, Schopenhauer und die Farbenlehre* (Leipzig, 1918)

Ostwald, Wilhelm, *Die Harmonie der Farben* (Leipzig, 1918)

Oud, J. J. P., *Mein Weg in De Stijl* (The Hague, 1960)

Overy, Paul, *De Stijl* (London, 1969)

Pit, A., *Het logische in de ontwikkeling der beeldende kunsten*, in the series Utrechtsche bijdragen voor letterkunde en geschiedenis, vol VI (Utrecht, 1912)

Podro, Michael, *The Manifold in Perception: Theories of Art from Kant to Hildebrand* (Oxford, 1972)

Read, Herbert, *The Philosophy of Modern Art* Greenwich, Connecticut, 1952)

Roland Holst, R. N., *Over kunst en kunstenaars* (Amsterdam, 1923)

Ruskin, John, *Aratra Pentelici* (London, 1890)

Schatborn, P., *Het legaat Roland Holst (1868–1938)*, catalogue of the exhibition in the Rijksmuseum, Amsterdam (13 April–24 June 1979)

Schippers, K., *Dada in Drachten*, catalogue of the exhibition at 't Coopmanschûs, Franeker, Friesland (20 November 1971–2 January 1972)

Schippers, K., *Holland Dada* (Amsterdam, 1974)

Schoenmaekers, M. H. J., *Beginselen der Beeldende Wiskunde* (Bussum, 1916)

Schopenhauer, Arthur, *The World as Will and Representation*, translated by E. F. J. Payne, 2 vols (New York, 1969)

Semper, Gottfried, *Der Stil*, reprinted in the series Kunstwissenschaftliche Studientexte, no III in 2 vols (Mittenwald, 1977)

Simmel, Georg, *Philosophische Kultur*, second edition (Leipzig, 1919)

Singelenberg, Pieter, *H. P. Berlage: Idea and Style* (Utrecht, 1972)

Smets, Marcel, *Huib Hoste, voorvechter van een vernieuwde architectuur* (Brussels, 1972)

Smit, C., *Nederland in de eerste wereldoorlog (1899–1919)*, 3 vols (Groningen, 1973)

Stace, W. T., *The Philosophy of Hegel* (New York, 1955)

Stam, Gunther, *The Architecture of J. J. P. Oud, 1906–1963*, exhibition catalogue (Tallahassee, Florida, 1978)

De Stijl, catalogue of the exhibition at the Stedelijk Museum, Amsterdam (6 July–25 September 1951)

van Straaten, Evert, *Theo van Doesburg, 1883–1931: een documentaire op basis van materiaal uit de Schenking Van Moorsel* (The Hague, 1983)

Troy, Nancy, *The De Stijl Environment* (Cambridge, Mass., and London, 1983)

Tummers, Nic., H. M., *J. L. Mathieu Lauweriks: zijn werk en zijn invloed op architectuur en vormgeving rond 1910* (Hilversum, 1968)

Viollet-le-Duc, E., *Entretiens sur l'architecture* [1863], Pierre Mardaga reprint (Paris, 1977)

Catalogue of *Les Vitraux des musées de Strasbourg* (Strasbourg, 1965)

Wattjes, J. G., *De verhouding van de bouwkunst tot wetenschap, techniek en kunst: rede uitgesproken bij de aanvaarding van het hoogleraarsambt in de architectuur aan de Technische Hoogeschool te Delft, op 27 September 1918* (Delft, 1918)

Werkbundes, Jahrbuch des deutschen: der Verkehr (Jena, 1914)

Werkbundes, Jahrbuch des deutschen: deutsche Form im Kriegsjahr; die Ausstellung Köln 1914 (Munich, 1915)

Werkbundes, Jahrbuch des deutschen: die Durchgeistigung der deutschen Arbeit (Jena, 1912)

Werkbundes, Jahrbuch des deutschen: die Kunst in Industrie und Handel (Jena, 1913)

Weyergraf, Clara, *Piet Mondrian und Theo van Doesburg* (Munich, 1979)

Wils, Jan, *De sierende elementen van de bouwkunst*, from the series De toegepaste kunsten in Nederland; een reeks monographieën over hedendaagsche sier- en nijverhiedskunst (Rotterdam, 1923)

Wolff, Kurt H., *Georg Simmel, 1858–1918* (Columbus, Ohio, 1959)

Wölfflin, Heinrich, *Principles of Art History: the Problem of the Development of Style in Later Art*, translated by M. D. Hottinger (New York, 1950)

Worringer, Wilhelm, *Abstraction and Empathy*, translated by Michael Bullock (London, 1953)

Worringer, Wilhelm, *Abstraktion und Einfühlung* (Munich, 1948)

Zevi, Bruno, *Poetica dell'architettura neoplastica: il linguaggio della scompositione quadridimensionale*, second edition (Turin, 1974)

de Zurko, Edward Robert, *Origins of Functionalist Theory* (New York, 1957)

Articles by other authors

Architectura, 'Driebondnummer', XXV, nos 39–40 (6 October 1917)

Architectura et Amicitia, members of, per 1 January 1918, *Architectura*, XXV, no 51 (22 December 1917), 391–94; corrections appear in *Architectura*, XXV, no 52 (29 December 1917), 406

Badovici, Jean, 'Les Constructivistes', *L'Architecture vivante*, III, no 8 (Autumn and Winter, 1925), 5–10

Badovici, Jean, 'Entretiens sur l'architecture vivante: l'urbanisme en Hollande', *L'Architecture vivante*, III, no 7 (Spring 1925), 10–13

Beckett, Jane, 'The Abstract Interior', in *Towards a New Art: Essays on the Background to Abstract Art, 1910–20* (London, 1980), 90–124

Beckett, Jane, 'Dada, Van Doesburg and *De Stijl*', *Journal of European Studies*, IX (1979), 1–25

Beckett, Jane, '"De Vonk", Noordwijk: an Example of Early De Stijl Co-operation', *Art History*, III, no 2 (June 1980), 202–17

Beckett, Jane, 'The Netherlands', in *Abstraction: Towards a New Art* (London, 1980), 39–57

Berlage, H. P., 'De historische ontwikkeling der ruimte: fragment uit *Schoonheid in samenleving*', *Bouwkundig Weekblad*, XLI, no 3 (17 January 1920), 11–16

Berlage, H. P., 'Slotvoordracht en samenvatting', in *Zeven voordrachten over bouwkunst gehouden vanwege 't Genootschap Architectura et Amicitia* (Amsterdam, 1908), 341–94

Blaauw, C. J., 'Een concreet slotwoord naar aanleiding van de laatste abstracties van den heer Van Doesburg', *Architectura*, XXV, no 6 (10 February 1917), 38–39

Boeken, A., 'Aanteekeningen bij het beeldhouwwerk van Csaky', *Bouwkundig Weekblad*, XLIII, nos 51–52 (December 1922), 507–11

Boeken, A., 'Huize Sevensteyn in Park Zorgvliet te 's-Gravenhage', *Bouwkundig Weekblad*, XLIII, nos 51–52 (December 1922), 496–504

Boeken, A., 'Staatliches Bauhaus in Weimar 1919–1923', *Bouwkundig Weekblad*, XLIV, no 52 (29 December 1923), 541–43

Booleman, Alex, 'Een woord ter introductie', *De Wiekslag*, I, no 1 (May 1917), 1

Booleman, Alex, review article 'De Stijl', *De Wiekslag*, I, no 8 (December 1917), 86–88

van Burkom, Frans, 'Kunstvormgeving in Nederland', in *De Amsterdamse School, 1910–1930*, in the series Monografieën van de Stichting Architectuur Museum (Amsterdam, 1979), pp. 71–108

Canter, Bernard, Editorial reply to Van Doesburg's open letter, *Holland Express*, X, no 37 (12 September 1917), 441–43

Canter, Bernard, 'Kunst: ter verklaring', *Holland Express*, X, no 38 (19 September 1917), 453–54

Canter, Bernard, 'Schilderkunst: vereeniging "De Sphinx", 1ste tentoonstelling, Leiden', *Holland Express*, X, no 5 (31 January 1917), 58–59; no 6 (7 February 1917), 70–71

Canter, Bernard, 'Thijs Maris', *Holland Express*, X, no 35 (29 August 1917), 411

Dake, C. L., 'Nieuwe richtingen in de schilderkunst: Cubisme, Expressionisme, Futurisme, etc. – Contra', in the series Pro en Contra, IX, no 1 (1914), 16–32

Deshairs, Léon, 'Une villa moderne à Hyères', *Art et décoration*, no 54 (1928)

van Doesburg, Nelly, 'Open brief aan den heer Jhr. W. F. A. Roëll, correspondent van *Het Vaderland*', *De Stijl*, VI, nos 10–11, Series XII (1924–1925), 151–52

Doig, Allan, 'De architectuur van De Stijl en de westerse filosofische traditie', *Wonen TABK*, 15/16 (August 1982), 44–57

Doig, Allan, 'Theo van Doesburg en Le Corbusier: rivaliteit, uitwisseling en ontwikkeling', *Wonen TABK*, 15/16 (August 1982), 28–36

Editorial, 'Amsterdam en Rotterdam in de crisis', *Bouwkundig Weekblad*, XXXIV, no 35 (19 August 1914), 425–26

Editorial, 'De "Bauhaus" tentoonstelling te Weimar', *Klei*, XV, no 21 (1 November 1923), 245–54

Editorial, 'Berichten', *Bouwkundig Weekblad*, XXIV, no 27 (4 July 1914), 334

Editorial, 'De Stijl', *Architectura*, XXV, no 36 (8 September 1917), 270

Editorial, 'De "Deutsche Werkbund" tentoonstelling', *Architectura*, XXII, no 32 (8 August 1914), 259–60; no 33 (15 August 1914), 261–62; no 34 (22 August 1914), 265–66; no 35 (5 September 1914), 273–74; no 39 (26 September 1914), 286–87; no 41 (10 October 1914), 298; no 42 (17 October 1914), 302–3; no 45 (7 November 1914), 315

Editorial, 'Een Hollandsche werkbond', *Architectura*, XXII, no 27 (4 July 1914), 221

Editorial, 'De huidige crisis en de particuliere architecten: het voorschotvonds der architecten', *Bouwkundig Weekblad*, XXXIV, no 46 (14 November 1914), 493–94

Editorial, 'Opening der "Deutsche Werkbund-Ausstellung" te Keulen, op Zaterdag, 15 Mei', *Architectura*, XXII, no 21 (23 May 1914), 172

Editorial, 'Prof. Behrens over moderne Nederlandsche bouwkunst', *Bouwkundig Weekblad*, XLIII, no 43 (29 October 1922), 424; no 44 (4 November 1922), 426

Editorial, 'Samenwerking tusschen industrie en kunst', *Architectura*, XXV, no 33 (18 August 1917), 251–57; no 34 (25 August 1917); no 35 (1 September 1917)

Editorial, 'Tentoonstellingen: tentoonstelling van de photographische opnamen der werken van Hermann Muthesius', *Architectura*, XXII, no 16 (18 April 1914), 127–28

van Eesteren, C., 'Amerikaansche torenhuizen', *Het Bouwbedrijf*, II, no 12 (December 1925), 442–45

van Eesteren, C., 'Haricots sans fil of Holland's geestelijke ondergang, 1923', *Mécano*, nos 4–5, white issue (1923), n.p.

van Eesteren, C., 'Tentoonstelling Prix de Rome bouwkunst', *Bouwkundig Weekblad*, XLIV, no 13 (31 March 1923), 144–47

van Eesteren, C., 'Uit de stad van Ford', *Het Bouwbedrijf*, II, no 2 (February 1925), 84–85

Elzas, A., 'Atelier met woning te Meudon-Val-Fleury', *De Stijl*, dernier numéro (January 1932), 36–37

Elzas, A., 'Een atelier met woning te Meudon-Val-Fleury', *De 8 en Opbouw*, no 17 (17 August 1935), 183–84

Elzas, A., 'Theo van Doesburg', *De 8 en Opbouw*, no 17 (17 August 1935), 173–82

Gerstner, Karl, 'Die Aubette als Beispiel integrierter Kunst', *Werk*, XLVII, no 10 (1960), 375–80

Gorin, Jean, 'Nature and Art in the 20th Century', *Structure*, second series, no 1 (1959), 23

Gratama, Jan, 'Kroniek LIX: de Duitsche Werkbund en zijn beteekenis voor Nederland', *Bouwkundig Weekblad*, XXXIV, no 26 (27 June 1914), 311–15

Gratama, Jan, 'Een oordeel over de hedendaagsche bouwkunst in Nederland', *De Bouwwereld*, XXI, no 28 (12 July 1922), 217–19

Gratama, Jan, 'Vacantiehuis te Noordwijkerhout', *Klei*, XII, no 2 (15 January 1920), 13–19

G. W., 'De Stijl-beweging in Duitschland', *Bouwkundig Weekblad*, XLIV, no 9 (3 March 1923), 103

H. A. C., 'Quelques considérations très actuelles sur le cachet artistique de l'Aubette', *Les Dernières Nouvelles de Strasbourg*, LI, no 54 (23 February 1928), 4

Heite, H. R., 'Dada in Drachten', *Trotwaer*, special number 9/10 (November 1971)

Hélion, Jean, 'Les Problèmes de l'art concret: art et mathématiques', *Art concret*, I, no 1 (April 1930), 5–10

van 't Hoff, Robert, 'Aanteekeningen bij bijlage XX', *De Stijl*, II, no 10 (August 1919), 114–16

van 't Hoff, Robert, 'Architectuur en haar ontwikkeling', *De Stijl*, I, no 5 (March 1918), 57–59; II, no 4 (February 1919), 40–42; no 5 (March 1919), 54–55

Hoste, Huib, 'Antwoord op een open brief', *De Stijl*, I, no 11 (September 1918), 135–36

Hoste, Huib, 'De roeping der moderne architectuur', *De Stijl*, I, no 8 (June 1918), 85–87

Hoste, Huib, 'Het vacantiehis te Noordwijkerhout', *De Telegraaf* (1 March 1919), evening edition

Huszar, Vilmos, 'Iets over *Die Farbenfibel* van W. Ostwald', *De Stijl*, I, no 10 (August 1918), 113–18

Huszar, Vilmos, 'Over de moderne toegepaste kunsten', *Bouwkundig Weekblad*, XLIII, no 7 (18 February 1922), 59–69

Jaffé, H. L. C., 'The Diagonal Principle in the Works of Van Doesburg and Mondrian', *The Structurist*, no 9 (1969), 14–21

Jaffé, Hans, 'The De Stijl Concept of Space', *The Structurist*, no 8 (1968), 8–11

Jelles, E. J., and C. A. Alberts, special issue 'Duiker', *Forum*, XXII, no 5 (1972)

'Jury rapport: prijsvraag winkel-galerij met café-restaurant aan de Laan van Meerdervoort te 's-Gravenhage', *Het Bouwbedrijf*, I, no 4 (October 1924), 165–69

Kalk, H. L., 'Excursie "Deutsche Werkbund" tentoonstelling', *Architectura*, XXII, no 26 (27 June 1914), 214

Le Corbusier (C. E. Jeanneret), 'Trois rappels à Messieurs les architectes', *L'Esprit nouveau*, I (n.d.)

Leering, Jean, 'De architectuur en Van Doesburg', in the Stedelijk Van Abbemuseum catalogue *Theo van Doesburg 1883–1931* (1968), 19–25

de Lillers, Edmée, 'L'Aubette salle par salle', in the catalogue of the exhibition *Theo van Doesburg: Projets pour l'Aubette*, Centre National d'Art et de Culture Georges Pompidou, Musée National d'Art Moderne (12 October – 12 December 1977), 10–19

Lissitzky, El, 'Proun', *De Stijl*, V, no 6 (June 1922), 81–85

Lotz, W., 'Die Aubette in Strassburg', *Die Form*, IV, no 2 (1929), 44–48

Macnamee, Donald, 'Van Doesburg's Cow: a Crucial Transition in the Structure and Reality of Art', *The Structurist*, 8 (1968), 12–23

Mieras, J. P., 'Manifest van "De Stijl", 1918', *Bouwkundig Weekblad*, XL, no 3 (18 January 1919), 17–18

Mieras, J. P., 'Prijskamp in de schoone bouwkunst', *Bouwkundig Weekblad*, XLIII, no 1 (7 January 1922), 2–8

Mieras, J. P., review article 'De Stijl', *Bouwkundig Weekblad*, XXXVIII, no 47 (24 November 1917), 273

Mieras, J. P., 'Tentoonstelling Prix de Rome bouwkunst', *Bouwkundig Weekblad*, XLIV, no 12 (24 March 1923), 144–47

Mondrian, P., 'L'Architecture future Néo-plasticienne', *L'Architecture vivante*, III, no 8 (Autumn and Winter 1925), 11–13

Mondrian, P., 'Het bepaalde en het onbepaalde', *De Stijl*, II, no 2 (December 1918), 14–19

Mondrian, P., 'Natuurlijke- en abstracte realiteit', *De Stijl*, II, no 10 (August 1919), 109–13

Mondrian, P., 'De nieuwe beelding in de schilderkunst', *De Stijl*, I, no 1 (October 1917), 2–8; no 2 (December 1917), 13–18; no 4 (actually no 3) (January 1918), 29–31; no 4 (February 1918), 41–45; no 5 (March 1918), 49–54; no 7 (May 1918), 73–76; no 8 (June 1918), 88–89; no 9 (July 1918), 102–7; no 10 (August 1918), 121–23; no 11 (September 1918), 125–31; no 12 (October 1918), 140–45

Mondrian, P., 'Projet d'une chambre exécutée pour Madame B. . . ., à Dresden', *Vouloir*, no 25 (1927)

Oud, J. J. P., 'Architectonische beschouwing: A. massabouw en straatarchitectuur', *De Stijl*, II, no 7 (May 1919), 79–82

Oud, J. J. P., 'Architectonische beschouwing big bijlage VIII', *De Stijl*, I, no 4 (February 1918), 39–41

Oud, J. J. P., 'Architectonische beschouwingen bij bijlage III', *De Stijl*, II, no 11 (September 1919), 127–32

Oud, J. J. P., 'Architectonische beschouwingen bij bijlage III', *De Stijl*, III, no 3 (January 1920), 25–27

Oud, J. J. P., 'Boekbespreking: Dr Otto Grautoff, *Formzertrümmerung und Formaufbau in der bildenden Kunst*', *De Stijl*, II, no 10 (August 1919), 113–14

Oud, J. J. P., 'Bouwkunst en kubisme', *De Bouwwereld*, XXI, no 32 (9 August 1922), 245

Oud, J. J. P., 'Glas-in-lood van Theo van Doesburg', *Bouwkundig Weekblad*, XXXIX, no 35 (31 August 1918), 199–202

Oud, J. J. P., 'Ingezonden' letter to the editor, *Holland Express*, X, no 40 (3 October 1917), 479

Oud, J. J. P., 'Kunst en machine', *De Stijl*, I, no 3 (January 1918), 25–27

Oud, J. J. P., 'Orientatie', *De Stijl*, III, no 2 (December 1919), 13–15

Oud, J. J. P., 'Over cubisme, futurisme, moderne bouwkunst, enz.', *Bouwkundig Weekblad*, XXXVII, no 20 (16 September 1916), 156–57

Oud, J. J. P., 'Uitweiding bij eenige afbeeldingen', *Bouwkundig Weekblad*, XLIII, no 43 (28 October 1922), 418–24

Penaat, W., 'De Duitsche Werkbund en een Hollandsche Driebond: Duitsche Werkbund', *Boukundig Weekblad*, XXXIV, no 28 (11 July 1914), 339–41; no 29 (18 July 1914), 356–58; no 30 (25 July 1914), 364–65; taken from *Het Orgaan van de Ned. Vereeniging voor Ambachts- en Nijverheidskunst*

Polano, Sergio, 'Notes on Oud: Re-reading the Documents', *Lotus International*, no 16 (September 1977), 42–54

Ringbom, Sixten, 'The Sounding Cosmos: a Study in the Spiritualism of Kandinsky and the Genesis of Abstract Painting', *Acta Academiae Aboesis*, Series A, XXXVIII, no 2 (1970), 1–226

Roggeveen, D., 'Ingezonden' letter to the editor, *Holland Express*, X, no 38 (19 September 1917), 455

Schoenmaekers, M. H. J., 'Over het wezen van het werktuig', *Nederlandsche ambachts- en nijverheidskunst jaarboek* (Rotterdam, 1922), 10–18

Schopenhauer, Arthur, 'The Metaphysics of Fine Art', in *The Essential Schopenhauer* (London, 1962)

Schwitters, Kurt, 'Dadaismus in Holland: Dada complet', *Merz*, no 1 (January 1923), 4–11

Schwitters, Kurt, 'Theo van Doesburg and Dada (1931)', translated by Ralph Manheim in *The Dada Painters and Poets: An Anthology*, edited by Robert Motherwell (New York, 1951), 273–76

Severini, Gino, 'La Peinture d'avant-garde', *De Stijl*, I, no 2 (December 1917), 18–20; no 3 (January 1918), 25–27; no 4 (February 1918), 45–47; no 5 (March 1918), 59–60; no 8 (June 1918), 94–95; no 10 (August 1918), 118–21

Speyer, Max, 'Indrukken van de Parijsche tentoonstelling', *Architectura*, XXIX, no 44 (31 October 1925), 386–88

Staal, J. F., 'Verslag van de 1397ste ledenvergadering van het Genootschap "Architectura et Amicitia" gehouden op Woensdag 10 October 1917', *Architectura*, XXV, no 42 (20 October 1917), 331

Staal, J. F., 'Verslag van de 1398ste ledenvergadering van het Genootschap "Architectura et Amicitia", gehouden op Woensdag 24 October 1917', *Architectura*, XXV, no 44 (3 November 1917), 339–43

Stamm, Günther, 'Het jeugdwerk van J. J. P. Oud 1906-1917', *Museumjournal*, XXII, no 6 (December 1977), 260–66

Verkruyzen, H. C., 'Ingezonden', *Architectura*, XXV, no 3 (20 January 1917), 17–18

Verkruyzen, H. C., 'De Nieuwe schilderkunst', *Wendingen*, I, no 2 (20 February 1918), 8–11

Welsh, Robert P., 'Theo van Doesburg and Geometric Abstraction', in *Nijhoff, Van Ostaijen, 'De Stijl': Modernism in the Netherlands in the First Quarter of the 20th Century*, edited by Francis Bulhof (The Hague, 1976), 76–94

Wescher, Herta, 'Entretien avec Nelly van Doesburg', *Cimaise*, XVII, no 99 (November-December 1970), 35–41

Wichman, E., 'Nieuwe richtingen in de schilderkunst: Cubisme, Expressionisme, Futurisme, etc. – Pro', in the series Pro en Contra, IX, no 1 (1914), 1–15

Wijdeveld, H. Th., 'Jaarverslag van de redactie', *Architectura*, XXV, no 50 (15 December 1917), 387

Wijdeveld, H. Th., 'Een verbond tusschen industrie, handel en kunst', *Architectura*, XXV, nos 39–40 (6 October 1917), 279

Wijdeveld, H. Th., 'Verslag van de 1385ste ledenvergadering van het Genootschap "Architectura et Amicitia" gehouden op Woensdag 20 December 1916', *Architectura*, XXV, no 2 (13 January 1917), 8–10

Wijdeveld, H. Th., '*Wendingen*', *Wendingen*, I, no 1 (January 1918), 1–2

Wils, Jan, 'Beeldhouwkunst', *Wendingen*, I, no 6 (30 June 1918), 12–15

Wittemans, F., 'K. de Bazel en de philosophie der bouwkunst', *Eenheid*, no 384 (13 October 1917)

Wolters, Théo, 'The Aubette, a Monumental Expression of De Stijl', *Cimaise*, XVII, no 99 (November–December 1970), 49–56

Index

255